INNS OF THE BLUE RIDGE

INNS OF THE BLUE RIDGE

Mountain Hospitality
in the Best Southern Tradition
from Virginia to Georgia.

An **EPM** Guide

Library of Congress Cataloging-in-Publication Data

Inns of the Blue Ridge : mountain hospitality in the best
Southern tradition from Virginia to Georgia. — 2nd ed.
    p. cm.
   "An EPM guide."
   Includes index.
   ISBN 0-939009-77-3
   1. Hotels—Blue Ridge Mountains—Guidebooks.
2. Blue Ridge Mountains—Guidebooks. I. EPM
Publications, Inc.
  TX907.3.B58I55 1993
  647.9475501—dc20   93-31131
                           CIP

Cover and book design by Tom Huestis
Cover photograph: The Bleu Rock Inn, Washington,
Virginia, by Cynthia Mahan

*Note: Because our maps had to be drawn small, locations of inns are approximate only.
Please consult local maps as well.*

CONTENTS

Inn at Monticello. *Charlottesville, Virginia*

THE ROAD TO MOUNTAIN MAGIC

As EPM staffers, we have spent years helping authors put across their views and advice about mid-Atlantic travel, offbeat outings and one-day trips. Now, with this book, it's our turn to express opinions. What follows is an independent report on the best inns, B&Bs, and country lodges in the Southern mountain states, starting in Virginia at the northern end of the Blue Ridge Mountains, running through West Virginia, North Carolina, Kentucky, Tennessee, and down through Georgia.

We took to the hills with lists of questions and open minds and have returned with a collection of favorites. In a nutshell, these are the places where we would like to stay ourselves. Because the seven of us collectively represent a range of interests, tastes and depth of pocket, our choices reflect a fairly broad selection. They range from a rustic hunting lodge without electricity where steaks are grilled outside, to a homey B&B where the chow is "self-help," to an internationally famous mansion where waiters take orders in hushed tones and prepare gourmet fare tableside.

In criss-crossing six states we visited more spots than are included here. We may have missed a diamond-in-the-rough here or there, and some new inn may have sprung up since we passed through. In any event, we want to hear from you if you have suggestions or amendments because we want to keep our evaluations fair and up-to-date.

We started this survey by getting in touch with each of the Chambers of Commerce in the large and small cities of the Southern Appalachian region. Most were very helpful, leading us to delightful places. Word-of-mouth from friends, relatives, innkeepers, locals and industry "inn" people led us to still more hideaways. Also, the excellent guide book written by Pat Hudson, *Inns of the Southern Mountains*, (which EPM published in 1985 but is now out of print), gave us many good leads. We are indebted to Pat for getting us interested in inns in the first place.

All of us had far more fun than we had anticipated. Though we found outstanding one-of-a-kind getaways and a multitude of activities to enjoy, it was the innkeepers themselves who bowled us over. Most of them had a story to tell and tell it they did!

Some of them were continuing a long-established family business and had generations of experience in their veins; others were venturing into the hospitality profession for the first time and expressed awe at the all-consuming demands of their new vocation; and many owners (and these deserve a special salute) had spent years of research, hard labor, money and time, completely restoring dilapidated, historic treasures to their original splendor and shine. Who can forget these proud faces! Innkeepers in general were so gregarious that at times during the interviews we found it hard to believe that only moments before we had been total strangers.

Special to Southern mountain inns, as you see, are the natural, warm friendliness of the innkeepers and their personal interest in guests. For this reason, we agreed to focus on the small places, excluding large country club and resort-type inns. No freebies or listing fees were asked of the inns. In most instances innkeepers knew in advance that we were coming.

We have not been rigid about the usage of "inn," " B&B," "country inn," knowing that the terms are used loosely and often ambiguously. We have labeled each establishment as the owners call it with the hope that our description will define what it is. Usually, the people in the business claim that an inn offers two or more meals plus lodging; B&Bs, lodging and breakfast only.

When making a choice, you should request a brochure from the inn and reserve rooms well in advance. Please confirm directions, rates, amenities and activities—these do change—and get a good state map. You can make your mountain getaway as full of action or as quiet as you like. Bring your walking shoes, camera, binoculars, favorite books, fishing poles, tennis racquets and golf clubs. Canoes, cross-country skis, bikes, and inner tubes are sometimes provided.

Everyone is advised to bring a spirit of adventure and an ear bent towards Appalachian history. The choice is yours. Ours is the pleasure of having shared our fun with you knowing that you'll find an abundance of your own.

Craig Avery	Suzanne Lord
Anita Back	Evelyn Metzger
Ed Bohling	Jon Metzger
Peter Exton	Janet Nelson

Fort Lewis Lodge. *Millboro, Virginia*

VIRGINIA

Abingdon

Convenience with charm

SUMMERFIELD INN

101 West Valley Street
Abingdon, VA 24210

Champe and Don Hyatt
(703) 628-5905

A portrait of Don and Champe Hyatt's children is the focal point of the living room at Summerfield Inn. The soft, warm colors of the painting inspired the color choices throughout the house. Champe, whose family has been in the hotel business, and Don, a retired dentist, acquired the early 1920s home in 1986. "We used the portrait's colors as a starting point," says Champe of the redecorating and remodeling. "About five years ago," she says, "we started visiting a lot of B&Bs. We thought Abingdon was a good choice for one, and a good draw," (because of the area's numerous scenic and cultural attractions).

Built by a well-to-do lumber dealer, the large, post-Victorian, two-story house with its hipped roof and dormers was occupied for many years by the Abingdon District Superintendent of the Methodist Church. It is in a quiet neighborhood just minutes from Interstate 81 and only blocks from the Martha Washington Inn and the internationally known Barter Theatre.

Summerfield's entryway is spacious and inviting. Pocket doors can close off a common area with television. Off the dining room

VIRGINIA

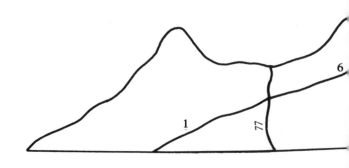

1	Abingdon	13	Lexington	24	Sperryville
2	Aldie	14	Lynchburg	25	Stanley
3	Castleton	15	Middleburg	26	Staunton
4	Charlottesville	16	Middletown	27	Steele's Tavern
5	Chatham	17	Millboro	28	Trevilians
6	Christiansburg	18	Monterey	29	Upperville
7	Culpeper	19	Orange	30	Vesuvius
8	Flint Hill	20	Paris	31	Warm Springs
9	Front Royal	21	Raphine	32	Washington
10	Harrisonburg	22	Scottsville	33	White Post
11	Hot Springs	23	Smith Mountain	34	Wintergreen
12	Leesburg		Lake	35	Woodstock

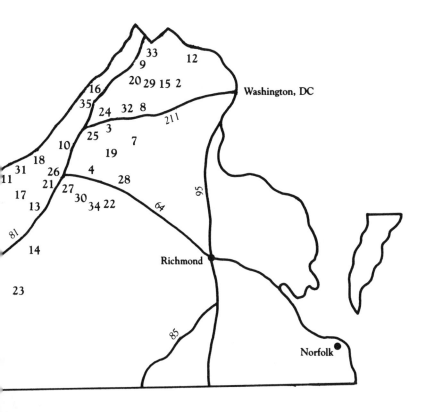

Summerfield Inn. *Abingdon, Virginia*

and guest pantry is a sunroom with wicker furniture and hanging plants. Often used for playing card games, it also offers visitors a great place to start the morning or enjoy some peace and quiet. The house furnishings are traditional, handsome and well appointed.

Each of the four guest rooms upstairs has its own bath, although not all are adjacent to the rooms. Feeding off a wide, angling hallway, the rooms are decorated with flower-patterned bedspreads and coordinated wallpaper and borders. A fabulous, four-poster walnut bed awaits some lucky guests. As with most homes of this period, there are few closets; an armoire adds a feeling of authenticity.

Guests can relax in rocking chairs and a wicker swing on the covered porch that runs across the front and along one side of the home. Various flags hang from each post of the porch, including one of a big goose with a peach-colored bow.

"There's no special reason for it," says Champe. "It's just pretty."

Location   *Abingdon. One mile from Exit 8, I-81. Take exit, follow Cummings Street to right on Valley Street. Inn is two blocks down on left*

Season	*March–November*
Dining	*Continental breakfast*
Children	*Over 12*
Pets	*No*
Payment	*Cash, check, MasterCard, Visa, AmEx*
Rates	*$65–$75 double occupancy; $60 for single*

An English Victorian in a small Southern town

VICTORIA AND ALBERT INN

224 Oak Hill Street
Abingdon, VA 24210

Don and Jeanette Darby
(703) 676-2797

A beautiful, turn-of-the-century three-story Victorian home, built in 1892 and renovated in 1988, the Victoria and Albert is located in the historic district and is within easy walking distance of many of Abingdon's fine attractions—restaurants, shops and the wonderful Barter Theater, the nation's longest running professional theater company.

The Victoria and Albert offers its guests spacious rooms furnished with reproductions, antique pieces and collectibles. Each of the rooms has a working fireplace, ceiling fan, cable television with VCR, telephone and comfortable surroundings. Two guest rooms share a bath and one has a private bath with marble-tiled flooring, fireplace and whirlpool tub. Guests are welcome to use the living room, dining room, three porches and the garden.

Don and Jeanette, resident owners, spent over two years searching for the "right spot" and the "right house" for their bed-and-breakfast dream. The town of Abingdon and the Victoria and Albert are a perfect combination. The Darbys offer guests everything they enjoy when staying at a bed-and-breakfast.

A full breakfast is served in the dining room near the fireplace, or it may be taken to the porch or the gazebo in the garden. There are bicycles for riding around town or the countryside, afternoon refreshments on the back porch, plenty of creaky, old wicker for sitting, fluffy bathrobes, stacks of books and magazines, and a small but growing VCR library.

Mount Rogers National Recreation Area is a short distance north on I-81. The Virginia Creeper Hiking and Bike Trail is three blocks away. Abingdon is a stone's throw from the state lines of Tennessee and North Carolina (and Blue Ridge Parkway) and within an hour of Kentucky and West Virginia. You can relax with a book from the county library across the street or browse the Hubbard's antique shop, a few blocks away on Main Street.

Location	*Abingdon. From I-81 Exit 17, take Cummings Street north past Main Street to the light at Valley Street and turn right. Go about three blocks to a left onto Oak Hill Street. The inn is on the right behind a white picket fence. Off-street parking is provided*
Season	*Year round, reservations recommended*
Dining	*Breakfast, afternoon refreshments*
Children	*No*
Pets	*No*
Payment	*Check, MasterCard, Visa*
Rates	*$70–$80 double occupancy*

Aldie

Sophisticated country

LITTLE RIVER INN

Box 116
Aldie, VA 22001

Tucker Withers and Monica Lee
(703) 327-6742

The popularity of Little River Inn is due not only to its six handsomely restored buildings (four of them accommodating some 20 overnight guests) but also to the inn's proximity to Aldie Mill and its accessibility to metropolitan Washington (only 35 miles east).

Since 1810, when the town of Aldie was settled around the gristmill, the population has remained fairly constant at 100. Nowadays 10,000 visitors flock to the village during the Aldie Harvest Festival in October. Many come at other times too, mining antiques, from funky to fine, in a total of nine shops.

Himself an antique dealer from Bethesda, MD, Tucker Withers restored a two-story brick house in the center of Aldie in 1982. He had bought the house from a family who had owned it since 1868 along with a walnut cupboard eight feet high that had been made for the family in 1810. "Because I wanted to have people in the house who would appreciate that piece," he grins, "I opened an inn."

The main house of five guest rooms was furnished with pieces dating from 1800 to 1860 and decorated by Withers's partner, Monica Lee. Linked to this building by a grape arbor are two separate cozy guest cottages called the Log Cabin and the Patent House, each with fireplaces.

Fourth on the renovation roster is Hill House. With much larger, more formal rooms, it sleeps two couples, six if the third pair beds in the library. Hill House has a fully equipped kitchen for those who like to cook away from home.

Withers designed Woodbyrn Guest House expressly for weddings and other parties. An 18th-century ordinary with walls 18 inches thick, stately Woodbyrn holds 75 to 125 guests depending on the weather. Parties at Woodbyrn are catered, as are those staged at Narrowgate, the sixth of Withers's renovations. A fine example of Flemish bond brickwork, Narrowgate was built on one of the original lots of Aldie and served as the town's first post office. Now it is rented, usually by the day, for small meetings of corporate and government executives. (A magnificent walnut table seats 20.) Until its renovation is completed, overnight guests are put up at the main part of the inn across the street.

A relentless restorer like Withers inevitably got involved in the renovation of Aldie Mill, owned by the Virginia Outdoors Foundation. He hopes to create a restaurant next to the mill. "After the restaurant," he says, "I'll rest."

Meantime he takes obvious delight in welcoming guests to the inn, many of them repeats. The inn's first guests, from Florida and Peru, still come back. Others come every year on their anniversaries. Conviviality ripples through the common areas of the inn, and guests are invited to help themselves to the wine, beer and mixers stocked in the kitchen.

Location	*On Route 50 where the Bull Run Mountains end—17 miles west of Dulles International Airport, 12 miles south of Leesburg, and five miles east of Middleburg*
Season	*All year*
Dining	*Full breakfast with room rate; catered dinners and luncheons*
Children	*Permitted at Woodbyrn Guest House if entire house is rented; babysitters available*
Pets	*No*
Payment	*Personal check, Visa, MasterCard*
Rates	*$80–$135, double occupancy*

Castleton

Neat and tidy country classic

BLUE KNOLL FARM

Rt. 1, Box 141
Castleton, VA 22716

Mary and Gil Carlson
(703) 937-5234

Opened under new management since April 1992, a spic-and-span blue and white-trimmed farmhouse sits at the end of a dead-end dirt road. Flowers, a few White Charlet cattle and a duck pond complete the picture-book-pretty scene. Nestled at the foot of Castleton Mountain and surrounded by pastures and rolling hills, this tidy time-capsule is several miles, turns and decades from Rt. 211. You may hear a cow moo, a cardinal call, or an evening choir of frogs, but not much else.

The impression of arriving at an meticulously kept house is reinforced when you meet Mary Carlson, who admits to answering to her sobriquet, "Mrs. Clean." When not applying Murphy's furniture oil to the handsome wooden tables and banister, she's uprooting dandelions with determined vengeance. Its hard to believe a retinue of resident elves has not been starching and bleaching the curtains and bedspreads in the four shining bedrooms. But don't feel intimidated by Mary's high standards, for she has created a homeyness that puts her city-weary guests at ease.

The one guest room downstairs, the library, boasts a nautical theme and has a working fireplace. Upstairs, the feminine, white, bright Rebecca's Room is furnished with antique dolls, quilts, children's clothing and an old-fashioned cradle. The Master Suite offers a jacuzzi tub, and the common room is a cozy area warmed in season by an 1877 wood stove. Mary attributes the high percentage of repeat guests to her premise that the secret to successful innkeeping is to treat guests the way you would want to be treated. "We make them feel welcome and comfortable without being intrusive." She adds that her quiet corner is succor for many young couples who want to escape for a few days the fast pace of professional, urban lives.

In all there are four sparkling bedrooms, each with king or queen size bed and private bath. If things get too quiet and the urge to splurge is irresistible, a five-star restaurant is not far away at the Inn at Little Washington. One should remember, however, that Mary's generous breakfast menu awaits in the morn: seasonal fruits, homemade nut/fruit breads, muffins or biscuits, egg casseroles or strata.

This is "real country." When seeking the solace of Blue Knoll, one is cautioned to follow directions and keep the faith that the road does indeed lead to a most charming and welcoming sanctuary in Virginia's Blue Ridge.

Location	*From I-66 west, take Exit 43A to Gainesville and head south on U.S. 29 through Warrenton. Take Rt. 211 west to Ben Venue and Rt. 729 S (15 miles). Follow 729 S to T-junction, turning left and staying on 729 towards Culpeper for about 2½ miles. Cross over small concrete bridge and turn right immediately onto Rt. 676, and right onto a gravel lane. Farm is ⅓ mile at dead end.*
Dining	*Full breakfast*
Season	*Year round*
Children	*Over 12 only*
Pets	*No*
Payment	*MasterCard, Visa, cash or check*
Rates	*$95–$125 per room per night*

Charlottesville

Monticello's neighbor

CLIFTON

Rt. 13, Box 26
Charlottesville, VA 22901

Craig & Donna Hartman
(804) 971-1800

Situated on 45 acres of rolling landscape that was once part of Thomas Jefferson's Shadwell estate, Clifton is a stately plantation property. It is also a versatile and accommodating inn that offers greater warmth and informality than one might first expect. Law-firm recruiters court prospects from the University of Virginia at receptions here; others have splashed on the lake with inner tubes and danced to *Big Chill* oldies on the terrace at twilight.

Originally owned by Jefferson's son-in-law, Thomas Mann Randolph, an early governor of Virginia, Clifton has been care-fully maintained rather than restored. That may contribute to the lived-in luxury one feels here.

The oldest portions of the inn were begun in 1799. The pine floors, paneled walls and fireplaces in every room have been preserved, giving rise to daydreams of walking in Jefferson's foot-steps and resting an arm on the mantel as he may have. Many large windows fill the rooms with light and look out onto lush greenery and trees. If lolling by the lake isn't inviting enough, croquet, tennis, biking, a lap pool and horseshoes are available. The Rivanna River is nearby.

Of the six guest rooms in the main house, a favorite is the Martha Jefferson. It is decorated in a hue of rich French vanilla—even the bed drapery, which can be drawn shut for cozy privacy. For greater privacy, there are separate cottages, including the Carriage House, furnished with articles and flooring from the estate of Meriwether Lewis, Jefferson's secretary and the great Missouri River explorer. All fourteen rooms have private baths, fireplaces and air conditioning. Three are actually suites.

In the morning, guests are treated to a full breakfast with delicious entrees such as blueberry pancakes and Virginia baked ham with fruit muffins and cornbread.

Location	*Near Monticello, just off US 250 East, on VA St. Rt. 729 in Shadwell*
Season	*Year round*
Dining	*Breakfast included. Prix Fixe dinners available daily by reservation.*
Children	*Yes*
Pets	*No*
Payment	*Checks (preferred), Visa, MasterCard, AmEx*
Rates	*$143–$193*
Other Considerations	*No smoking*

Down the road from Jefferson's gem

THE INN AT MONTICELLO

Highway 20 South, Route 19, Box 112
Charlottesville, VA 22902

Carol and Larry Engel
(804)979-3593

Gracious but not pompous, elegant without pretension, The Inn at Monticello and its hospitable veranda sit back from the road like a Southern host, greeting old friends and welcoming newcomers to the glories of Charlottesville. The country clapboard manor dating from the mid-1800s is barely visible from the road during spring as the dogwoods create a lacy curtain through which one barely spies the lush manicured lawn, vibrant azaleas and seductive porch rockers.

Owners Carol and Larry Engel couldn't have chosen a more appropriate quote to introduce their brochure—and themselves—than Thomas Jefferson's claim that "You know our practice of placing our guests at their ease. . . ." Carol's wry sense of fun, good taste and natural warmth make guests feel they are returning to a familiar scene. She anticipates what the uninitiated need to know about the area's many attractions by keeping handy in the parlor information on local attractions and a book of menus and prices from local restaurants to help plan the evening out. You're warned not to overindulge at dinner since a gourmet country breakfast awaits you next day. Some of Carol's delicacies are crab quiche, orange yogurt pancakes topped with berries, freshly brewed hazelnut coffee and homemade breads.

Five spacious, immaculate and beautifully decorated rooms, all with private baths, have their own special features: one a canopy bed, others, working fireplaces or private porch. Down comforters encourage winter visitors to sleep late. Fine reproductions and period antiques remind you of local history and Jefferson's omnipresent and enduring influence. Indeed, Monticello is just minutes away and Ashlawn, James Monroe's home, a stone's throw farther. Those wanting to explore vineyards, historical sites (including the magnificent University of Virginia), famous gardens and antique shops find this inn centrally located for a day's foray in any direction.

Guests in a lazy mood need not feel guilty napping in the hammock or sipping ice tea between croquet matches. Afternoon wine is served on the porch as is breakfast, weather permitting.

Location	*From I-64, take Highway 20 heading south and go 0.3 miles after stoplight. Inn entrance is marked with a sign on right, just past sign for Constitution Route*
Season	*All year-round*
Dining	*Breakfast. Picnic lunches prepared with advance notice*
Children	*Over 12 only*
Pets	*No*
Payment	*Visa, MasterCard, cash, check*
Rates	*From $95 to $130 plus tax, double occupancy. Deduct $10 for singles and add $25 for third person*

Country charm close to town

SILVER THATCH INN

3001 Hollymead Drive
Charlottesville, VA 22901

Vince and Rita Scoffone
(804) 978-4686

Hospitality resides at the Silver Thatch Inn from the early morning breakfast greeting to the after-dinner farewell. That the Scoffones, who bought the charming clapboard home in 1992, are newcomers to Charlottesville and innkeeping, is not obvious in either regard: Vince knows the area almost as well as a native and can advise you on area's offerings, and Rita greets visitors as if they were her dearest friends. She loves people and it shows.

One of the oldest buildings in this part of Virginia, dating back to 1780, the Silver Thatch was built by Hessian soldiers who were captured during the Revolutionary War. The two-story cabin they put up on the site of a former Indian settlement, now part of the inn, is known as the Hessian Room. Note the handsome oak floors, original beams and log wall remains on the staircase. The central part of the inn (1812) once served as a boys' school, and the final wing and cottage were added in 1937 and 1984 respectively.

Today the inn, framed with charming gardens and retaining an aura of plantation elegance, includes seven guest rooms, a restaurant with three intimate dining rooms and a cozy bar. Each room, three in the main building and four in the cottage, is named for a Virginia-born president and has its own unique motif and personality. All have private baths and several have fireplaces.

In the intimate, candlelit dining rooms, Modern American cuisine is beautifully presented under exacting standards. A sample of daily entrees includes veal, unusual seafood and vegetarian dishes, the salmon, with a variety of sauces, being the chef's signature dish. The Inn has received the coveted Wine Spectator Award for Excellence for its selection of fine domestic and Virginia wines.

Silver Thatch Inn. *Charlottesville, Virginia*

Close to the excitement of downtown Charlottesville (and the famous homes of presidents Jefferson, Madison and Monroe) but tucked into a private, quiet setting, Silver Thatch is a romantic relic from Virginia's early history with all the comforts and amenities for a contemporary, discriminating clientele.

Location	*From Washington, D.C., take I-66 to exit at Gainesville, U.S. Route 29 South. Go one mile past Charlottesville airport road and turn left at traffic light onto Rt. 1520. From Richmond take I-64 West to U.S. Rt. 250 West. Follow this to U.S. Rt. 29 North and proceed five miles, turning right at the Inn sign at Route 1520.*
Dining	*Continental Plus breakfast included; dining room open Tuesday through Saturday 5:30 to 9:00 P.M. Average dinner $35.00 per person*
Season	*Year-round except December 24 and 25*
Children	*Well-behaved children over five are welcome for both lodging and dining*
Pets	*No*
Rate	*$105 to $125*
Payment	*Visa, MasterCard, checks, cash*

Elegant little hotel in town

200 SOUTH STREET INN

Charlottesville, VA 22902

Brendan Clancy
(804) 979-0200 or (800) 964-7008

As times change, a building's use can change, and what goes on inside can affect its character in extremes. This is certainly true of the main house of 200 South Street, which in its lifetime has been both splendid and sullied in reputation.

In its early days, the 1856 structure was home to Thomas Jefferson Wertenbaker, son of a close friend to the former president, and then served as primary residence to members of the Valentine family of Richmond, for whom the famed Valentine Museum is named. Later it served as a girls' finishing school. Oh, but how its personality changed afterward. It isn't told if any of the young ladies who received training here signed on when the place became a brothel. The mantels and floors have seen it all.

Today, after a complete restoration, the house has regained its pride. Two buildings make up the present property, which is one block from Charlottesville's pedestrian mall and within walking distance of other parts of the historic district. A Victorian "cottage" (1890s) complements the older main house, and between them there are 17 rooms and three suites, all with modern private baths. Some have fireplaces and whirlpools.

The inn is lavishly, expensively, decorated. The canopy beds, fine furnishings, English and Belgian antiques and sparkling white tile and whirlpools may give some guests a feeling that the interior is overdone, setting a somewhat impersonal tone in comparison to the warmth of other inns. However, others who groove on these things will love the ceramic dalmatian-leopard baring his teeth and claws beneath a large gilded mirror in the hallway.

To regain your balance, sip some tea or wine in a wicker chair out on the neo-classical veranda. If it's still morning in warm weather, that's a nice place to have your breakfast too. There are many restauranteurs in the area eager to feed you at other mealtimes.

Location	*Charlottesville: Coming from Richmond take Exit 23 from Rt. 64; follow signs for Charlottesville. At third traffic light turn right onto South Street. Inn is one half block on right*
Season	*Year round*
Dining	*Continental breakfast plus*
Children	*Yes; crib available. No charge for children 12 and under*
Pets	*No*

Payment *Checks, Visa, MasterCard, AmEx*

Rates *$90–$170*

Colonial coach-stop inn

WOODSTOCK HALL

Rt. 10, Box 297
Charlottesville, VA 22903

Munsey and Jean Wheby; Clarence and Mary Ann Elder
(804) 293-8977

What a delight! An historic house restored to museum quality without the feeling that every room should have a velvet cord across the doorway. This colonial coach-stop inn has been returned to its original beauty and use.

The sycamores of Woodstock Hall were hardly more than saplings when a French nobleman stayed a night there in June 1796, after visiting Thomas Jefferson at Monticello. In his travel journal, the Duc de la Rochefoucauld wrote about the inn "with pleasure," describing it as "so good and cleanly."

A generation later, Edgar Allen Poe may have passed occasional nights in the enlarged tavern beneath the same trees, by then well established. A student at the University of Virginia in 1826, he often took long hikes through these hills; Woodstock Hall was a convenient place to stay.

More than 160 years have passed since Poe wandered by, and those sycamores shade the inn still. After a century of disuse, travelers are once again welcome.

Woodstock Hall is perhaps above all a triumphant example of historic preservation, and certainly a rescue of major personal effort by its owners, Munsey and Jean Wheby and Clarence and Mary Ann Elder. When the two couples bought the dilapidated eyesore in 1984, a developer's bulldozer was virtually snarling at the steps. Half a million dollars and two and a half years later the inn reopened, a state and national historic landmark.

Consisting of two sections, the original 1757 Georgian struc-ture and a Federal wing added in 1808, Woodstock Hall has been lovingly, and meticulously, restored. A muted glow has returned to the old pigment deep in wood and the unpolished heart-of-pine floors. The new paint colors are the same as those found closest to the wood surface—the first colors—and that includes the gold exterior, warm like honey against a backdrop of what Poe called "ragged mountains." Most of the floors are original, as are the mantels, wainscotting and wrought-iron hinged doors. The central hall has holders for Katy bars (as in "Katy, bar the door!"), and the Georgian part of the house features a rare stair-well with its own window.

The inn has three upstairs suites and one in the summer kitchen, an outbuilding. All have private baths and working fireplaces with wood available. The inn is centrally air condi-tioned. The rooms are complete with period furnishings, in-cluding a king-size adaptation of a Federal canopy bed. The original blue stain has been saved on the mantel of one suite. Rental includes use of the Federal parlor, sitting rooms, tavern keeping-room and the inviting patio beneath the trees.

Breakfast is served in the stenciled, check-floored keeping-room. The menu varies from day to day, sometimes including sherried eggs and fruit croissants. Tea is served in the afternoon. Although dinner is not offered, it can be specially arranged for groups occupying the whole house. There are many fine restau-rants in nearby Charlottesville.

It is one thing to peer into history from behind a velvet cord; it is quite another to become a part of it. Your visit continues the purpose of Woodstock Hall begun more than 230 years ago, and that's what makes it so special.

Location	*West of Charlottesville, 1.8 miles south of I-64 Exit 114 (Ivy), just ten minutes from University of Virginia and downtown area*
Season	*Year round*
Dining	*Breakfast; afternoon tea; champagne is offered to honeymooners and anniversary celebrants*
Children	*Not under age 8*
Pets	*No*

Payment   *Check, cash*
Rates   *$95–$130 per night, depending on suite desired*

Chatham

Books, bears and high tea

HOUSE OF LAIRD

335 South Main Street
P.O. Box 1131
Chatham, VA 24531

Cecil and Ed Laird
(804) 432-2523

It was on a Friday night when Ed and Cecil Laird came upon an ad in *Southern Living* for an 1880 mansion on Main Street in Chatham, VA. On the following Monday they flew from their home in southern California to have a look at it; before that day was over, they had bought it and were on the move East.

It takes the visitor only a few minutes of savoring the exquisite place the Lairds have created out of the old mansion to confirm that they made a great purchase. Also, they have made many wise decisions in furnishing and decorating it. The House of Laird is filled with antiques, Oriental rugs and all sizes of amusing stuffed bears. Despite the massiveness of some of the furniture, there's a lightness and sweet-scented airiness that permeates every room of the house.

The unusually fine antique pieces, half of which are English, bespeak Cecil Laird's background. She grew up in Lexington, VA, she will tell you, but her family lives in England. (One does not mention the handsome antiques in the presence of her husband without her teasing about his ultimatum: "No more antiques!") A pair of tall, slender sideboards at the end of the commodious entry hall are stocked with sherry, wine and other complimentary drinks and snacks generously proffered by the host. If you arrive late in the afternoon, you can be welcomed with an English high tea, an option which must be planned for in advance.

Guests whose tastes run to books are captivated by the Library Suite on the main floor. Here, as in each of the three bedrooms upstairs, there is a working fireplace. The Library Suite, however, has not one but two fireplaces, one in each of its two rooms. The lavishly draped four-poster bed befits a bride and groom or a couple celebrating an anniversary.

Guests who come here are people who generally bypass hotels. They may plan to visit Poplar Forest, Thomas Jefferson's country retreat, or Appomattox. Or they may be seeing their children at Hargrove Military Academy or Chatham Hall. Chatham, the girl's school, is known nationally for its most famous graduate, artist Georgia O'Keefe.

The Lairds encourage their guests to bring their own bicycles. There is space to park them, along with cars, in the Carriage House at the back. If you plan to bike you can count on a hearty breakfast that starts with Ed's "Smoothie," his own blend of juices and strawberries. If you don't intend to work off breakfast but want to enjoy its sumptuousness to the full, better leave your calorie counter in the car. Cecil makes all the breads herself!

Location	*Two hours south of Charlottesville on U.S. 29 Business, Main Street, Chatham*
Dining	*Continental breakfast served between 7:00–10:00 A.M., full breakfast between 8:30–10:00 A.M.*
Season	*Year round*
Children	*Well-behaved children over the age of ten*
Pets	*No*
Payment	*Credit cards, check, cash*
Rates	*From $38 to $78*

Christiansburg

An inn house with "presence"

THE OAKS

311 East Main Street
Christiansburg, VA 24073

Margaret and Tom Ray
(703) 381-1500

This elegant, cheerful 1889 country manor is not what one thinks of as classic Victorian, dark and somber. The yellow Queen Anne style house radiates a warm glow. Turrets rising to the third floor, and large double-hung windows open the rooms to an abundance of natural light. An extra bonus is the intangible bouyancy inside that owners Margaret and Tom Ray attribute to the "presence," a sense of well being and optimism left over from when the original owners, Major William Pierce and his large family, lived here. This aura of good will extends throughout the house, even to the regal oaks outside, hundreds of years old. Like welcoming arms, the ancient branches spread across the lawn embracing an area nearly as wide as the tree's formidable height.

Consistent with this "presence" of hospitality, Margaret and Tom Ray set their priorities for the maximum comfort and pleasure of their guests. Particularly proud of her luxurious linens, which she irons herself, Margaret puts out extra thick, fluffy towels and robes, and splurges on designer sheets, lace spreads, crocheted canopies and stunning quilts.

The five rooms—each decorated around a different theme—are furnished with antiques and accented with the Rays' personal collections and art (some by architect Tom) acquired from years of travel. All have telephones, spacious private baths and discreetly hidden fridges. In several rooms, the wallpaper itself approaches art: exquisite and imaginatively applied.

The Julia Pierce room on the second floor, named for the major's wife, witnessed the birth of seven Pierce offspring. (Five generations of the family have visited the house since the Rays took charge in 1989). Bathed in soft peach tones, the room has

The Oaks. *Christiansburg, Virginia*

a handsome hand-painted slate fireplace, turret windows, gay wicker furniture and a large bath and jacuzzi for two. One flight up, in the opulent Lady Melodie's Turret, the skylight, fireplace and windows tempt guest to linger over sunset views. Bird watchers should choose the Bonnie Victoria Room from whose king, canopied bed, one looks to the garden and oaks.

The common areas include an wrap-around porch, garden gazebo with hot tub, sunroom, parlor, study and entrance hall, which the Rays light at dusk with candles.

Food fanciers find their favorite room candle-lit and the table set with sterling silver, china and fresh flowers to complement a gourmet low-cholesterol breakfast that might include rum raisin French toast or buttermilk pancakes in praline syrup with toasted pecans.

With all this luxury priced very reasonably, it is no wonder The Oaks has a three diamond AAA rating, three star Mobil and four crown ABBA, and in 1992 was named among the top twelve inns of the year.

Location   From I-81 take Exit 114. At bottom of ramp turn left if coming from the south and right if coming from the north onto Main St. Continue about 2 miles to fork at Park and Main; bear right on Park and left into the Oaks

Season   Year-round

Dining   Full breakfast

Children   14 years and older

Pets   No

Payment   Visa, MasterCard, AmEx, Discover, check

Rates   Double occupancy, Sunday through Thursday, $95 to 110 (corporate rate $75); Friday and Saturday $105–120

Culpeper

All aboard for a step back in time

FOUNTAIN HALL

609 South East Street
Culpeper, VA 22701-3222

Steve and Kathi Walker
(703) 825-8200 or (800) 476-2944

Now that US 29 bypasses Culpeper, things have settled down to a more relaxed pace in this farm country town. Tourists, college students, business travelers and everybody else now speed by on the outskirts, leaving Main Street to the locals and visitors who like the feel of small towns that retain a character all their own. Undisturbed by rapid growth, Culpeper and Fountain Hall take you back to a time when more people traveled by rail than air. You can still get there by train, and they still serve malts at the pharmacy soda fountain.

Built as a simple Country Victorian home in 1859, Fountain Hall wasn't the grandest home in town when Jackson Lee Fray, a prominent businessman, bought it in 1923. But according to a local tale, making it so played an important role in the new owner's love life. In a pre-nuptial agreement with the mayor—his future father-in-law—Fray agreed to provide his new bride with the "biggest house in Culpeper." He went all the way to Philadelphia to find an architect to design the present Colonial Revival building using much of the original structure. All the old fireplaces, the foundation and most of the walls were incorporated in the new design. The house you now see apparently satisfied the "biggest" requirement!

The small-town feel is emphasized when you arrive at Fountain Hall and see that it is both nestled into an old established neighborhood and on the edge of town. Out the back is a dairy farm and the railroad tracks. Furnished mostly with antique pieces from the 1800s to 1950s, the inn exudes homey comfort. Three of Fountain Hall's five guestrooms have porches. Other rooms include a den, drawing room, dining room, breakfast room and a bright conservatory filled with plants. In the winter months the fireplace is lit making the den a cozy place to gather. The grounds are meticulously kept. Formal gardens and a variety of trees surround the property. Flower beds and vegetable gardens flourish most of the year.

Innkeepers Steve and Kathi Walker cater to the needs of travelers who want the finest accommodations and a good night's sleep. Each room is tastefully restored and decorated in antique decor. All have a phone and offer private bath facilities. The sun-lit breakfast room is the morning gathering place for enjoying home-baked croissants and freshly brewed coffee. Fresh fruits, hot and cold cereals, a variety of teas and friendly conversation will brighten the start of your day.

Culpeper is a part of the Main Street Program developed by the National Trust for Historic Preservation, which seeks to keep the architecture and flavor of America's small towns intact. A walking tour of historic Culpeper is available. Several large Virginia wineries are nearby, and also Commonwealth Park, a riding facility that is the site of major horse shows. Twenty minutes away is heavily wooded South Wales Golf Course, a public course where the wildlife is plentiful and you might have to aim your drive to avoid deer in the fairway.

In addition to its preserved small town atmosphere, Culpeper is the home of Ace Books and Consignments, a book browsers paradise. Organized in categories similar to a general bookstore, Ace offers roughly 200,000 books on just about every subject.

For those who like trains, Culpeper is a stop on Amtrak's Cardinal and Crescent lines. Fountain Hall is only six blocks from the station, and shuttle service is available.

Location	*Historic Culpeper*
Season	*Year round*
Dining	*Breakfast*
Children	*Yes; must be supervised at all times. Cribs available*
Pets	*No. Local kennels available*
Payment	*Visa, MasterCard, AmEx, Discover, check, cash*
Rates	*$65–$115* *$50 (Business rate)*

Flint Hill

Back to school

THE FLINT HILL PUBLIC HOUSE

Rt. 522, P.O. Box 605
Flint Hill, VA 22627

Robin and Conrad Koneczny
(703) 675-1700, (800) 551-4142

The Flint Hill Public House accommodates its guests in an imaginatively renovated 1900 school house that served as a grammar school until 1964. After standing vacant for a decade, the building was converted into a residence, then a restaurant, but the character of its original purpose remains: one can almost hear the animated echo of children laughing on their way to recess, ebullient and free.

Two of the larger class rooms on the first floor are now comfortable, popular dining areas: The Colony Room, a more formal, sophisticated setting, and the Public Room, where local farmers mix with city visitors and both feel at home. While the menu spans traditional favorites (grilled trout, crab cakes and steaks), more classical cuisine is offered on weekends, such as pheasant breast and pan-seared salmon. A separate menu is prepared for Sunday brunch, served 11:00 A.M. to 3:00 P.M. Smoking is allowed only in the Parlor, an informal gathering spot/watering hole where appetizer-portions complement friendly chatter and cold beer. The wine list, which pays special honor to Virginia selections, has been lauded "complete and comprehensive."

Upstairs, two large spacious rooms furnished with period antiques, and each with queen size bed and bath across the hall, accommodate overnighters. A large common sitting area allows for reading, writing or TV viewing. A conference room on this level accommodates 16 for meetings or 26 for private dinner parties.

At the back of the school, guests gather on the deck to dine al fresco while taking in the view of the surrounding five acres of land, well kept gardens and panorama of the Blue Ridge Mountains. In keeping with traditional Virginia hospitality, the management stresses warmth and friendliness. A general feeling of relaxation prevails, and while the staff has a respect for schedules and duties, there is never a sense of being rushed.

Location   *Take I-66 West to Exit 27 (second Marshall exit), bear left over I-66 and turn right onto Rt. 647. Go about 17 miles and turn right onto Route 522. Flint Hill Public House will be on the left in the center of Flint Hill*

Season   *Year round*

Dining   *The full breakfast included in room rate is usually* *orange French toast with bacon or sausage, home fries, fruit and juice, but other fare is available with notice. Lunch and dinner served daily to the public*

Pets   *With a cash deposit of $250 held until departure*

Children   *Well behaved and supervised*

Payment   *MasterCard, Visa, check, cash*

Rates   *$75–$95 double occupancy*

Front Royal

Main Street hospitality with international flair

CHESTER HOUSE BED & BREAKFAST

43 Chester Street
Front Royal, VA 22630

Bill and Ann Wilson
(800) 621-0441 or (703) 635-3937

The stolid, stately exterior of Chester House, a Georgian-style mansion in Front Royal's historic district, does not prepare the first-time visitor for the light, lofty spaciousness of its center hall and the lovely rooms surrounding it: formal living room, sunken dining room, garden/game room, TV parlor and portico. One's spirits rise, as well as one's eyes, as he takes in architectural details, the quality of which one rarely sees today outside of museum houses.

An international lawyer, Charles Samuels, who helped write the Versailles Treaty following World War I, bought the property at public auction in 1897. It had been the childhood home of his mother, and he replaced the original building in 1905 with Chester House, which she used as her residence and he, as a vacation/retirement home. Samuels ordered chandeliers and statuary from Europe and many mantels. The most outstanding mantel, intricately carved from white Italian marble, is the showpiece of the dining room. He had the house so well insulated and cooled that even now the Wilsons use air-conditioning only for the bedrooms upstairs.

Seven wide windows with billowing white curtains afford a romantic view from upstairs of the terraced boxwood gardens below at the back. Called the Royal Oak Suite, this bedroom has its own sitting room. Another suite, the Shenandoah, can be rented as two separate rooms if desired.

The Wilsons regard 99 percent of their guests "like family," who, after being treated so warmly, come back time and again. Several come from Canada and Europe. It was fitting that the Chief Justice of the Supreme Court of Norway visited this house built by an international lawyer; he came with his wife shortly after she had been appointed the first woman president of Oslo University. Says Bill: "It's like going traveling and sitting in your own living room at the same time."

Ann Wilson, a former veterinary technician, has a sister who is a midwife in New Zealand, and at one time Bill was a production supervisor in a plant in Australia. He has had seven different careers, from manufacturing to stock brokering. (Ann interjects: "The family joke used to be that when Ann got bored she redecorated; when Bill got bored he quit his job.")

Having, with his talented wife, decorated and maintained this beautiful place for five years, he shows no sign whatsoever of wanting to do anything else. Of all his experiences, being an innkeeper, he swears, demands "the longest hours, the most work and is the most rewarding and least stressful."

When it's time for dinner or entertainment, guests can stroll to the newly renovated Main Street of Front Royal where there are several restaurants, or take in a summer evening concert at the gazebo in the Village Common. Incorporated only two years after the American colonies declared independence, Front Royal in May 1862 was the opening battle of General "Stonewall" Jackson's storied Valley Campaign. Civil War buffs will want to visit the Confederate museum just down the street from the mansion. Next door there is the cottage inhabited by Belle Boyd, the colorful Southern spy.

Location	From I-66 take Exit 6 south on Rt. 340 to Main Street. Turn left on Main. From Skyline Drive, go north on Rt. 340, turn right on Main St. and take second left onto Chester Street
Season	Year round
Dining	Continental breakfast. Complimentary tea, wine and cheese
Children	Over the age of 12
Pets	No
Payment	Visa, MasterCard, AmEx, cash, checks
Rates	$60 to $105 for rooms; $170 for Shenandoah suite

Harrisonburg

Board as beautiful as the beds

THE JOSHUA WILTON HOUSE

412 S. Main Street
Harrisonburg, VA 22801

Roberta and Craig Moore
(703) 434-4464

"Roberta and Craig Moore will spoil you," they say, "with complimentary wine or beer and a gourmet breakfast including homemade pastries, fresh fruits and steaming coffee." They spoil you with even more than food in this handsomely restored Victorian house on S. Main Street. In the heart of historic downtown Harrisonburg, within walking distance of James Madison University, the house was built originally around 1888 by Joshua Wilton who had moved south from Canada to open a foundry and hardware business. In addition to bringing electricity to the little city (current population is 35,000), Wilton built a solid, imposing brick house with turrets, porch and gingerbread trim.

Inside, the doors are heavy oak, the floors parquet. The Moores, in their restoration, maintained the grandness of the original, avoiding the heaviness often seen in old Victorian houses. The five guest rooms and baths upstairs are luxurious, yet light and airy. They are especially inviting after one of Chef Craig's "button-popping" meals downstairs. John Barrett, columnist for "Dining Out," *Richmond Times Dispatch*, claimed this was the best restaurant he'd eaten at in a whole year.

While Craig reigns at the range or outside at the grill, Roberta presides over the salads, breads and desserts. She creates a *creme brulee* so ethereal, in the words of *Bon Appetite*, it "could steal a Frenchman's allegiance."

The three dining rooms are open to the public. They have been so popular with residents and visitors that the Moores, in the same year they added a baby to their household, added a cafe at the back in the sun room and on the terrace. Dinners here range from $6.95 to $13.95, featuring beef, fish and pasta dishes. Dinners in the formal dining rooms range from $16.95 to $20.95 and are served Tuesday to Saturday starting at 5:30 P.M. It need hardly be added that reservations are required.

Location	*From Washington, D.C. take I-66 to I-81 towards Roanoke. Take Exit 245 west on Port Republic Rd. to Main Street. Turn right and go about 1 mile*
Season	*Year round*
Dining	*Continental breakfast included; restaurant open for dinner Tuesday to Saturday.*
Children	*Ten and over*
Pets	*No*
Payment	*MasterCard, Visa, AmEx, checks, cash*
Rates	*$85–$100*
Other Considerations	*Restricted smoking*

Hot Springs

All that's fit and more. . .

KING'S VICTORIAN INN

Route 2, Box 622
Hot Springs, VA 24445

Liz and Richard King
(703) 839-3134

It seems fitting that the man who built and owned the mansion now known as King's Victorian Inn was Dr. Henry S. Pole, a holistic physician who is said to have acquired an unequaled knowledge of the health-promoting benefits of the nearby spas. Everything about this magnificent place promotes peace of mind and ease of body.

Set in a grove of old maple trees on three lovely acres in Bath County, the doctor's mansion shuts out the clang of contemporary life. Its turrets and bay windows outside and the exquisite antique furnishings, stained glass and tiled fireplaces inside give off an air of 19th-century refinement. Yet there is nothing stuffy about this magnificent restoration done by its present owners, Liz and Richard King.

Their inviting wraparound porches lined with rocking chairs bid you to sit awhile and ease into the gentler pace of this peaceful valley. As you sit and sip (refreshments are served as soon as you arrive), you come to feel what true Southern hospitality is all about. You may be regaled with a story or two about the good doctor. He had 12 children, and he was the first resident of the area to buy an automobile, a noisy contraption that disturbed the local peace. The neighbors tried unsuccessfully to have autos outlawed on Bath County roads. (It should be noted, however, that there are still no traffic lights anywhere in the county.)

The mansion must have had other noisy moments after Dr. Pole sold to A.E. Dudley. Dudley renamed the place "Manor Terrace" and filled it variously with the bustle of a restaurant, barber house, leather shop and rooming house. When Liz and

King's Victorian Inn. *Hot Springs, Virginia*

photo by Anita Back

Richard King found the place during a vacation trip in 1987, it had been a quiet family dwelling for more than two decades.

Although the Kings have altered the interior somewhat, much remains as it was originally, such as six fireplace mantels. Most recently they have remodeled the old ice house behind the main dwelling into a pleasant guest cottage with its own little kitchen and porch. Counting the cottage, they now have five commodious units (three with private baths) that can accommodate 12 guests in all.

If you drag yourself away from the comfort, you can walk along the trails to downtown Hot Springs. Lunch at the Cafe Albert or dine at Sam Snead's Tavern. Only 150 yards away at the Homestead Hotel, the nationally-known resort, there are three 18-hole championship golf courses. Also available at the Homestead are dining and dancing, tennis, horseback and carriage riding, skeet shooting, spas, and winter skiing and skating.

Location   *From I-81 in Staunton, VA, take Route 250 West to Buffalo Gap, Route 42 west to Goshen, Route 39*

west to Warm Springs, Route 220 south four miles on right. There's a sign in front and name on mail box.
From I-64 in Covington, VA, take Route 220 north to Hot Springs. Continue past Sam Snead Tavern. Inn is third house on the left (about one mile).

Season	*Year round. Closed Thanksgiving and Christmas*
Dining	*All-American (hearty) breakfast included*
Children	*Not recommended for small children; no cribs*
Pets	*No*
Payment	*Checks, cash, travelers' checks*
Rates	*From $79–$125; $25 extra for 3rd person in room*

Hospitality has always been here

VINE COTTAGE INN

P.O. Box 918
Hot Springs, VA 24445

Pat and Wendell Lucas
(703) 839-2422 or (800) 666-VINE (8463)

The Vine Cottage Inn, located in Hot Springs, VA, in the midst of beautiful Bath County, has been receiving overnight guests since it was built in the early 1900s. Large and rambling with many angled gables and a wraparound porch, the three-story inn is a non-intimidating contrast to its neighbor just steps away, the huge Homestead resort. Although the proximity to the resort has its advantages—inn guests may use the resort's famous Cascades golf courses as well as its skating, skiing and other recreation facilities—the main attraction of a stay at Vine Cottage is its homeyness. "Our philosophy," say innkeepers Pat and Wendell Lucas, "is to make our home available to you. We want you to feel as relaxed and comfortable at Vine Cottage as you do in your home." The Lucases' home is enriched by the interesting mementoes and stories they acquired while living in other parts of the world, including Europe, the Far East and the Mid-East.

Together with their two daughters, Phaedra and Ashley, the family came to Hot Springs in 1984 when they acquired the inn.

By then the inn's hallmark of hospitality was etched in time. One innkeeper, Mrs. Sally, had become famous in the area in the 1930s for her brand of conviviality and her good cooking. Aware that old-style country inns aren't for everyone anymore, the Lucases look for "travelers who seek simple comfort and hospitality, quiet and tranquility, charm and quaintness." This you'll find in each of the inn's 13 refreshing, country-style guest rooms. Two rooms called "dorms," can sleep six people each and are popular with skiing and golfing groups. The others are single and double rooms, all with a sink and nine with private baths and claw-footed tubs. A spacious, inviting sitting room, with fireplace, TV and loaded bookshelves, is on the first floor. "Sticky" buns and sweet bread are part of the country continental breakfast served. Dinner can be prepared with advance notice.

Many inn guests enjoy taking the "waters" at either Hot or Warm Springs. The namesake of Bath County, the springs date back to 1761 when a gentleman's pool was opened in Warm Springs. With temperatures reaching 96 degrees, Warm Springs now has two bath houses. The Hot Springs, now in the Homestead Spa, reach 106 degrees and feature other heat- and water-induced delights including a whirlpool, a steam room, an exercise tank and, for those who like it dry, a sauna.

Location	*On US 220 North from Covington, VA*
Season	*Open year round except December 24 and 25*
Dining	*Continental breakfast, dinner on order*
Children	*Yes*
Pets	*No*
Payment	*Cash, MasterCard, Visa, personal or business check*
Rates	*Single ranges from $40–$55, double ranges from $55–$85. Breakfast included in room rate*

Leesburg

For history buffs and lovers of tradition

LAUREL BRIGADE INN

20 West Market Street
Leesburg, VA 22075

Ellen Flippo Wall
(703) 777-1010

Innkeeper Ellen Wall says when her father, Roy Flippo, began his tenure as the operator of the Laurel Brigade in 1949 "rooms were $3.00 for a single and $6.00 for a double. A steak dinner was $2.95 and chicken, $2.50. Today the taxes on the building are more than my father paid for it." Obviously everything costs more today—including lodging and meals at this inn—but history buffs and lovers of tradition will want to sample the goings-on here.

Located one hour from Washington, DC, in the heart of historic Leesburg, this landmark dates back to 1759 when it began offering bed and board to people traveling between Winchester and Alexandria. Records show it standing on Lot Number 30 in the original town plan. The stone structure you see today was built in 1820 to replace the original log house and was described then as "a tavern, the finest in Leesburg." A wing was added in 1825—as legend has it—to entertain the Marquis de Lafayette when he visited James Monroe at nearby Oak Hill.

Beginning in 1854 travelers had to stay elsewhere because a local physician, Dr. A.R. Mott, acquired the inn for his residence. Many of the building's best improvements were made while Dr. Mott lived here, and they remain among the inn's highlights. These include the addition of French marble mantel pieces, the installation of unusual Swiss door fixtures and the planting of lovely gardens at the rear of the inn. The building on Lot 30 didn't return to serving the public until Ellen's father purchased it at public auction following the death of the last of the Mott family.

The inn's restaurant, which can serve up to 175 people, is an enormous draw. The facilities are often used for civic club events, parties and weddings. The main dining room alone seats 100 people and serves traditional American food including locally grown fruits and vegetables. All the bread and pastry baking is done on the premises. Overnight lodging is available in eight guest rooms, each of which has a private bath and air conditioning. The rooms are furnished with a collection of antiques and period reproductions and are comfortable, albeit plain. There are no phones or TVs.

Sightseers should stop by the Visitors' Center located at 16 W. Loudoun Street. Among the bits of history to be picked up on a visit to Leesburg is the source for the inn's name. The Laurel Brigade was a Confederate cavalry group whose commander and many of its members came from the Leesburg area. The brigade made the last cavalry charge of the Civil War near the Appomattox Courthouse, but refused to surrender. They chose instead to ride to Lynchburg, and there they disbanded.

Location	*The inn is in the heart of the historic district, one half block west of the intersection of King St. (Business Rt. 15) and Market St. (Business Rt. 7)*
Season	*Year round; Closed Mondays*
Children	*Yes*
Pets	*No*
Payment	*Cash, travelers' check, personal check*
Rates	*Range from $50–$85, double occupancy*

A brick beauty graciously restored

THE NORRIS HOUSE INN

108 Loudoun Street, SW
Leesburg, VA 22075

Pam and Don McMurray
(703) 777-1806

The Norris House Inn. *Leesburg, Virginia*

Built in 1806 and located only one hour northwest of Washington, DC, in downtown historic Leesburg, the brick Federal-style home with its handsome green shutters, ornamental windows and elaborate dentil molding, was owned by the Norris family from 1850 until conversion to an inn in 1983. The inn was recently acquired by Don and Pam McMurray, former business executives who have spent a year lovingly renewing, refurbishing and expanding.

Complimentary beverages await arriving guests. The entire house is open to them. The library, one of the favorite rooms, has built-in bookcases that typify the exceptionally fine woodworking found throughout the inn. Each of the six guest rooms has a comfortable sitting area and all are beautifully decorated.

They share three baths. Two rooms have working fireplaces with fires laid for guests.

The recent expansion of the inn includes The Old Stone House next door, purported to be Washington's headquarters during the French and Indian War of 1753–54. The new facilities are used for a lovely Tea Room with service on the weekends and during special events. The expanded area also includes additional functional rooms that make the inn an ideal setting for business retreats or family reunions. The expanded garden area provides a lovely respite and serves as a spectacular setting for many special events.

The inn is conveniently located within walking distance to several fine restaurants. Pam and Don also invite you to dine alfresco in the inn's garden by prior arrangement.

Location	*From Dulles International take Route 28 north to Route 28 north to Route 7 and northwest to Leesburg. From Washington, DC, take Route 7 west into Leesburg. Keep left at the fork and then drive four blocks to the inn on your right*
Season	*Year round*
Dining	*Full country breakfast, tea, alfresco and catered dinners by prior arrangement*
Children	*Yes, except weekends*
Pets	*No*
Payment	*Personal check, cash, Visa, MasterCard*
Rates	*$70–$140, double occupancy*

Lexington

Far more than a farm house

FASSIFERN

Rt. 5, Box 87
Lexington, VA 24450
Ann Carol and Arthur Perry
(703) 463-1013

The Fassifern B&B rests on property once part of a 1,500-acre farm owned by Thos S. White, a Civil War veteran, prominent merchant and farmer. White had acquired the land when he married Sallie Cameron after the war. Known then as Fassifern Stock Farm, it derived its name from the Cameron clan chief's house on Loch Eli in Scotland. The main house you see today, built in 1867 on the same foundation of an older structure, has been renovated and converted together with two outbuildings to provide attractive and relaxing accommodations for travelers.

The handsome three-story house is far more than what you might expect of a house once associated with a working farm. Now in the midst of 3½ acres of pastures, lawns and pond, shaded by century-old maples and oaks, the home has taupe painted brick, a formal green terne-plate roof, distinctive cornices and moldings and a second-story bay window that illuminates a hall-way seating area. Located on Route 39, which is a scenic byway and a part of the TransAmerica Bike Trail, this B&B is but a half mile away from the entrance to the Virginia Horse Center. And it is only two miles from the center of historic Lexington.

Innkeepers Ann Carol and Arthur Perry are continuing the course begun by Fassifern's previous owners. Restoration was completed in 1986 and outbuildings converted in 1987. Ann Carol's mother, Frances Smith, purchased Fassifern in 1989 for her daughter and son-in-law to operate. Thus, it was a turnkey operation, leaving Ann Carol and Arthur to concentrate on their knack for innkeeping. Special touches in the rooms such as fresh flowers, baskets of toiletries and lots of reading materials linger long in guests' memories of this delightful place. The Perrys are also eager to offer suggestions on area sightseeing.

Each of the four guest rooms in the main house has a private bath. Behind the main house is the Dependency. Inside, the Colonel's Quarters has a queen-sized bed and full bath. The Pond Room has a double bed, shower, private entrance and deck. All rooms are air-conditioned. Granola, three-grain muffins, bread pudding, apple crisp and country ham spread are only part of the expanded continental breakfast.

Location	*Fassifern is located on Rt. 39 near the US 11 and I-64 interchange. From I-81 take Exit 52 West (I-64) near Lexington. Take Exit 13 (US 11 North) and travel 50 yards before turning left on Rt. 39 toward Goshen. Fassifern is three-quarters of a mile on the left*
Season	*Year round (closed Thanksgiving, Christmas Eve & Day, and New Year's Eve & Day)*
Dining	*Expanded continental breakfast*
Children	*No*
Pets	*No*
Payment	*Cash, personal check, major credit cards*
Rates	*Single: $65; double: $79 & $87; 3rd person in queen-sized guest rooms add $25*

Hard to choose which one

HISTORIC COUNTRY INNS OF LEXINGTON

11 North Main Street
Lexington, VA 24450

Don Fredenburg
(703) 463-2044

Peter Meredith's family developed a love for the town of Lexington over many years. Like his father, Peter Sr., and his son,

McCampbell Inn. *Lexington, Virginia*

Richard, Peter came to know the Shenandoah Valley town well as a student at the Virginia Military Institute. (All three Merediths are graduates of the Institute's Civil Engineering School.) It was only natural for the family to become involved in restoring three of the town's most venerable buildings: the Alexander-Withrow House and the McCampbell Inn, across from each other on Main Street, and Maple Hall, six miles north of town. The three inns, each designated Virginia Historic Landmarks, are now known collectively as the Historic Country Inns of Lexington.

In 1969, a group of caring Lexingtonians formed the Historic Lexington Foundation to save a three-story 1789 house from demolition and to restore its exterior. One of Lexington's oldest buildings, named for its first and last owners, the **Alexander-Withrow House** was later purchased from the Foundation by Mr. and Mrs. Carlson Thomas who refurbished the interior and opened it as an inn. The Merediths acquired the inn in 1978. Built as William Alexander's family residence and store and later used as a bank and a school, the building now offers six suites, beautifully appointed with 18- and 19th-century antiques. Distinctive yet not pretentious, each suite features refreshment centers stocked with coffee, tea and juice, individual temperature controls, phone and private bath. Of special interest is the building's basement, exposed to the outside when Main Street was lowered in 1850, and the "diapering" in the exterior brickwork. Ask about it if you don't know.

The Historic Lexington Foundation was also instrumental in preserving the **McCampbell Inn**. Built by John McCampbell in 1809, and added on to in 1816 and 1857, the large three-story brick building was later used as a jewelry store, a doctor's office and the town's telegraph and post office before being converted to the Central Hotel in 1907. The Foundation purchased the old hotel in 1972 and restored its exterior. Ten years later the Merediths acquired the property, gutted it and re-designed the interior. They re-named it in honor of its original owner. With several entrances and verandas, the McCampbell Inn offers 14 guest rooms and two suites furnished similarly to the Alexander-Withrow House and with the same amenities. The reception desk for both inns is in this building, as is McCampbell's Great Room where guests come to enjoy an expanded continental breakfast and an evening glass of wine.

Maple Hall, north of Lexington on Route 11 and high on a hill surrounded by mountains, was restored and opened as the third of the Historic Inns by the Merediths in 1985. The stately, three-story red-brick plantation house with impressive white columns and entrance stairways, was built by John Beard Gibson in 1850 on the 257-acre Maple Hill Plantation. The property stayed in the Gibson family until the Merediths purchased it. They bought 56 acres of the wooded hills and pasture land and a small brick building believed to be the original plantation house. Antiques abound in each of the inn's 13 beautifully decorated guest rooms, and there are working fireplaces in most. Unlike the downtown inns, Maple Hall serves an evening meal and Sunday brunch. Its three lower-level, intimate dining rooms shimmer with fine crystal and silver on dark blue tablecloths. Available by reservation to inn guests and the public, the a la carte menu (changed weekly) includes such choices as Chicken Pecan, Filet Mignon, Coquilles Saint Jacques and Lemon Pork. The continental breakfast is served either in a conservatory breakfast room or on the inn's shady patio. Across from this patio sits the venerable small brick building restored as a guest house. Suitable for a family get-together or mini-conference center, it provides three bedrooms with baths, a living room and a full kitchen.

Maple Hall may be the best choice of the three inns for those who enjoy outdoor activities. There are a tennis court and swimming pool on the grounds, a stocked ½-acre fishing pond and several miles of easy walking trails. All three of the inns tempt history buffs. Among the sites near Maple Hall are Cyrus McCormick's home, Wade's Mill (a 19th-century flour mill still active today), the Blue Ridge Parkway and Goshen Pass. In town and within easy walking distance of one another are the Stonewall Jackson Home and Museum, the George C. Marshall Museum and the Robert E. Lee Chapel and Museum.

A new addition is the **Pond House** with two guest rooms and four suites—all with fireplaces—and common living rooms for gathering.

Location	*The Alexander-Withrow House and McCampbell Inn are located on Main Street in downtown Lexington. Maple Hall is at Exit 53/ Milepost 195 off I-81 at Rt. 11 North*
Season	*Year round*
Dining	*Expanded continental breakfast*
Children	*Yes*
Pets	*No, but arrangements for kenneling may be made in advance*
Payment	*Visa, MasterCard and personal check*
Rates	*Single occupancy: range from $80 to $115 for inn rooms, $135 for Maple Hall Guest House. Add $15 for each additional person in room, $5 for children 12 and under*
Other Considerations	*No smoking requested in Maple Hall*

Historical, theatrical, gastronomical

LLEWELLYN LODGE AT LEXINGTON

603 S. Main Street
Lexington, VA 24450
Ellen and John Roberts
(703) 463-3235 or (800) 882-1145

When you are passing through the Shenandoah Valley and come to the town of Lexington, look up Ellen and John Roberts and stay at their B&B, the Llewellyn Lodge at Lexington. These two are guaranteed to help you get the most out of your visit to this area. Ellen is a 20-year veteran of the airline, travel and hospitality business and John is a knowledgeable, local Lexingtonian—which means he can lead you to things of importance, like the best fishing holes.

The B&B they run, on Main Street in an old residential neighborhood and within easy walking distance of the historic district, is an ideal spot from which to enjoy many of this town's most interesting sites. You will want to have your most comfortable shoes with you so sore feet won't keep you from walking to and through the sites associated with three of America's greatest generals: the home of Stonewall Jackson, the Robert E. Lee Chapel and Museum, and the Museum and Library of George C. Marshall. Small, quiet, with a relaxed atmosphere, the B&B is well-suited for overnight visitors to the Virginia Military Institute or Washington and Lee University, both nearby. It is also popular with area real estate shoppers who make it their overnight choice. All guests are treated to beverages and canapes upon arrival, compliments of Ellen and John.

Built in 1936, and remodeled in 1980 and again in 1985, the three-story colonial house, painted oyster gray, is furnished with antiques and period pieces collected from different parts of the world. Newly painted throughout and with central air conditioning, the B&B offers six guest rooms, each with private bath, extra-firm beds and soothing ceiling fans. Other parts of the house available for guests' use include an attractive living room with fireplace, a separate TV room, a dining room and an outdoor deck where, in good weather, the B&B's full gourmet breakfast is served. Tasty eye-openers range from omelettes and Belgian waffles to homemade muffins.

When you are through absorbing history, you can go hiking on the Chessie Trail, bicycle riding on country roads, canoeing on the Maury River, tubing and picnicking at Goshen Pass, trout fishing in any of several clean streams, skiing at Wintergreen and golfing and tennis playing at the Lexington Golf and Country Club. Of special interest are the Virginia Horse Center and the Lime Kiln Arts Center. The latter, once a lime kiln, now an outdoor theater, presents regional historical theater and concerts. "Take your own picnic dinner," say Ellen and John, "and have a most memorable evening under the stars."

Location *Three miles off I-81 on Rt. 11 South*

Season *Year round*

Dining *Full breakfast*

Children *Yes, if well-behaved, over 10 years of age*

Pets *No*

Payment *Personal check, Visa, MasterCard, AmEx*

Rates *Single: $55–$68, double: $65–$80. Each extra person add $10*

Lynchburg

Return to a finer yesterday

LYNCHBURG MANSION INN

405 Madison Street
Lynchburg, VA 24504

Bob and Mauranna Sherman
(804) 528-5400; (800) 352-1199

In the decade before the Civil War, Lynchburg, Virginia, was one of two cities that enjoyed the highest per capita wealth in the nation. Within the Garland Hill District (one of six districts in this city of 65,000 that are on the National Register of Historic Places), many of its old mansions remain.

One of these monuments to riches at 405 Madison Street (formerly known as Quality Row) has become the Lynchburg Mansion Inn Bed and Breakfast. The owners, Bob and Mauranna Sherman, moved here from Washington, D.C., in 1990 and, with a crew of 15, spent six months restoring the place to its original splendor.

Built in 1914 for James R. Gilliam, Sr., president of five coal companies, the Lynchburg Shoe Company, and six banks throughout Virginia, the Gilliam Home is a mixture of Spanish Colonial and Georgian Revival. It was the last of the great mansions built on Garland Hill.

If surroundings can make you feel like a solidly successful entrepreneur of the early twentieth century, this one surely can. To enter it, you ascend massive concrete steps that rise to a six-columned entry portico. Inside, a 50-foot grand hall takes your eye even higher—up heavy wooden columns pieced together from solid cherry like so many thin slices of a pie. The rich cherry wood continues in massive sliding doors and in wainscoting surrounding the parlor off the hall at the right and the library at the left. The staircase, cherry with oak, winds up three stories and encases 219 (count them!) spindles.

The dining room with its elaborate table and sideboard befits a king. So does the breakfast served on gold-rimmed china: fruit course, crumpets, quiche, Belgian waffles with maple syrup, bananas and walnuts; the menu varies. The room is sometimes used (with outside caterers) for teas and wedding receptions.

There are four commodious bedrooms each with bath; the largest is actually a suite off the library downstairs, the original master bedroom which opens onto the veranda. It has a mini-bar and kitchen for business entertaining and is handicapped accessible. Each upstairs guest room is sumptuously decorated: the Victorian Gilliam Room, the Country French Room and the wicker-and-bamboo Nantucket Room. Each has a hidden TV set, telephone and thick bathrobes for the trip to the spa on the terrace below.

Lynchburg Mansion Inn. *Lynchburg, Virginia*

Guests are often corporate executives, parents of students at any of Lynchburg's four private colleges or tourists visiting such sites as Poplar Forest, Thomas Jefferson's country retreat; Red Hill, the last home and burial place of Patrick Henry; Appomattox and other Civil War sites. The Jones Memorial Library in Lynchburg is one of the nation's leading genealogical research centers. The Fine Arts Center houses one of America's oldest continuous theater groups. As if that were not diversion enough, there are self-guided tours of the historic areas and shopping—at both the high and low ends—at antique and outlet shops.

Location	*Lynchburg is easily accessible from I-95 and I-81 and major routes 460 and 29. From Rt. 29, exit Main Street (downtown). Continue on Main to Fifth Street (Business Rt. 29) and turn left onto Fifth and right onto Madison Street; go one block to inn*
Season	*Year round*
Dining	*Full breakfast included*
Children	*Well behaved*

Pets   *No*

Payment   *MasterCard, AmEx, Visa, Diners Club, check, cash*

Rates   *$89–$119*

Middleburg

Horses, hunters and heroes

THE RED FOX INN & MOSBY'S TAVERN

Box 385
Middleburg, VA 22117

Turner and Dana Reuter, Jr.
(703) 687-6301 or (800) 223-1728

What began as Chinn's Ordinary in 1728, a midway stop for colonial travelers (such as young George Washington) riding the turnpike between Alexandria and Winchester, has metamorphosed into a compound of three buildings holding 19 attractive hotel rooms plus an art gallery and Mosby's Tavern, an informal modern restaurant, pub and banquet facility with meeting rooms and ballroom.

Located in the center of Middleburg, at the heart of Virginia's world-renowned horse country, the main building of the Red Fox Inn is the original stone structure, with 30-inch walls, built by Joseph Chinn almost three centuries ago. It was named The Beveridge House in 1812 and served under that name during the Civil War both as a tavern and hospital. While strategy was planned at dinner meetings upstairs in what is known today as the Jeb Stuart Room, wounded soldiers were cared for downstairs in the tavern rooms. Known since 1937 as the Red Fox Inn, the main building includes seven dining rooms, five of them on the second floor, as well as guest rooms. Not to be missed at the rear of the first floor is a service bar made from the field operating table used by the surgeon who ministered to the men of General Stuart's cavalry.

The Stray Fox Inn, located a short stroll away from its headquarters at Red Fox Inn, was also an inn in the early 1800s, and its stable boarded the change of horses for the stagecoach run. Stray Fox has eight inviting rooms with stenciled floors and walls, hooked rugs and original fireplace mantels. All have room service (continental breakfast between 8:00 and 10:00 A.M.). Some overlook a handsome patio paved with the original bricks of the stable's courtyard and, in one corner, an aviary of exotic birds, a passion of Mr. Reuter's along with his 19th-century sporting-scene paintings and bronzes. The gallery housing his art is the little building (open Monday–Friday) that was the Stray Fox stable. Stray Fox Inn, it should be noted, got its original name, Stray Shot, when a misfired cannonball struck its foundation during the War Between the States.

One of the rooms at the side of the Stray Fox Inn sports a tiny romantic screened porch. And the largest, the Belmont suite, is large enough to do justice to a gorgeous grand piano and a stairway leading to a bedroom upstairs—an ideal setting for a small private wedding.

The McConnell House Inn, connected to the Stray Fox and the Red Fox by a pergola walkway, got its first name, "Pill Box," by virtue of having housed the local country doctor. It has five rooms. You'd hardly expect to find lodging here—or at any place in the compound—during the month of May when the horse racing peaks. Other times you'll find peace and quiet at the fireplaces, under the canopied beds or in the six-foot tubs of these luxurious rooms.

For conviviality you walk up the street to Mosby's Tavern at the corner of Marshall and Madison streets. The painting on the Tavern's sign depicting the dashing Col. Mosby on horseback swooping down to rescue a damsel, though not truly in the style of Virginia's famous guerrilla raider, puts you in mind for seeking out Mosby Raider types at the long, man-styled oak bar. Nowadays you find national TV and political personalities in the booths at the back. The food is American/Mexican, served at lunch (weekend brunch) and at dinner "till late."

Back at the more formal Red Fox Inn main building, the food includes a wide choice: pastas, veal, chicken, filet mignon, lamb, crabcakes, salmon ($18 to $27 for daily specials). A nice come-on is the whole Maine lobster ($9.95) served on Friday nights. America hasn't had it so good since 1728!

Location	*2 East Washington Street, Middleburg, VA. From Washington, DC, take Rt. 66 west to the Winchester Rt. 50 exit near Fair Oaks Mall. Continue on Rt. 50 west for 26 miles directly to Middleburg. From the Shenandoah Valley, Take Rt. 81 and exit at Winchester onto Rt. 50 east for 30 miles to Middleburg*
Season	*All year*
Dining	*Continental breakfast with room rates; dinners and luncheons at Red Fox Inn and Mosby's Tavern*
Children	*Yes with advance notice; cots ($25) cribs ($10)*
Pets	*No*
Payment	*Visa, MasterCard, AmEx*
Rates	*$135 to $225, double occupancy*

Genuine gentility

WELBOURNE

Middleburg, VA 22117
Nat and Sherry Morison
(703) 687-3201

Welbourne, a grand southern mansion sitting atop 550 acres of farm land about six miles west of Middleburg, invites its guests to take "a step back in time."

When you enter the center hall you know from the paintings, the bibelots and worn Oriental rugs that this house has been occupied for many years by people of a patrician lifestyle. Your mind wants to change the spelling of Welbourne to Well Born.

The seventh generation of the Morison family lives here now, and they treat their guests as kindly as members of the family. They offer a choice of six commodious rooms in the main house (each with private bath) plus three cottages. Being parents of young children themselves, Nat and Sherry Morison extend a genuine welcome to youngsters and also pets. "The children of the guests who come here," says Sherry, "are not the kind who scream and otherwise annoy other people. There has never been a breakage with a child." Pets are allowed to stay in the bedrooms with their owners.

At 6:30 every evening guests are invited to join the Morisons (gratis) for cocktails in the Victorian parlor. Conversation flows so easily at times that restaurant managers in Middleburg, who are holding dinner reservations, will call to remind the Morisons that the so-and-so party is due at such-and-such a time. The chatting may revolve around a literary light such as editor Maxwell Perkins, molder of authors Thomas Wolfe and F. Scott Fitzgerald, all three of whom have stayed at Welbourne.

Sherry also spends time with her guests at the long breakfast table. The fare is hearty Southern: scrambled eggs, fried tomatoes, grits, fresh rolls—"enough to last you till dinner."

Fingering a slight tear in the silk taffeta upholstery of one of her chairs, Sherry described Welbourne this way: "People do not come here for perfection." Her easy informality amid the fading grandeur helps one understand why one guest, on discovering that there were 50 retired horses roaming the fields around the lovely old house, inquired somewhat enviously whether the Morisons also took in human retirees.

Location   *Go west on Rt. 50 out of Middleburg. After 3.5 miles turn right on Rt. 611. Go another 1.5 miles and turn left on Rt. 743. When the macadam road turns to dirt, keep following it for another 1.2 miles to the Welbourne driveway on the left*

Season	*All year*
Dining	*Breakfast only*
Children	*Yes, any age*
Pets	*Yes*
Payment	*Personal checks; no credit cards*
Rates	*$85.20 (house) to $95.85 (cottages) based on double occupancy; full breakfast and tax included; fireplaces are $10 extra per day, if used*

Upscale manor on main street Middleburg

WINDSOR HOUSE RESTAURANT AND INN

2 West Washington Street
Middleburg, VA 22117

Jacqueline Watson
(703) 687-6800 Metro 478-1300

A New Yorker introduced to the horse country of Middleburg by her late husband, Jacqueline Watson believes, as the seal of the town of Middleburg proclaims, that "the glory of the countryside belongs to God." She does her mightiest to augment it.

Entering the blue-and-white suite on the second floor of her inn is like approaching the guest room of a loving, well-traveled aunt who wants nothing so much as to share her beautiful things. The drifts of pillows across the white cutwork spreads under the canopy of bed (inviting immediate surrender) vie for your attention with the extra thick terryrobes, hanging in wait, and the glow of the fire reflected in the crystal decanter of welcoming sherry. The second suite, equally romantic, invites quiet-by-the-fire dining with your own lacy private table, but who would want to when they could dine fireside downstairs in any of three cozy rooms on Chef Robert Mayer's Crispy Long Island Duck with lingonberry sauce or Filet Mignon with Sun Dried Tomato Sauce.

His popular fare consists of numerous adaptations of contemporary American/French cuisine.

Located at the center of historic Middleburg bustling with avid shoppers, Windsor House serves three meals and drinks to the public every day plus afternoon tea and Sunday brunch. (Overnight guests take breakfast in their private rooms, of which there are four including the suites.) Dinners and special parties are often accompanied by a guitarist or a trio of classical musicians. The walled back garden is "tressed" with flowers, as Mrs. Watson puts it—large shade trees and umbrella tables ideal for wedding parties, board meetings and other small events.

Whether the group is small or large, this proprietor has the experience to handle it. Formerly the director of social events for the American Institute of Architects in Washington, she has handled 2,000 people as confidently as she has restored and decorated. We suspect that the House of Windsor has never been more attractive since it was built in 1824, including the 40 years in the 19th century during which it also served as an inn.

Some women get their pleasures from furs and jewels, says Mrs. Watson, but hers come from pleasing her guests. Best to make reservations early.

Location	*Capital Beltway (495) to Rt. 66 west to Rt. 50 west (Dulles exit). Rt. 50 west to the center of Middleburg. Located on right just past only stoplight in town*
Dining	*Breakfast included in rate*
Season	*All year*
Children	*Well behaved permitted*
Pets	*No*
Payment	*MasterCard, Visa, personal checks*
Rates	*$115 to $225; weekly rates available*

Middletown

You can hear the stagecoach coming

THE WAYSIDE INN SINCE 1797

7783 Main Street
Middletown, VA 22645

Maggie Edwards
(703) 869-1797
FAX: (703) 869-6038

The Wayside Inn in downtown Middletown, first known as Wilkinson's Tavern, was a stagecoach stop along Valley Pike, one of the early roads cut through the rugged mountain wilderness. (Valley Pike is now Route 11.) During the Civil War, soldiers from both the North and the South stayed here. All were treated well, and it is likely for this reason that the inn was not damaged during the conflict, even though Stonewall Jackson's Valley Campaign passed within a few miles.

After the war, the inn was called Larrick's Hotel for its new owner, Jacob Larrick. In the early 1900s the inn sold to Samuel Rhodes who changed the name to the Wayside Inn and added a third floor and wings with clapboard siding on either side of the original brick structure. The 1960s saw Washington financier and antique collector Leo Bernstein take over and continue the inn's tradition. Bernstein completely restored the inn, furnishing it with hundreds of antiques, many rare. A 1985 fire gutted ten rooms, but the inn was lovingly restored again and now proudly approaches its 200th year in operation.

A white-columned front porch runs the length of the long building studded with rocking chairs and hanging flower baskets. A raised seam metal roof adds to the charm. Inside, 24 guest rooms, each with private bath, special soaps, generous towels and individual climate control, are available. Two rooms designed as suites have a living room in addition to a bedroom. Many guests request the same room year after year while other repeat visitors opt to sample the variety found here. Furniture ranges from four-poster beds with canopies to French Provincial

The Wayside Inn. *Middletown, Virginia*

and Greek Revival pieces. As in other antique-laden inns, many of the furnishings are available for purchase. Not for sale is a weathered chunk of wood displayed in a case. It is said to be part of the cherry tree chopped down by George Washington.

Virginia cuisine, including peanut soup, spoon bread, country ham, game, seafood and homemade desserts, is served in seven cozy dining rooms. Exposed brick and natural wood add lots of atmosphere as do the serving people in their colonial costumes.

The Wayside Inn hosts many meetings, banquets, weddings and receptions. A five-room conference center in an adjacent building, circa 1724, was opened for use in May 1989 to serve small groups up to 40 people. A log pavilion, spacious patio and terrace can accommodate up to 250 people for cocktail parties, wedding receptions or sit-down dinners.

Inn guests receive discounted admission to Half Moon Beach, four miles away. The woodland recreation park features swimming, paddle-boating, canoeing, picnicking, fishing and hiking. The area's historic and scenic sites include Abram's Delight, Stonewall Jackson's Headquarters, Cedar Creek Battlefield, Belle Grove Plantation, Skyline Drive, Luray Caverns and the Shenandoah National Park. After a day's sightseeing many guests head for the Wayside Theatre, one of the region's best.

Location	*Take Exit 302 off I-81. Follow Rt. 11 south into town; located on the Main Street*
Dining	*Breakfast, lunch, dinner ($60 for two)*
Season	*Closed during January*
Children	*Yes*
Pets	*No*
Payment	*AmEx, Visa, MasterCard, Diners Club, cash, personal checks*
Rates	*$65–$125 per night (double occupancy)*

Millboro

The call of the outdoors

FORT LEWIS LODGE

Star Route A, Box 21A
Millboro, VA 24460

John and Caryl Cowden
(703) 925-2314

The Fort Lewis Lodge is easily accessible yet removed from main roads and far from a town of any size in western Virginia's Allegheny Mountains. The lodge derives its name from the small stockade Colonel Charles Lewis built on this property in 1755 to shelter his family from Indian raids. Lewis died fighting the Shawnee Indians, Britain's ally, in the 1774 Battle of Point Pleasant, considered to be the first battle of the American Revolution. Now part of 3,200 acres of lovely fields, forests and streams—there is even a Black Angus farm here—the lodge features countless outdoor activities ideal for a family reunion, a group retreat or a private getaway.

From April to October you'll likely see hiking boots and walking sticks, a trout fly or two sticking out of someone's hat and bicycles being readied for a day trip through the countryside. People of all ages come to enjoy a dip in the lodge's "swimming hole," a safe, five-foot-deep pool in the river complete with a raised wooden deck. Naturalists will enjoy bird-watching, wildflower walks or spelunking in nearby limestone caves. The more adventuresome can camp under the stars with accoutrements provided by the lodge and take pictures from any of more than 50 wildlife observation blinds.

During November and December this lodge is paradise for the serious hunters. White-tail deer, wild turkey and pheasant hunting is exceptional, and the lodge has a top-notch hunting staff ready to take you to the game. Many activities here center around the hunt, and interested parties should inquire in advance about details. You can expect everything that contributes to a successful outing: well-managed habitat, the best facilities and guides.

Many visitors choose to combine hunting with fishing. Trout and smallmouth bass are waiting to tug at your line in the Cowpasture River that flows through the lodge's grounds.

There are numerous points of interest nearby (Civil War battle sites, the Museum of American Frontier Culture, the Virginia Horse Center, Garth Newell Chamber Players and Warm Springs Baths chief among them). It's hard to see, however, why anyone would want to stray from the lodge. Given the beauty of the surroundings and the lure of its activities, the lodge's only limit, as its brochure aptly puts it, is that "there are just 24 hours in a day."

All of this has been well thought out and put together by a delightful young couple, John and Caryl Cowden. In 1986, John and Carol decided to restore the circa 1850 gristmill on their farm and use it for a family-style restaurant and lounge. The adjacent lodge has 12 well-appointed cheery and attractive guest rooms. Eight rooms have private baths. All the furniture is handmade from cherry or walnut. Attached to the lodge is a renovated four-level silo. Recently, the Cowdens added three "in-the-round" bedrooms, with private baths. On the fourth level a glass-panelled observation room overlooks miles of pastures and valleys.

In 1993 the Cowdens reconstructed two authentic hand-hewn log cabins that date from the 1870's. Complete with oversize bath tubs and fireplaces, these cabins are ideal for those looking for a romantic getaway.

Location	*12 miles north of Millboro Springs on Rt. 625*
Season	*Mid-May through mid-October*
Dining	*Breakfast and dinner included*
Children	*Yes*
Pets	*No*
Payment	*Visa, MasterCard*
Rates	*$120–$145, double occupancy. MAP (dinner and breakfast included)*

<table>
<tr><td>Other
Considerations</td><td>Beer and wine service is available. Because of its special nature, the lodge does not encourage one-night reservations</td></tr>
</table>

Other Considerations *Beer and wine service is available. Because of its special nature, the lodge does not encourage one-night reservations*

Monterey

A bargain—any time of year

HIGHLAND INN

Main Street, Box 40
Monterey, VA 24465

Michael Strand and Cynthia Peel
(703) 468-2143

Visit the Highland Inn in March to see maple syrup being made at Monterey's Maple Syrup Festival. Or come any time of the year for that matter. We found this to be one of the best bargains around—truly a spot for all seasons.

Even when it is steamy and hot elsewhere, it is pleasantly cool here. Air conditioning is never needed—but heat is—at this lovely, pristine mountain retreat located 45 miles west of Staunton in "Virginia's Switzerland," Highland County. The county, has a population of fewer than 3,000 people (the town of Monterey doesn't have 300 full-time residents yet). It boasts not only the highest mean elevation of any county east of the Mississippi, but also has more than three million acres of unspoiled national forestlands, including the George Washington National Forest.

Another pride of the county, the large, three-story, white clapboard Highland Inn with green steep-pitched tin roof, was built in 1904 for $6,000. Now a Virginia Historic Landmark and on the National Register of Historic Places, it features two floors of gingerbreaded, East Lake-style wraparound porches with antique rocking chairs. Michael and Cynthia, who purchased the inn in 1990, have been refurbishing each of the 17 guest rooms, all of which have private baths. Recent improvements include a new parlor complete with an antique upright piano, new carpet in each guest room and a freshly decorated dining room. There is a new wood stove in the tavern. Modern conveniences are tastefully camouflaged behind old country charm. The clean, comfortable rooms feature some iron bedsteads, original to the building, plus Victorian and Edwardian antiques.

The inn's popular restaurant is famous for its fresh mountain trout, prepared to order, and maple pecan pie. You can also sample Virginia wines in the Black Sheep Tavern.

Special packages are available for interested fishing, hunting or skiing fans. Or you can simply pay a visit, and see life as it used to be—county fairs, street dances, clean air, no phones, relaxation.

Location	*On Main Street (Rt. US 250)*
Season	*Year round*
Dining	*Complimentary continental breakfast served seven days a week. Dinner served Wednesday through Saturday; Sunday brunch*
Children	*Yes*
Pets	*No*
Payment	*Cash, check, Visa, MasterCard*
Rates	*$45–$64, includes continental breakfast. Average cost of dinner for two: $25*

Orange

Easy to miss, but don't

HIDDEN INN

249 Caroline Street
Orange, VA 22960
Barbara and Ray Lonick
(703) 672-3625

A cheerful blue, red-trimmed farmhouse dating from 1890, the Hidden Inn is aptly named. Just off a busy intersection, the inn is obsured from the street by large trees and eight acres of grounds. Despite its proximity to downtown Orange, the scene is surprisingly private. Cats sleep on porch rockers and guests read on their balconies as though they were in the country, but interesting shops and good restaurants are just a few minutes' walk away and Montpelier, James Madison's home and gorgeous gardens, just a ten-minute drive.

Full-time innkeepers Barbara and Ray Lonick focus all efforts on providing their guests with maximum comfort and pampering. Buying the inn in 1987 they wanted to create a romantic getaway for honeymooners as well as for weekend escapees from the city (no telephone or TV in guest rooms). Ray, a retired executive and still an organized manager, is the best source for information on what to do and see, where to dine and dance, hike, bike, shop and canoe. He even has trail maps for guests who are bicycling through to such scenic areas as nearby Lake Anna.

All ten guest rooms have private baths, a few with jacuzzi or whirlpools; some have fireplaces and/or private verandas overlooking the garden. Furnishings are country Victorian: quilts, wicker, chintz and canopied and brass beds. You may choose from five rooms in the Main House, one in the Carriage House, including the honeymoon suite in the Garden Cottage, or three in the Caroline House, with the options of a separate living room and small kitchen.

A full country breakfast is served in a large, pretty dining room at tables set with china and sterling for two: juice, fresh fruit, entree (such as eggs, pumpkin pancakes, French toast, sausage, bacon), muffins, coffeecake and Hidden Inn coffee. Barbara shares her special pecan chocolate chip cookies over tea in the living room from 4 to 5 P.M. and, with a 24-hour notice, the Lonicks will prepare a five-course candlelight dinner (under $100 with wine for two) starting with artichokes Romano and ending with a Decadent Dessert.

Location	*On Rt. 15 just south of Orange*
Season	*Year round*
Dining	*Full breakfast, tea, picnics and dinner with advance notice.*
Children	*Yes*
Pets	*No*
Payment	*Visa, MasterCard, cash, check*
Rates	*From $59 single occupancy to $ 159 for deluxe suites; extra person sharing room $20*

In the favored land of presidents

WILLOW GROVE INN

Route 1, Box 30
Orange, VA 22960

Angela Mulloy
(703) 672-5982

In 1987, when Angela Mulloy was converting the Willow Grove manor house into an inn, she heard from a woman who offered

Willow Grove Inn. *Orange, Virginia*

her some chairs. The woman, about 90, was Nancy Lyne Coleman, who had grown up at Willow Grove. The chairs were original to the house.

Arrangements were made for a visit. Mrs. Coleman came and slept in the room that had been hers as a child. She was touched that all the rooms in the house had been repainted with the same colors she remembered from her childhood. How could Angela have known? She can only say that while decorating she would think about a room's palette, then sleep on her decision, and awake knowing what colors to use.

Since that first visit, Mrs. Coleman and two of her siblings have become great friends of the Inn, and are regular guests, often recounting stories of their early years. Aside from the addition of modern bathrooms, the manor house, on 37 acres, has remained structurally unchanged since about 1830. Originally a modest frame dwelling built for Joseph Clark in the late 1770s, it was completely remodeled by his son in the mid-1820s. A brick, Classical Revival wing is similar to several pavilions designed by Thomas Jefferson for the University of Virginia. An imposing Tuscan portico reflects more Jefferson influence, contrasting sharply with the simpler Federal style interior. Among other things, the original fireplace mantels have been preserved.

A cannonball removed from the eaves of the house, along with Union uniform buttons found on the property and scattered breastworks, suggest the home was under siege during the Civil War, when General Lee met with his command on nearby Clark's Mountain.

Willow Grove has three guest rooms and two suites, all with private baths. Each suite has two bedrooms. Angela has maintained an antebellum decor throughout. The two rooms and one of the suites are on the third floor, which has access to a veranda. On the fourth floor, formerly the attic, is the third room and other suite. Mrs. Coleman often played up here as a child, enjoying the wonderful, dizzying view from the fan window.

A full country breakfast is served to inn guests in the Clark's Tavern, the old root cellar now a dining room. Dinner is also available there and can also be enjoyed in the more elegant atmosphere of either of two second-floor dining rooms. Menu selections include freshly made pastas, local trout, duck, game birds and seafood.

A trip to Willow Grove should include a visit to Montpelier, the recently opened home of James and Dolley Madison, which is nearby. Zachary Taylor was born in Orange County, and a short distance away are Monticello and Ash Lawn, homes of Thomas Jefferson and James Monroe, respectively. Also, since this is Virginia wine country, local vineyards encourage visits (and a sampling of their wares).

Location	*Just north of Orange on US 15*
Season	*All year*
Dining	*Breakfast, dinner. Closed Mondays, Tuesdays and Wednesdays*
Children	*Yes*
Pets	*No*
Payment	*Check, MasterCard, Visa*
Rates	*$95–$135 per night. Weekday rates: Double occupancy with dinner, $95. Special rates for packages, such as winery tours*

Paris

Lafayette would be proud

THE ASHBY INN & RESTAURANT

Route 1, Box 2/A
Paris, VA 22130

John and Roma Sherman
703-592-3900

If it's a spectacular meal, gorgeous view and a good night's rest you seek, you can have it all at The Ashby Inn, barely more than an hour's drive from Washington.

Before John and Roma Sherman bought their building in November 1984, they did a "fairly pragmatic" search along the Eastern Shore, through western Maryland and Pennsylvania. Not until they got to the tiny village of Paris, VA, (pop. 47), once called Pun'kinville and renamed to honor the Marquis de Lafayette, did they discover a house that really piqued their interest. Built in 1829 across the street from the original Ashby Tavern, the house had possibilities; but it wasn't until they walked out back and beheld the view of the Blue Ridge foothills that they knew they had found "a magic location."

By now the Shermans have acquired three buildings for the inn, and a fourth dating from 1790 that has been restored for use as their private residence. In addition, they have created one of the finest restaurants in northern Virginia, one that draws as may as 130 people to its famous Sunday brunches.

Whether one dines outside on the large terrace or watches the sun set from a little balcony off the Fan room (named for the Palladian window) or greets the morning through a dormer window on the third floor, one is drawn to that magnetic view. For the sleep-overs, there are ten bedrooms. The Fan, Fireplace, Victorian and New England have private baths. The dormer rooms on the floor above share a bath but each has a sink. Rates include a tremendous breakfast that allows you all the fresh eggs you can eat laid by hens that belong to a member of the kitchen staff.

As much as possible of the outstanding food served here is made from locally grown produce. Sherman will not allow a tomato in the kitchen that is not grown on his premises. Chef Eric Stamer imports the salmon for his gravlax, which he serves about once a week throughout the year. It comes from Norway, but the dill for it is grown in the Sherman garden along with other herbs that flavor such house specialties as homemade sausage and broiled backfin crabcakes.

People visit here primarily to eat, limiting activity to nothing more strenuous than croquet and horseshoes or darts and drinks in the taproom. The taproom, as befits a room that was once a country kitchen, is the coziest spot of all. It has a full bar and an unusually fine wine list—at least 50 varieties selected and discriminately described by John Sherman, a former *Newsweek* correspondent who now writes speeches for clients and faxes them to Washington or New York.

The Ashby Inn's most recent additions are the four rooms located two doors down the street in the village's original one-room schoolhouse. Each room includes a queen-size canopy bed, fireplace and private balcony.

Location	*Paris, VA. From the Beltway (495) take Rt. 66 west to Exit 5 (marked Delaplane/Paris); continue 7.5 miles north on Rt. 17, then left on Rt. 701, which runs into the village*
Dining	*Hearty breakfast included in room rate*
Season	*Year-round except New Year's Day, July 4, Christmas Eve and Day*
Children	*Well-behaved children over 10*
Pets	*No*
Payment	*MasterCard, Visa, personal checks, cash*
Rates	*$80 to $175 double occupancy*
Other Considerations	*Women's bath can accommodate a wheel chair. No smoking in rooms, only in one dining room*

Raphine

The art of country living at its best

OAK SPRING FARM AND VINEYARD

Rt. 1, Box 356
Raphine, VA 24472

Pat and Jim Tichenor
(703) 377-2398

Innkeepers Pat and Jim Tichenor are the kind of people one would like to have as neighbors. They can do almost anything and do it with eclat. They spark a party and know when to leave their guests alone. They think nothing of importing 1,000 old bricks from Richmond and building a new walk. They find a run-down chest of drawers at an auction and create a handsome bathroom commode out of it. They make jams and serve gourmet green grapes from their own vineyard. They wallpaper an entire house together and stay happily married.

A retired military couple, the Tichenors have lived in many parts of the world, as their collection of antiques attests. Above the mantel in their own bedroom, for example, is a remarkable collection of Saudi Arabian guns. Adjoining a second bed in the largest guest room is a magnificent Log Cabin quilt made in Kentucky by Jim's grandmother. One appreciates the instinct of hosts who would share such treasures with guests not known to them. Yet in seven years of innkeeping, Pat says, not one of their guests has ever harmed anything. One guest's compliment explains why: "You have created a work of art here."

In their 1826 plantation house, the three bedrooms upstairs (each with private bath) and two cozy sitting rooms convey the message that here, surrounded by muted country sounds (no TV) and coaxed into repose by nodding fresh flowers, you can easily let go.

In the morning you discover that every room has a view of some part of Oak Spring Farm's 40 acres, most of them in hay and alfalfa but as many as five acres in grapes. The grape harvest, which guests are welcome to watch, runs from the end of August well into October. More than 20 tons a year are marketed to wineries near Charlottesville. Fruits in the orchard include peaches, apples, pears and plums, any one of which may be served at the full breakfast included in the tariff. If you spot the swoop of a bluebird through the dining room window, your day is destined to be blessed with happiness.

There is always plenty to see and do at a working farm. In this area of the Blue Ridge between the historic cities of Lexington and Staunton, other attractions also abound. The Museum of American Frontier Culture is nearby and the popular Virginia Horse Center. Guests often take their dinner in any of several restaurants in Staunton, 20 minutes away, before returning to the farm.

Built originally in 1826, the plantation house has had only three previous owners. There are signs, moreover, of much earlier habitation on the land. Artifacts have been found going back 5,000 years, and the farm is a registered archaeological site.

In the presence of such timelessness, it is easy to picture a man and wife who come every summer to visit. A Navy Captain and Commander, they like to sit quietly on the porch swing and wait for the fireflies to begin their show in the massive oak tree at the edge of the lawn. The fireflies start their dance down low and flit elegantly upwards, lighting up the whole tree as they go. It is hard to imagine a place better suited for people who love the country and who want to relax and enjoy it.

Location	*Located on Country Route 706 just east of U.S. 11. From the north on I-81, take Exit 54 and follow Rt. 606 east to Steele's Tavern. Turn right on U.S. 11 and proceed to next crossroad (706) and turn left. House is 50 yards on right. From the south on I-81, take Exit 53A, go three miles on U.S. 11 to Red Barn and turn right on 706*
Season	*Year round*
Dining	*Full breakfast included*
Pets	*No*
Children	*16 and older*
Payment	*MasterCard, Visa, check, cash*
Rates	*$55–$65*

Scottsville

Vineyard inn, roses too

HIGH MEADOWS INN

Route 4, Box 6
Scottsville, VA 24590
Peter Sushka and Mary Jae Abbitt
(804) 286-2218 or (800) 232-1832

If you're game you can stain your hands with the juice of Pinot Noir grapes by joining the August harvest at High Meadows Inn. Of course, guests don't have to help pick the four tons of wine grapes at this working vineyard, although meals and wine are free to those who do.

High Meadows innkeepers Peter Sushka and Mary Jae Abbitt have created a relaxed atmosphere reminiscent of British country inns, and they welcome visitors whose only aim is to break away from the frenetic life of big cities. In addition to its grapevines and the attractions of the Blue Ridge and nearby Charlottesville, High Meadows offers a stream and two ponds that attract birds and other wildlife, paths to saunter along, and a tearoom surrounded by famous roses of antiquity.

The inn is actually two historic homes connected by a long two-story hall; there is no other dwelling like it in Virginia. The original home, a fine example of Federal design, was built by Scottish immigrant Peter White in 1832. Fifty years later, new owner Charles Harris built a stylish Victorian Italianate country house only ten feet from the older home. He fully intended to raze the White house, but his wife refused to leave it. Carpenters and masons working on the new structure pointed out the qualities of the old house, including the hand-carved wood mantels. After a five-year stand-off, Mr. Harris satisfied everyone by creating the "grand hall" that connects the two buildings along their backside length.

The unified building has a total of 17 rooms, including seven guest rooms, the grand hall, a Victorian music room, a parlor and two dining rooms. There are four porches. The guest rooms have small private baths and are complete with antiques and scrapbooks that tell the stories behind the furnishings. A 1905 Queen Anne manor house with five rooms and mountain views has been added on the north meadow. There is also a teahouse and a streamside gazebo on the inn's 50 acres.

Anyone who delights in the aroma of fresh flowers will love High Meadows' rose garden. Species grow there that gained fame as partisan emblems during the War of the Roses and others that once were cultivated at the palace of Napoleon's Empress Josephine. Salet, a moss rose that blooms consistently, gives off a blossom scent so strong it will perfume the hand that holds it.

Peter, who is an enthusiastic chef, concentrates on Northern European cooking—chicken, veal, pasta, venison and, in season, pheasant. A six-course gourmet dinner is served on Saturday nights and four-course dinners on Friday and Sunday with, naturally, house wine. High Meadows specializes in European supper baskets. Monday through Thursday, in lieu of formal table dining, guests may request one of these large hampers containing china, crystal, wine, several hot entrees, salads and desserts, a book of poetry and a rose! The picnic will be delivered to a designated spot, such as the gazebo or pond.

Wine, roses, elegant private suppers. Could it be that Cupid appears often at High Meadows?

Location	*On Rt. 20, 17.6 miles south of I-64 Exit 121 at Charlottesville. A sign hangs at the entrance*
Season	*Year round*
Dining	*Full breakfast. Friday and Sunday dinners— $20–$25 per person. Saturday dinners—$35 per person. Weekday supper basket—$40 per couple*
Children	*On weekdays*
Pets	*In three rooms by prior arrangement. Pet deposit: $10 for small, $15 for large*
Payment	*Check, cash, Visa, MasterCard*

Rates $85–$145 per night, per couple. Includes breakfast and evening wine tasting

Other
Considerations Two-night minimum on spring, fall and holiday weekends; 15 percent gratuity for food service. No smoking

Smith Mountain Lake

Acme in the foothills

THE MANOR AT TAYLOR'S STORE

Route 1, Box 533
Smith Mountain Lake, VA 24184

Lee and Mary Lynn Tucker
(703) 721-3951 or (800) 248-6267

When you come to stay at the Manor at Taylor's Store, located just five minutes from Smith Mountain Lake and only 20 minutes from Roanoke, you can expect the consummate B&B experience. So complete is the offering from innkeepers Lee and Mary Lynn Tucker that you will likely want to return time after time to enjoy something you missed on a previous visit.

Taylor's Store, built as a trading post in 1799 later became a community center and, in 1818, a post office. It stood in front of the Manor near what is now Route 122. The store was dismantled in the early 1970s by owner Dr. Henry Lee, who used some of its bricks in the renovations he had undertaken on the Manor house. The Manor house dates back to the 1820s when it was the center of a tobacco plantation. Originally brick, it was lost to a fire around the turn of the century but was re-built on the same foundation, this time with wood siding.

When the Tuckers found the house in 1986 on one of many Sunday drives spent searching for a B&B site, they knew instantly that this was the one. They picked up where Dr. Lee had left off on his renovations, rebuilding chimneys, painting and landscaping. They added a circular driveway, new heating and air conditioning and a sun room, and outfitted the home for guests.

The two-story house, with column-like corner trim, has a handsome front entry flanked by large white columns with a gabled overhang that includes a round-spoked window. Inside, six memorable and contrasting guest rooms, are available. All exquisitely decorated and furnished, they have large windows, hardwood floors with handwoven and Oriental rugs and wonderfully wide, one-piece crown molding. Each room's name suggests its decor. The Victorian Suite has tapestries and lace and a full-size walnut bed. A garden level private entrance takes you to the appealing English Garden Suite, complete with indoor sitting porch, view, antique wicker furniture and brass bed. And the Colonial Suite features Williamsburg blue, a queen-size canopied bed and a private balcony.

In a house as historically appointed as this one, you may be surprised to find a large-screen TV, pool table, guest kitchen, exercise room and hot tub. They are in the downstairs great room, tastefully presented, screened if necessary—all thoughtfully provided for enjoyment of the guests. If you haven't yet tried a hot tub soak you may be seduced! If you're a piano player you are welcome to play the grand in the parlor off the entry way. A full breakfast designed for the health conscious is served to you in the dining room at a long oval table lined by Queen Anne chairs. For large families or couples traveling together, the Christmas Cottage, casual and separate from the Manor house, offers three bedrooms, two baths, its own kitchen, den with stone fireplace and a big deck.

A short walk over the estate's rolling 120 acres takes you past six private spring-fed ponds. You can paddle a canoe, fish, swim (docks have been installed), or just take in the fresh mountain air. For winter, the Tuckers have cleared a cross-country skiing trail and for drinking enjoyment, they have started a vineyard.

The Manor hosts small conferences and retreats. Outdoor concerts have been held here as have Virginia wine festivals.

Mary Lynn is the President of the B&B Association of Virginia, a support network, among other things, for innkeepers charged with promoting Virginia's B&B industry. If the Manor at Taylor's Store is any indication, there couldn't be a better leader for the association. Mary Lynn and her husband know the way to go.

Location	*From Roanoke take 220 south to 122/40E, follow signs for Booker T. Washington Monument. Taylor's Store is 1.6 miles past Burnt Chimney intersection, on the right. From Blue Ridge Parkway, exit at 460E, 24E or 220S to 122*
Dining	*Breakfast; picnic lunches available*
Season	*All year*
Children	*Only in cottage*
Pets	*No*
Payment	*MasterCard, Visa, personal checks*
Rates	*Cottage $90 per night, double occupancy; $20 each additional person. Suites $75–$105*

Sperryville

Unbuttoned hunt country

THE CONYERS HOUSE

Slate Mills Road (Rt. 1, Box 157)
Sperryville, VA 22740

Sandra and Norman Cartwright-Brown
(703) 987-8025

The road to The Conyers House, Rt. 231, passes through some of the most beautiful stretches of farmland in the state. Beyond the gentle, rolling pastures, the Blue Ridge Mountains beckon and beguile. No wonder Sandra and Norman Cartwright-Brown fell in love with the site and jumped at the chance to buy the old farmhouse in 1979. The Conyers House was named after its builder, Bartholomew Conyers, in 1810. Another older house was moved and integrated into the structure in 1815. The latter was built by Hessian soldiers after the Revolution. Since then, various eclectic additions have included porches, stairways, narrow corridors and bedrooms. It took two years of extensive renovation and more additions before the present owners could open the inn in 1981.

For the first-time visitor the impression of arriving at an 18th-century inn is reinforced by the boisterous greeting of several Jack Russell terriers, as essential to a hunt country setting as the horses themselves. An avid horsewoman and active member of the Rappahannock Hunt, Sandra may well be found cleaning tack or organizing a ride with guests. She is an enthusiastic guide, willing to take even novice equestrians in tow. Two-hour trail rides are available by reservation.

Stepping inside the inn, one feels the comfort of old things: worn wood, Oriental rugs, soft sofas, country antiques and silver trophies. The library is the gathering spot for guests after a day's outing. It is here that sherry is served at fireside before dinner, books read, the piano played. Despite the aura of country gentility, Sandra insists people come to The Conyers House for rural informality and to escape button-down city stress. "No one should wear high heels here or they will fall through the porch planks," she warns.

The inn offers rooms in both the Main House and two private cottages. One of the latter is the Hill House with woodburning stove, private bath with jacuzzi and porch with mountain view— perfect for honeymooners. The six rooms in the Main House are filled with rich carpets, handsome souvenirs from the owners' extensive travels, and inherited antiques, many with interesting histories.

Uncle Sim Wright's Suite is in the older part of the house with an antique bed and four posts seven feet high. Amusing stuffed animals peer down on guests from corner niches. Helen's Room boasts a hand basin from the White House. Another room offers towels monogrammed for Clare Booth Luce (that Sandra purchased in her favorite Georgetown thrift shop). Sunny Grampie's room welcomes the weary with a family rocking chair seven generations old. Under the eves is the cozy low-ceilinged Attic room with a private deck for star gazing.

Although a major attraction of the inn's location is its proximity to the famous gourmet restaurant, the Inn at Little Washington, The Conyers House serves its own candlelit seven-course dinner, complete with sherry and canapes before dinner and wines for $135 per couple (includes four wines, gratuity and tax). Menu specialties include local trout and venison and super-rich chocolate dessert.

The average couple staying here is 38 years old, affluent and appreciative of a getaway weekend in the country, the opportunity for physical exercise, fine food and sophisticated conversation.

Location	*About 1½ hours from Washington, DC. Take 495 to 66 west, exiting on 29 south to Warrenton. From here take Rt. 211 to Sperryville. Turn left at the Sperryville Emporium and left at the blinking light (Rt. 522). From Rt. 522 turn right onto Rt. 231 and drive about eight miles to a left turn on Rt. 707. The Conyers House is about six-tenths of a mile on the left*
Dining	*Breakfast and tea included in room rate; lunch and dinner available by reservation*
Season	*All year*
Children	*Not suitable for children*
Pets	*Yes, in the Spring House and Cellar Kitchen rooms only (non-shedding, small dogs only, please)*
Payment	*Cash or check. No credit cards*
Rates	*$100 to $195 double occupancy per night*

Stanley

A great place for horsing around

JORDAN HOLLOW FARM INN

Route 2, Box 375
Stanley, VA 22851

Jetze and Marley Beers
(703) 778-2209

Innkeepers Jetze and Marley Beers claim their inn is not just for horse lovers, but the opportunity for equestrian recreation is obviously a main attraction of this handsome colonial farm. Set on 145 acres of rolling hills, trails and meadows with sweeping views of the Shenandoah National Park, Jordan Hollow Farm looks like a calendar scene of Americana.

A large barn accommodates resident horses (which guests can use) as well as the horses which guests bring along for trail riding or carriage driving. Marley Beers offers rides in her lovely wagonette by prior appointment. A mini-barnyard is home to a number of friendly goats, sheep and ducks, as well as to Rhonda, the Rhodesian Ridgeback. Rhonda frequents the pub each evening.

With the exception of Arbor View Lodge, which houses 16 guest rooms with private baths, and Mare Meadow Lodge—a hand-hewn log lodge with four guest rooms, each with a whirlpool tub and fireplace—the buildings date from the original farm and have been restored with careful attention to authenticity. Now covered with wisteria vines, Arbor View Lodge, built in 1984, and its lovely deck blend in with the older structures.

The farmhouse (the log cabin rooms are 200 years old) has several dining areas and houses the office, kitchen and some bedrooms. One dining room is decorated with fascinating masks and wall hangings from Africa. Dinner is carefully prepared to order and features delicacies such as quail, chicken and trout flavored with African and mideastern spices. Seasonal fruits and vegetables are lovingly prepared.

The Watering Trough, a pub renovated from a stable, is the

social center and common meeting area. Here Jetze Beers plays "master of the trough," introducing guests to each other and organizing chess and other games. The inn also has five miles of walking trails. There is a swimming pool in a park across the street.

In addition to horseback riding, guests come to hike in the Shenandoah National Park, visit the Luray Caverns and New Market Battlefield, and explore nearby antique shops. Skiing opportunities are within an hour's drive.

"Country Continental" is how Dutch-born Jetze, describes the atmosphere at his inn. "Our clientele are mostly repeats and direct referrals. It's their country hideaway." Conscious of maintaining high standards of service, Jetze leaves a questionnaire in every room querying guests on the quality of service they experienced and welcoming suggestions for improvement. This personal care is one reason he can boast the highest occupancy rate in the Shenandoah area. Make reservations well in advance.

Location	*From the Washington area take I-66 West, Rt. 29 to Warrenton and Rt. 211 to Luray. From Luray go south on Rt. 340 six miles and turn left on Rt. 624 and left again on Rt. 689. Go over the bridge and turn right on Rt. 626. You will see a sign on the right for the farm*
Dining	*Breakfast, box lunches, dinner. For those not staying in the inn, average dinner for two without drinks is $40. (Dinner is included in room rates.)*
Season	*All year*
Children	*Well-behaved, properly supervised children are welcome*
Pets	*Horses only*
Payment	*Cash, personal checks, Visa, MasterCard, Diners Club and Carte Blanche*
Rates	*$140–$180 per double per night, MAP (includes 2 breakfasts & 2 dinners.)*

Staunton

A first-class operation

THE BELLE GRAE INN

515 W. Frederick Street
Staunton, VA 24401

Michael Organ
(703) 886-5151

Every conceivable amenity is delivered at the Belle Grae Inn, perched high above Frederick Street in historic downtown Staunton. The beautifully restored Victorian mansion, which overlooks the pair of double hills for which it is named, Betsy Bell and Mary Gray, is as multi-dimensional as it is polished and elegant.

Two different restaurants, 15 individually designed guest rooms, business meetings, mini conferences, private parties and weddings are all looked after by a very friendly staff. A lovely veranda and courtyard with wicker rockers as well as a handsome parlor, sitting and music rooms with fireplaces invite use. Guests have access to full health club facilities complete with an indoor pool and tennis and golf within four blocks of the inn. Plus there are off-street parking, handicapped accessibility, necessary business equipment, transportation and planned activities for spouses, not to forget music for special events and even staff wardrobe changes to complement wedding color schemes.

As if that were not enough, innkeeper Michael Organ seasons the pot with long-established Shenandoah hospitality. "We want our guests to feel like they're returning home," he says, recalling the Scotch-Irish who migrated to the Shenandoah Valley from Pennsylvania in the 1700s. "They settled here in Augusta County because it reminded them of their homeland in Scotland. As traders, merchants and farmers they were hosts to explorers traveling west. It is with the same sense of homeland and hospitality that we welcome guests to the inn."

Michael purchased and restored the circa-1870 mansion in 1983. The restoration project deservedly received the Historic

Staunton Foundation's Preservation Award. Over the past nine years six neighboring 1880s homes have been restored adding four rooms, five suites, a guest house, a gift shop and a very private conference cottage to the Belle Grae family.

The guest rooms, all of which have private baths and air conditioning, are on the second floor of the old inn, in an adjacent 1860s town house and in a recently restored pre-Civil War railroad house. Pleasing to the eye, they are decorated with such antiques and family keepsakes as four-poster, canopy, sleigh, Murphy and antique brass beds. Many bathrooms have brass fixtures and original claw-footed tubs. Most rooms have fireplaces.

Visitors have a choice for dining. There is the refined Old Inn dining room where regional cuisine meals with many courses and fine wines are served by candlelight. And there is The Bistro, Staunton's only indoor/outdoor cafe. Art deco in style and more casual than the Old Inn, it features a view of the town's rooftops, light fare and bar. A full American breakfast is included in the room rate as is tea, crumpets and shortbread, served every afternoon at 4:00, by reservation.

The inn takes pride in its special packages, tailored for guests' budgets and tastes and centered around an activity or event of the month. Past activities have included a Maple Sugar Festival, touring historic homes of Staunton, a jousting tournament in Natural Chimneys, a sing-along with the Statler Brothers on July 4th and bidding on quilts at the Mennonite Relief Sale, the largest quilt auction east of the Mississippi.

Location	*The inn is just three miles off I-81 (Exit 222) and I-64 in Staunton. Follow 250 west to the center of town. At 254W, which is W. Frederick Street, turn left. Parking is at rear or alongside*
Season	*Year round*
Dining	*Breakfast is served daily; lunch Sunday; dinner, Wednesday through Sunday*
Children	*Yes, 10 years and older*
Pets	*No*

Payment   *Cash, travelers' check, personal check, Visa,*
MasterCard, AmEx and Diner's Club

Rates   *$69–$139 per night, double occupancy*

In search of quiet history

FREDERICK HOUSE

Box 1387
Frederick and New Street
Staunton, VA 24401

Joe and Evy Harman
(703) 885-4220 or (800) 334-5575

Frederick House, across the street from Mary Baldwin College in downtown Staunton, is actually five town houses that have been combined into a small hotel and tearoom. The adjoining townhouses, built in 1810, 1850 and 1910 respectively, were purchased in 1983 by Joe and Evy Harman, who quickly became award-winning restorers. Evy now runs a nearby jewelry store while Joe mans the hotel. Joe, who was born in Staunton, says, "Our guests come for all imaginable reasons," and adds that "Most are in search of history."

You will find plenty of history in Staunton (pronounced Stanton), the oldest city in Virginia west of the Blue Ridge Mountains. The Shenandoah Valley city boasts many sites, including Woodrow Wilson's birthplace, Stuart Hall and the museum of American Frontier Culture, all easily accessible via an excellent self-guided walking tour beginning at the Frederick House's front door. For non-historic activities, you'll find the Staunton Athletic Club next door, with an indoor heated swimming pool and gym available for an extra charge. Fine restaurants, antique shops and gift, craft and fashion boutiques are all within walking distance. And driving, hiking and biking tours in the nearby Blue Ridge and Allegheny Mountains are popular. Should you ever run out of things to do, see Joe. He can provide a wealth of information.

The Frederick House itself is a source of historic note. Its oldest part, the 1810 townhouse, is believed to have been designed by Thomas Jefferson. The hotel's 14 guest rooms, six of which are suites with sitting rooms, give off a feeling of history too. They are elegantly furnished with antiques and period pieces. All rooms have a private bath, cable TV, phone, ceiling fan, air conditioning, oversized beds, and private entrances. The guest rooms are very quiet because the walls have been well sound-proofed. One cannot even hear street noises. Yes, as you may have imagined, this means children are welcome.

A full breakfast is served in Chumleys Tea Room, located in one of the five town houses.

Location	*From I-81 take Exit 222 (Rt. 250) and go west 2.7 miles. The hotel is on the corner of Frederick and New Streets*
Season	*Year round*
Dining	*Full breakfast included. Dinner is available at McCormicks Restaurant and Pub adjacent to Frederick House*
Children	*Yes*
Pets	*No*
Payment	*MasterCard, Visa, Diner's Club, Discover, AmEx*
Rates	*Range from $55 to $95, double occupancy*
Other Considerations	*Smoking is not permitted. Conference facilities available*

Steele's Tavern

Move over, Grandma

THE OSCEOLA MILL COUNTRY INN

Steele's Tavern, VA 24476

Paul Newcomb
(703) 377-MILL (6455) Phone and FAX
(800) 242-RELAX (7352) Reservations

The Osceola Mill Country Inn is "a place to make you feel as if you'd been to Grandma's." This claim about the family-run inn centered between Lexington and Staunton, Virginia, in Steele's Tavern is accurate. Innkeeper Paul Newcomb and his young sons, Drew and Adam, are as fun loving, helpful and sincere as the best of grandparents!

If you let Paul know your preferences and schedule ahead of time, he'll help you plan your entire trip to the area. If you are honeymooning (and reserve far enough in advance to get the Mill Store), they offer breakfast in bed or a romantic private dinner by the fireplace—or will follow your cue and leave you alone. They encourage you to make music in the music room or enjoy games and conversation with other guests in the parlors. And, just as Grandma does, they provide good, home cooking. Says Paul, "Guests seem to like our lack of phony ambiance. . ." He adds a telling oddity: "We're doing something unique in our marketing, but I don't know what it is. About 60 percent of our guests are first time inn-goers. When you consider the fact that only about two percent of the traveling public in Virginia use inns, that's remarkable." It speaks well for the inn's hospitality and reasonable rates.

Accommodations are spread among three different buildings, which were once a gristmill compound. Part of the McCormick Farm, where the agricultural revolution began with the invention of the reaper, the mill was operated by the McCormicks and several other families from 1849 through 1969. The large 27' x 42" Fitz over-shot steel waterwheel could still turn, reminding visitors of its original use.

The Newcombs searched five months and drove over 40,000 miles before settling on this site in 1986. After extensive renovations they opened five rooms in the three-story Mill and a honeymoon cottage in the Mill Store in May 1987. Each of the Mill's guest rooms has a private bath and furniture made in Virginia. For children, there are toys and playground equipment near the pool. As Paul puts it, "honeymooners, and those practicing or remembering, delight in the 'Mill Store.'" Very popular and often booked a year ahead, it has a private entrance and deck, vaulted ceilings and a large stone fireplace and whirlpool tub side by side. The Mangus House, built in stages from about 1840 as the miller's house, was restored by the Newcombs in 1988 to offer seven additional rooms, each with deluxe private bath. Much more traditional and kid-free, this three-story frame farm house has views of the Blue Ridge Mountains.

A full breakfast is included in the room rate. Hearty, home-cooked dinners served around large oak tables are available most weekends to inn guests only, for around $20 per person. You need to reserve in advance. Dinner is generally served to all about 6:00 P.M. The inn also has its own pool, babbling brook and over 100 running feet of rocking-chair porches.

Shoppers who sally forth, especially antique addicts, are cautioned, by "You'll probably need a truck to get home. You can't go more than a few miles in any direction from anywhere without discovering some intriguing shop." Also among their recommendations are outings on the National Bike Trail which goes right past the inn's door or along the Blue Ridge Parkway just atop the hill. Good rental bikes are available. On the other hand, if it weren't for the worlds of history, education, recreation, exploring and entertainment within minutes of the Mill, the innkeepers claim, "you might never leave!" Just like Grandma's.

Location	*Inn is located two miles east of Exit 205 on I-81 and four miles west of Blue Ridge Parkway milepost 27 on VA 56*
Season	*Year round*
Dining	*Full breakfast daily and dinner most nights*
Children	*Yes, in Mill and Mill Store only*

Pets   *Boarding for pets and horses nearby*

Payment   *Cash, travelers' check, personal check*

Rates   *(Double occupancy) weekends, holidays, October: first night $109; weeknights (except October), first night $89; significant reductions for longer stays; $20 for each extra person in room. Mill Store rates range from $139 to $169 for the first night with discounts for additional nights*

Trevilians

Plantation inn

PROSPECT HILL

Trevilians, VA 23170

Michael Sheehan
(703) 967-0844
Reservations (800) 277-0844

When the Civil War ended in 1865, William Overton took off his Confederate uniform and went home, only to find the family plantation of nearly 1,600 acres overgrown and most of his slaves departed. In the difficult years that followed, the Overtons began taking in guests to help make ends meet. By 1880 additional bedrooms had been added to the manor house and the slave quarters were enlarged to accommodate guests. Thus began the innkeeping tradition at Prospect Hill.

Today, the grounds have shrunk to a manageable 45 acres, but there are ten different buildings, including the manor house, slave quarters and dependencies that have been adapted for housing visitors. The youngest of these is more than 100 years old, and the oldest, a cabin of hand-hewn logs and pegs, is nearly

Prospect Hill. *Trevilians, Virginia*

300. The converted outbuildings include the summer kitchen, smokehouse, carriage house and groom's quarters, coach house, overseer's cottage and Sanco Pansy's Cottage, an 1880 structure named for a loyal slave who, in turn, had been named after Don Quixote's devoted servant Sancho Panza. Sanco Pansy is buried on the property, along with 75 other slaves.

Ivy climbs the old poplars, beeches and magnolias that shade the grounds here and stir the mind with images of the past. Worn millstones dot the property, reminders of the plantation's days as a large wheat and corn producer. After their usefulness at the mill had ended, the stones were given new life as decorative pieces. Some are imbedded in the front walk.

The central section of the manor house dates from 1732, converted from an existing barn after the original owners' log cabin had burned down. Over the next century, Prospect Hill gradually grew and the manor house was enlarged, until its size peaked under the Overton family ownership.

When the dinner bell sounds, guests gather with the innkeeper's family in the two manor house dining rooms. There is no menu as Prospect Hill follows the old fashioned tradition of serving their guests what they serve their family. This is usually a five-course dinner of appetizer, soup, salad, meat course and dessert, all with a French accent. Special diets are always accommodated. Supreme de Volaille, Chateaubriand and Fillet de Porc Farci are examples of the main courses served.

Location	*Fifteen miles east of Charlottesville. From I-64 Exit 136 go south ½ mile on US 15 to Zion Crossroads. Turn left onto eastbound US 250; go one mile to a left onto Rt. 613. Go three miles to inn on left*
Season	*Year round, except December 24–25*
Dining	*Breakfast and dinner daily*
Children	*Yes*
Pets	*No*
Payment	*Check, MasterCard, Visa*
Rates	*Weekends: $195–$280 per couple, per night (includes breakfast and dinner). Weeknights (Monday–Thursday): 10 percent discount on weekend rates. Non-guests can dine for $40 per person*

Upperville

Gemütlichkeit on a silver platter

1763 INN

R.D. 1, Box 19D
Upperville, VA 22176

Uta and Don Kirchner
(703) 592-3848 or (800) 669-1763

At this refined country inn, a complex of six buildings situated on 50 farming acres originally surveyed by George Washington and given to him by Lord Fairfax, guests bathe in two-person whirlpools, step out onto thick Oriental rugs and dry off in front of fireplaces. As if that weren't history and opulence enough, guests can learn about the Confederacy's popular guerrilla leader, Colonel John Mosby, from prints and other memorabilia in the sitting room next to the bar. Since the inn was visited during the Civil War by both Union and Confederate soldiers, there's a choice of ghosts to look for during the night.

One lucky couple gets to sleep in a canopied king-size bed in the "Mosby Room," the largest of the 16 bedrooms. The scale of the room grandly accommodates a museum-size portrait of President Franklin D. Roosevelt, which once hung in the Embassy of Mexico.

The 16 other bedrooms are not as large but equally remarkable. Two rustic log-cabin cottages, nestled like chalets on the wooded hills behind the main building, offer complete privacy and, yes, whirlpools, Oriental rugs and fireplaces. The log cabins are originals moved from West Virginia and reconstructed by Uta's husband, Don. The stone barn, converted into seven rooms, is ideal for family reunions, wedding parties and business seminars. Businessmen may need to know that there are telephones and televisions in these rooms. And meeting planners might enjoy assigning certain guests to the "Wild Animal Room" (so named for the stuffed wild turkey, buffalo head, elk hide and bearskin that adorn the room).

Both avid travelers and collectors, Don and Uta Kirchner share their best finds with their guests, such as crystal chandeliers from Istanbul and Czechoslovakia and Meissen china from Uta's native Germany. Her blue and white Meissen dominates the decor of the five-table "George Washington" dining room. Even cozier than this is the wee "French Room" with its three tables and Quimper ware, and the "German Room" (also three small tables) with its low-hanging lights, family pictures and cuckoo clock on the plate rail.

The inn is open year round, air conditioned throughout. Hearty breakfasts are served every day, but dinners and some luncheons are served Thursday through Monday only, plus holidays. The German-American cuisine is a la carte, primarily schnitzels, salmon, flounder and shrimp—and desserts made fresh daily. Overseen by an Austrian-born chef, the food is made to Old World standards and served punctiliously.

At the inn there are a hillside swimming pool, tennis court, strolling 'mid thousands of jonquils, and a fish pond (bring your own poles). Golf is available to non-members at the 18-hole Shenandoah Country Club. There are horse races and the nationally famous Upperville Horse Show, antiquing, wine-tasting and, only five minutes away, hiking in Sky Meadows State Park adjoining the Appalachian Trail. The new Cherokee Ski Resort in nearby Linden that opened in January 1991 fills out the year's calendar of available recreational activities.

Location	*2½ miles west of Upperville on US 50*
Season	*Year round*
Dining	*Breakfast included with room. Lunch served Saturday and Sunday. Dinner served Wednesday through Sunday. Reservations recommended*
Children	*Yes, but inn caters to adults*
Pets	*No*
Payment	*Check, MasterCard, Visa, AmEx*
Rates	*$95–$165 double occupancy (includes box of firewood; additional boxes, $5)*

Vesuvius

Fine lodging and lovable animals

IRISH GAP INN

Rt. 1, Box 40
Vesuvius, VA 24483

Dillard Saunders
(804) 922-7701

Eighteen miles from Lexington, Virginia, and just off the Blue Ridge Parkway between Mileposts 37 and 38, you'll find the Irish Gap Inn. On 360 acres of mountain-top woodlands and fields of wildflowers—complete with pond swimming and fishing as well as a bevy of lovable pets and wild animals—the inn offers a standout setting. Built between 1985 and 1987, it presents distinctive lodging. The country furnishings are elegant, and the designer fabrics and wallpaper are beautifully coordinated.

The inn, built on a site once occupied by a log cabin, features oak beam, timber frame construction. Its old pine floors convey a lived-in feeling that belies the building's newness. The five guest rooms are called the Fox Hunter, Rabbit Garden, Heart, Woodland and Master Suite. Furnished with English, American and European antiques and reproductions, each room has a private bath, refrigerator, wet bar and color TV as well as a private porch with flower-filled window boxes, rockers and swings. The Heart Room, as one might expect, is popular with honeymooners.

The innkeeper's love for animals provides wonderful entertainment for guests. The prize French, English and Holland Lop rabbits will soak up all the attention you can give them. Other pets may become jealous, so save a friendly pat or two for the goats, chickens, horses, llama and seven dogs that roam about the inn. Other local attractions popular with inn guests include quilt-hunting at antique and art and craft stores; visiting Natural Bridge, one of the world's seven natural wonders; taking in an

Irish Gap Inn. *Vesuvius, Virginia*

equestrian event at Lexington's Virginia Horse Center; and golfing and skiing at the Wintergreen resort.

Location	*At intersection of the Blue Ridge Parkway and country road #605 (between mileposts 37 and 38)*
Season	*April–mid November*
Dining	*Full breakfast (included in room rate) and dinner by reservation*
Children	*12 and older*
Pets	*No*
Payment	*Cash, check, MasterCard and Visa*
Rates	*Single: $78–$98, Double: $98–$118*
Other Considerations	*Three handicapped-accessible rooms available. No alcohol sold*

Warm Springs

All-inclusive getaway

THE INN AT GRISTMILL SQUARE

Box 359
Warm Springs, VA 24484

The McWilliams family
(703) 839-2231

Five 19th-century buildings surrounding a stone-paved square comprise the Inn at Gristmill Square, located on Warm Springs Mill Stream in the center of Warm Springs, Virginia. Created in 1972 and run by the McWilliams family since 1981, the inn gives guests the feeling they have walked into a small village complete in itself. It almost is. With three tennis courts, a pool and a sauna in addition to an award-winning restaurant, proximity to natural spas and the best of the outdoors in lovely Bath County, this is an especially attractive, all-inclusive getaway.

The centerpiece of the complex, in the converted gristmill, is the Waterwheel Restaurant whose gourmet mountain trout, salmon, veal and duck specialties have earned top marks. Built in 1900 (other mill buildings here have dated back to as early as 1771), the gristmill's inner workings were removed in the renovation process, leaving huge exposed timbers as well as numerous levels and nooks and crannies for private parties and intimate dining. Guests may choose wine from the inn's wine-cellar where bottles are displayed in the gears of the waterwheel. For drinks, the Simon Kenton Pub adjoins the restaurant.

The remaining buildings—the former hardware store, a converted silo, a private home now called the Steel House and, the last structure to be restored, the Miller's House—offer in total 14 appealing guest rooms. As you might expect, in the Miller's House the guest rooms are called The Oat, Barley, Rye and Wheat Rooms. Single-room accommodations as well as multi-room suites are available and each is decorated differently with furnishings ranging from antique to contemporary. All rooms have a private bath, refrigerator, cable TV and phone. Eight rooms feature fireplaces where a fire is laid everyday from October to May. Rates vary. Top priced are two apartments, each with two bedrooms, a full kitchen and living room. Especially noteworthy is the tower apartment, which has a turreted circular living room with tiles laid concentrically from the center. A continental breakfast is brought to each room between 7:30 and 10:30 A.M.; guests get to savor the luxury even more by specifying the exact time they wish to be served.

The Warm Spring Pools, complete with two circular bath houses designed by Thomas Jefferson and only a stone's throw away, are among the popular "must-do's" when here. Guests can play golf at the famous Cascades courses, or go horseback riding, fishing, hunting and hiking. In winter, there's skiing nearby at The Homestead resort.

Location   *The inn is on Rt. 645 in the center of Warm Springs*

Season   *Year round*

Dining   *Continental breakfast everyday, brunch on Sunday and dinner daily May–October, Tuesday–Sunday November–April*

Children   *Yes*

Pets   *No*

Payment   *Personal check, Visa, MasterCard, Discover*

Rates   *Range from $80–$135 based on double occupancy. Includes continental breakfast. Modified American Plan also available*

Many things in a pastoral setting

MEADOW LANE LODGE

Star Rt. A, Box 110
Warm Springs, VA 24484

Cheryl and Steve Hooley
(703) 839-5959

Meadow Lane Lodge, four miles west of Warm Springs, VA, is many things to many people. With such an abundance of wildflowers, birds, farm animals, graceful wild creatures and outdoor sports to enjoy, no guest comes here for the exact same reason as another. But one thing is certain: you will be hard pressed to find a better setting to savor gentle R and R than on this lodge's 1,600 acres of woods, mountains, fields and streams. Says innkeeper Philip Hirsh, "The inn is more like a club than an inn." Repeat guests make it a vacation place. Magnificent scenery, pure water and unpopulated surroundings are the background for a relaxed, carefree time in a home away from home.

Life wasn't always so carefree in these parts. Indian raids on settlers' property became increasingly common and dangerous in the mid-1700s. William Warwick, the owner of the land that now makes up Meadow Lane's estate, built a stockade-type fort around his log cabin for protection in 1754. The fort became one of many strategically strung along the Allegheny Mountains from Bedford, PA, to Greensboro, NC, and was overseen by George Washington on orders from Virginia Governor Dinwiddie. Named in honor of the Governor, the fort site can be seen today on the lodge's grounds. Also on site is an Indian burial ground and a log slave cabin dating from the late 18th or early 19th century.

The Meadow Lane property has been in the Hirsh family since the 1920s. First a thoroughbred horse breeding farm, it later became a cow/calf cattle operation. Philip and Catherine Hirsh, who conceived, built and operated Gristmill Square in the village of Warm Springs, then turned the estate, including the expansive farm house and numerous outbuildings, into a country escape counterpart to their other "in-town" inn. The Hirshes sold Gristmill Square in 1981 to focus on Meadow Lane—and you get to pleasure in the results.

There are 11 delightful guest rooms, all blending contemporary comfort with antiques and art. Clean and simple, and each with a private bath, the rooms range from doubles and suites with living room and fireplace to private, antique-filled cottages. A full country breakfast featuring Southern dishes popular at the beginning of this century is served buffet-style from a 1710 oak sideboard in the lodge's dining room.

Guests need not leave the grounds for recreation. Among the favorites here is croquet—which is taken seriously. The lodge is a member of the United States Croquet Association and boasts a beautiful court. For the casual player, space is available as well. There is also a dynaturf (rubber) tennis court. Proper shoes for croquet and tennis are a must. Swimming can be enjoyed in either a private pool or in a six-foot deep hole of the Jackson River, two miles of which meander through the lodge's grounds. Very scenic and known for good smallmouth bass, rock bass, pickerel and panfish fishing, the river is stocked by the Hirshes with brown trout. As a result, a daily fee is charged for fishing.

Highly recommended is the short stroll from the lodge to the cliffside overlook deck. From there you can watch a beaver bog below and observe deer and birds in their natural surrounds. Popular with children is a barn complete with goats, donkeys, ducks, turkeys and peacocks.

Location	*Lodge is four miles west of Warm Springs on Rt. 39*
Season	*Year round*
Dining	*Full country breakfast, dinner Friday and Saturday April–October*
Children	*Yes*
Pets	*Discouraged*
Payment	*AmEx, Visa, MasterCard and personal check*
Rates	*Double occupancy range from $90 to $115. The Francisco Cottage rate ranges from $110 to $230 depending on number of bedrooms used, days of week and time of year*

Washington

Between a rock and a soft place

THE BLEU ROCK INN

US 211/P.O. Box 555
Washington, VA 22747

Bernard and Jean Campagne
(703) 987-3190

Brothers Bernard and Jean Campagne, owners of the well-known
La Bergerie Restaurant in Alexandria, VA, come from a large
Basque family. Hearsay is that they chose the Virginia countryside for their second restaurant (and first inn) because it reminded
them of the family farm in the Pyrenees. Seven of the 90 acres
surrounding the Bleu Rock Inn are planted in grapes, a beautiful
foreground framimg the magnificent mountain scenery beyond.
The vineyard produces the grapes for the inn's Cabernet Sau-
vignon, Chardonnay and Seyval wines listed on the menu.

The house itself, a sparkling white and blue farmhouse dating
from the last century, has been renovated, polished and added
on to in such unpretentious good taste that the natural setting
and cozy feeling of a home have been preserved. The relaxed
and gracious greeting at the desk, where last-minute guests can
be heard begging for reservations, is a pleasant contrast from the
cold civility one often receives at other gourmet establishments.

One suite is designed to accommodate the handicapped. Most
of the five cheery bedrooms have balconies and a view of the
mountains, but the best panorama is from the terrace. From that
vantage point the eye is drawn over the pond stocked with bass
and catfish, to the Old World beauty of the vineyard beyond
and then to the dramatic peaks of the Blue Ridge. It is an
exhilarating spot for a wedding party as the terrace can be used
for dancing in good weather. Three dining areas leading to it
can accommodate a sit-down dinner for at least 68 guests. Each
dining room is intimate and charming. The walls are whimsically
painted with floral designs. Opened as recently as May 1990, the

Bleu Rock Inn has been so successful that there are plans to expand and build tennis courts.

Dining here is first class and the "rock" on which the reputation of the inns rests. A chef with more than fifteen years experience, Scott Carr calls his cuisine "American Regional," combining ethnic foods with the freshest produce available in season. The full breakfast included in the tariff may offer muffins, fresh fruit, raspberry pancakes, and/or a special Bleu Rock omelette: ham, Monterey Jack, Shiitake mushrooms. Dinner favorites are Shenandoah Applewood smoked trout, Cajun shrimp brochette, grilled swordfish with ginger black bean sauce, seafood bisque, French pastries and homemade ice cream. A popular Sunday brunch, (which can be enjoyed on the terrace in good weather), for around $17.00 includes three courses. The magnificent view of the Blue Ridge (cover) is free.

Location	*From Washington, DC, take the Beltway (495) to I-66. Follow I-66 to exit 10-A (22 miles), Gainesville. Take Rt. 29 south to Warrenton. From Warrenton take 211 west (25 miles) past Washington, VA, to the inn on a knoll on the right*
Season	*All year*
Dining	*Breakfast included in room rate. The restaurant is open every night except Monday. Dinner from 5:30 to 9:00 P.M. On Sundays, brunch is served from 11:30 A.M. to 3:00 P.M. and dinner until 9:00 P.M.*
Children	*Well-behaved children over ten years of age are welcome*
Pets	*Accommodations can be arranged for small animals*
Payment	*Visa, MasterCard, AmEx, personal check, cash*
Rates	*From $125 to $150 double occupancy. Average Dinner for Two: Around $60 for a three-course meal for two, excluding alcoholic beverages. The total bill will fluctuate depending on your cocktails and wine selection*

One of a kind

THE INN AT LITTLE WASHINGTON

Middle and Main Street
PO Box 300
Washington, VA 22747

Patrick O'Connell and Reinhardt Lynch
(703) 675-3800
FAX (703) 675-3100

"The best," "the most magnificent," "the ultimate," "number one," "perfect"—hardly the words one would use to describe a country garage with a community basketball court upstairs. But this was the structure chosen in 1978 by owners Lynch and O'Connell for their restaurant, which in time became their inn. Now the building—metamorphized beyond belief—houses one of the most famous and prized establishments in the US.

The awards go on and on: AAA Five Diamond Award; Mobil 5 Stars; a perfect score from the Zagat Hotel Survey; and the only inn in North America designated "Relais Gourmand" by the world reknowned Relais & Chateaux organization. If these titles mean little or nothing to you, they translate as great food in a kingly setting. Less than 70 miles from the capital in "the other Washington," this inn and its gourmet food are so famous that Californians have been known to fly in for dinner, spend the night and return to the West Coast after breakfast the next day.

They come primarily for the food, food so acclaimed by critics that it has become the standard by which would-be rivals are judged: superb food – sophisticated, original, mostly French – served by waiters who are meticulously screened and given a year's training. A wine list matching the breadth of the menu would please the most discriminating oenophile.

And if all this were not enough, the eight rooms and two suites upstairs, along with the newly added guest house, are draped, papered, cushioned and cloaked in extravagant English-country style. They draw accolades and superlatives such as "luxurious," "romantic," "sumptuous." Tones of salmon and green and Victorian furnishings dominate the decor. Velvet couches, exquisite antiques, gilded mirrors and extravagant amounts of fabric were brought over by the English decorator who did the entire inn. Without ever sacrificing the effect of elegance, she brilliantly mixed traditional materials, art-deco stenciling, and faux marbling making a joyful, vibrant, and youthful statement.

In the romantic privacy of the bedroom, thick terry robes, baths designed for royalty, fresh fruit and flowers await the overnight guest. And then there is that view of the Blue Ridge Mountains.

Truly, the Inn at Little Washington is "thing of beauty"—a once-in-a lifetime experience for the senses and spirit. Make reservations at least three months ahead for a room; two months for dinner during the weekend.

Location	*From DC take I-66 west to Exit 10-A Gainesville; Follow Rt. 29 south to Warrenton; take Rt. 211 west for 23 miles. Turn right on 211 Business to Washington, VA. The Inn is one half mile ahead on the right*
Season	*Year round; closed Tuesdays June–September, November–April*
Dining	*Breakfast for hotel guests; dinner for public. The prix-fixe five-course dinner is $78 per person except Saturday when it's $93. Drinks are additional*
Children	*Over 10 only*
Pets	*No*
Payment	*Cash, personal check, MasterCard, Visa*
Rates	*From $240–$480 per night double occupancy Sunday–Thursday; $340–$580 Friday and Saturday*

Rooms with a view

SYCAMORE HILL HOUSE AND GARDENS

Rt. 1, Box 978
Washington, VA 22747

Kerri and Steve Wagner
(703) 675-3046

For a view you will never forget, comparable to what eagles see of the Blue Ridge Mountains meeting the valleys, rivers and orchards of Rappahannock County, try the vista from Sycamore Hill. Even though you traverse one steep mile up Menefee Mountain on a gravel road that cuts through a wildlife sanctuary—you are unprepared for the panorama that pulls you through the house to the windows and veranda. From here one looks *down* on tiny planes gliding like white gulls across the farms beyond. In spring especially, framed by dogwood and redbud, the visual impact is stunning and spellbinding.

After rubbing your eyes and absorbing the drama below and beyond, you can concentrate on the bright, warm interior. Soft shades of peach and green create a tranquil but sophisticated tone for the contemporary decor—an up-beat contrast to the traditional antiques and Victoriana popular in many country inns. The fact that an artist/photographer and horticulturist live here and that their origins are Western is evidenced by the clever, unorthodox arrangement of eye-catching objects, warm-hued rugs from Arizona and pots of blooms and greenery everywhere.

Intriguing paintings and witty sketches on the walls are the works of internationally published illustrator Steve Wager. Wife Kerri is the gardener, cook and overseer of this three-bedroom bed-and-breakfast and beautiful grounds. It is she who produces the mouth-watering morning feasts of apple puff, shrimp souffle, French toast with raspberries, fried trout, homemade muffins and breads. If this is not ample fare for starting the day or you need a snack later, cookies and mints are in your room for nibbling. In the evening, you're minutes away from Little Washington and some of the finest restaurants in the East.

Outside on the surrounding 52 acres of woods and extensive

gardens, strollers who can resist the mesmerizing trance of the veranda can count a good variety of wildflowers and birds, including bluebirds who have been encouraged to nest in specially designed houses. All rooms have private baths and views of the mountain majesty surrounding them. No smoking policy.

Location	*From Washington, D.C., take I-66 west to Gainesville, Rt. 29 to Warrenton and Rt. 211 west 22 miles. Make a right U-turn on 683 onto entrance road, past library, and follow gravel road up mountain.*
Season	*All year-round*
Dining	*Full breakfast*
Children	*Over 12 only*
Pets	*No*
Payment	*Visa, MasterCard, cash, check*
Rates	*$100 to $130 plus tax per night per room*

White Post

Country French at its American best

L'AUBERGE PROVENCALE

P.O. Box 119
White Post, VA 22663

Celeste and Alain Borel
(800) 638-1702 or (703) 837-1375

"You can take the man out of the country, but you can't take the country out of the man." Thank goodness. The man in this case is Chef Alain Borel, owner with his wife Celeste of L'Auberge Provencale. And the country is France, more specifically its justly famous province on the Mediterranean.

If you haven't been to Provence or have lacked the time to read the best-selling *A Year in Provence*, you can get a faithful sense of its charms right here near Front Royal and the Skyline Drive. The experience may seem expensive to some, but not for a special occasion such as a visit here would be.

You pass through the inn's gates under the flying colors of the Stars & Stripes and the Tricolors and are coaxed forward by the sight of the solid stone farm house, "Mt. Airy," built in 1753, in the midst of verdant pastures and munching cows and four ponds visited morning and night by Canada geese.

How did Chef Alain find a place that all but duplicated the scene of his childhood in Avignon in Provence? He had come on vacation from Key West, FL, where he had a restaurant, flying his own plane over Virginia's seductive hunt country, when he spotted this treasure below. That was a little more than a decade ago, and by now the manor house has two additions ringed by orchards, herb, flower and vegetable gardens.

There are ten guest rooms in all, each with private bath, five with fireplaces and all furnished with Victorian antiques, hand-painted bathroom and fireplace tiles, plus yards and yards of fabric printed with traditional Provencal colors and patterns. The first floor of the manor house holds three dining rooms that together seat 75 at one sitting. The largest one, a floral symphony of peach and green, is dominated by octagonally-shaped window walls overlooking the mountains. The five-course gourmet dinners, served in all the dining rooms to the public as well as overnight guests, are fix priced at $48 a person, plus wines. It should be noted that the wines come from a well-stocked cellar where French wines co-mingle with Virginia and California wines. On Sundays, from 11:30 A.M. to 2:00 P.M., there's an a la carte brunch menu for visitors who come to the country for the day only.

No guest should miss the carved birds that lead up the stairs to the bedrooms and are displayed for sale in the gift shop at the end of the additions to the manor house. These intriguing birds are crafted of reeds in Spain and brought over regularly by the Chef's father (the family's third in four generations of chefs). In the shop animals of all sorts and sizes, affectionately named by the staff, join the birds. One giraffe, life size and carved from wood, did not stay long even though he cost $600. Among many wooden horses, there is one carved from an ancient beam of a Spanish castle. For those who like art at their luncheon or dinner tables, there are hand-painted ceramic plates and bowls that many people would fly all the way to the Mediterranean to find.

How fortunate are their guests that the Borels hold the country close to their hearts and share it with eclat.

Location	*From I-66 West take Exit 23 (Route 17 North). Go 9 miles on Route 17 to Route 50. Turn left to first traffic light (intersection of Route 50 and Route 340). Turn left again and go one mile to inn on right*
Season	*Year round*
Dining	*Gourmet breakfast included in rate*
Children	*Well behaved children over 10 are welcome*
Pets	*No*
Payment	*MasterCard, AmEx, Visa, Diners, checks, cash*
Rates	*$125 to $190, plus $20 for additional person in room; extra on Saturdays and holidays*

Wintergreen

Rustic resort inn

TRILLIUM HOUSE

P.O. Box 280
Wintergreen, VA 22958

Betty and Ed Dinwiddie
(804) 325-9126 or (800) 325-9126

Couples who have trouble agreeing on something to do together might find a solution in the Trillium House locale. If one loves a country club atmosphere of golf and tennis, and the other the wildness of mountains and rivers, both can be satisfied. And that's just a beginning. Skiing, antiques, vineyards, historic sites and museums are some of the other attractions.

Trillium House is a classy yet rustic lodge set along the 17th fairway of the mountaintop golf course at Wintergreen resort. Its location enables guests to take advantage of the amenities of the large commercial resort, the vast natural surroundings of the George Washington National Forest and Blue Ridge Parkway, as well as countless other diversions. Returning to the homey comfort of this fine country inn at day's end is just another added pleasure.

Centered around a huge stucco chimney and hearth, Trillium House, though modern, is built of weathered cedar that blends with its surroundings. The interior walls and ceilings are white, accented by the dark woodwork of beams, stairs, bookcases and especially windows. The overall effect is warm and pleasing and makes for a nice alternative to the condominium lodging otherwise available in the resort vicinity.

The five common areas, including a library and a garden room, are spacious, especially the 22-foot high great room. Birdwatchers may have difficulty concentrating on meals in the dining room: lots of windows afford superb views into the surrounding foliage. All 12 guest rooms have private baths, but you get a television only by request. The idea is to take advantage of the 11,000-acre resort.

Breakfast, a part of the room rate, is served all week long. Dinner by reservation is available only on Fridays and Saturdays, although the quality of the selection suggests the innkeepers enjoy serving good food. For example: shrimp-stuffed tomatoes, Moroccan chicken breasts, fresh figs baked with blue cheese and walnuts and grilled veal with tomato-basil butter.

Location	*Forty-three miles southwest of Charlottesville at Wintergreen. The resort entrance is on state route 664 east of the Blue Ridge Parkway, west of US 29 and south of I-64. Specific directions depend greatly on where you are coming from; call 1(800)325-9126 for instructions*
Season	*Year round*
Dining	*Breakfast included in room rate, dinner extra, Fridays and Saturdays by reservation*
Children	*Accepted with non-disruptive behavior expected*
Pets	*No*
Payment	*Check, Visa, MasterCard*
Rates	*$90–$105 double occupancy. Suites $120–$150*
Other Considerations	*Resort facilities available for extra charge. Dinner for two $50–$55*

Woodstock

Anxiety Antidote

THE COUNTRY FARE

402 N. Main Street
Woodstock, VA 22664

Bette Hallgren
(703) 459-4828

Visitors to the small, cozy Country Fare, one of the oldest homes in the Shenandoah Valley, receive a very warm welcome from Innkeeper Bette Hallgren. She shares the home with fall foliage lovers, skiing couples, travelers passing through, business people and a number of dedicated cyclists. "Impatient DC residents," according to Bette, also frequent her B&B. They have found a dose of Bette's hospitality in the quiet of the valley makes a perfect antidote for city woes. It is only two hours removed from Washington.

Bette came down from Boston in 1985 after reading about the old log and brick house in the *Preservation News*. Known originally as the Ott House, the two-story home was started in 1772, probably by Jacob Ott Sr. On a log foundation, the "four square" home, flanked on either end by stone fireplaces, was similar to many early homes in Woodstock. It once had a porch and front entrance on Main Street. Jacob Ott Jr. added the back portion in the 1840s. "The Otts had four spinster daughters who sat in front of four front windows in rocking chairs watching carriages traveling by," smiles Bette. The house served as a hospital during the Civil War and stayed in the Ott family until 1936. An authentic log building erected at the rear of the house in the 1940s was used for many years for antique auctions.

Previous owners are responsible for some of the B&B's beautiful decorating including the Williamsburg paint colors and wallpapers. Furnished with Bette's antiques and collectibles, the B&B has original hand stencil designs throughout. Each of the three guest rooms has a window unit air conditioner and ceiling fan.

One room has a private bath and double bed, and a second room with a double bed and a third with a queen bed share a full bath. A continental breakfast featuring home-baked breads, herbal teas, fresh fruit (in season), and, on cold winter Sundays, strata and other egg casseroles, starts your day.

When here, it's worth a short walk to visit the Woodstock Museum on West Court Street, for a look at some local history. The museum also sponsors an excellent self-guided walking tour of Woodstock, of which Country Fare (The Ott House) is a part. Bring your walking shoes and head out to see the birthplace of Lt. Charles B. Gatewood, the man credited with negotiating the surrender of the Apache Indian Chief Geronimo; the Tollgate Keeper's House, a reminder of the day when Route 11 was known as "Valley Pike" and tolls were collected every five miles; and The Old Courthouse, the oldest courthouse west of the Blue Ridge in continuous use as a court building, its original part dating back to 1795.

Location	*On Route 11, running parallel to I-81, in the town of Woodstock. From the north, the B&B is located at the first traffic light; from the south, it is located at the fifth traffic light*
Season	*Year round*
Dining	*Continental plus breakfast only*
Children	*At innkeeper's discretion*
Pets	*No*
Payment	*Personal check, traveler's checks or cash*
Rates	*From $45–$65, double occupancy*
Other Considerations	*No smoking in the guest rooms*

Scenes of wild Indians and Old Stonewall

THE INN AT NARROW PASSAGE

US 11 South
Woodstock, VA 22664

Ellen and Ed Markel
(703) 459-8000

When innkeepers Ellen and Ed Markel bought this 250-year-old log house in the northern Shenandoah Valley 90 minutes from Washington, DC, and two miles south of Woodstock, VA, it was little more than a shell. It had neither water nor electricity, but it did have a rich history lively enough to quicken even reluctant history students. "We fell in love with it," says Ellen, "because it has such an interesting past and we felt someone should restore it for the future."

They did so—with a vengeance. What they accomplished in just four years of restoration work is amazing.

One of the first cabins on the Virginia frontier, the Inn at Narrow Passage was built in 1740 and soon began welcoming—and protecting—stagecoach travelers who came along Wilderness Road (the Valley Turnpike and today's Rt. 11). Hostile Indians commonly attacked at the narrow passage of the roadway between the Narrow Passage Creek and the Shenandoah River.

During the Civil War, in March 1862, the inn served as Stonewall Jackson's headquarters when North and South met head on in valley fighting. His troops camped by the river and on the grounds surrounding the inn. In the late 1800s the building was used as a girls' boarding school before falling into disrepair in the early 1900s.

Guests conjure up the inn's past sitting on large porches overlooking the Shenandoah River or lounging in any of 14 guest rooms. Most with private bath and working fireplaces, the rooms are furnished with antiques, queen-size beds and hand-crafted colonial reproductions such as the rag and braided rugs on the pumpkin pine floors. Exposed log walls (uncovered by the Markels) and stenciling throughout complete the very warm, attractive atmosphere. The room in which Stonewall Jackson slept has

119

The Inn at Narrow Passage. *Woodstock, Virginia*

a handmade quilt topped by a canopy of hand-tied fisherman's knots. The inn also has a large, paneled colonial dining room and a common area where guests gather at a huge limestone fireplace. Two new wings, one attached and the other connected by a covered walkway, have been added, along with a well-equipped conference room accommodating about 25 guests. The tin and pewter lamps that hang everywhere can't be missed. So many guests inquired about where they could buy some that the innkeepers have opened a small gift shop to meet the demand.

A hearty fireside breakfast at the inn is Ellen's specialty and includes juice, eggs, bacon, French toast, sausage, blueberry muffins and apple cake. Lunch and dinner are served to groups by special arrangement.

All kinds of guests come here from fall-color fans to Civil War buffs to those, as Ellen puts it, "who are just tired of staying in impersonal motels." They enjoy outings to nearby historic battlefields and plantations, caverns, wineries, music festivals and, during the season, to the ski slopes at Bryce. Some head no farther than to the inn's back door where they find hiking and fishing along the river.

Location	*The inn is located two miles south of Woodstock on US 11 South (I-81, Exit 283)*
Season	*Year round*
Dining	*Breakfast. (Lunch and dinner by special arrangement for groups)*
Children	*Yes*
Pets	*No*
Payment	*Visa, MasterCard, check*
Rates	*$55–$95, double occupancy; includes full breakfast*
Other Considerations	*No smoking in guest rooms*

Beekeeper Inn. *Helvetia, West Virginia*

WEST VIRGINIA

Berkeley Springs

Massage manor

THE COUNTRY INN

207 S. Washington St.
Berkeley Springs, WV 25411

Jack and Alice Barker
(304) 258-2210 or (800) 822-6630

The slogan on the Country Inn's brochure is "Retaining the Best of the Past." In line with this promise, the inn maintains a southern gentility and relaxed tempo while providing personal attention and superb service. The Colonial brick buildings and gracious porches and gardens adjoining the village green recall another time when terms like "stress" and "fast track" did not connote the hectic pace of today. Jack and Adele Barker's personal interest in managing their inn brings guests back year after year. "Guests come first," they say, and they mean it.

Indeed, despite the 70-room capacity of the inn, guests receive individual catering from the attentive and well-trained staff. Mr. Barker, who bought the inn in the early 70s, adds a personal touch by cooking breakfast for guests on Sunday mornings.

The rooms offer a variety of accommodations and prices, from a European-style room with bath and toilet down the hall to rooms with half baths, full baths or suites. The honeymoon suite occupies the entire fourth floor. Most rooms are decorated in Colonial or Victorian style with colorful wallpapers. Many have

WEST VIRGINIA

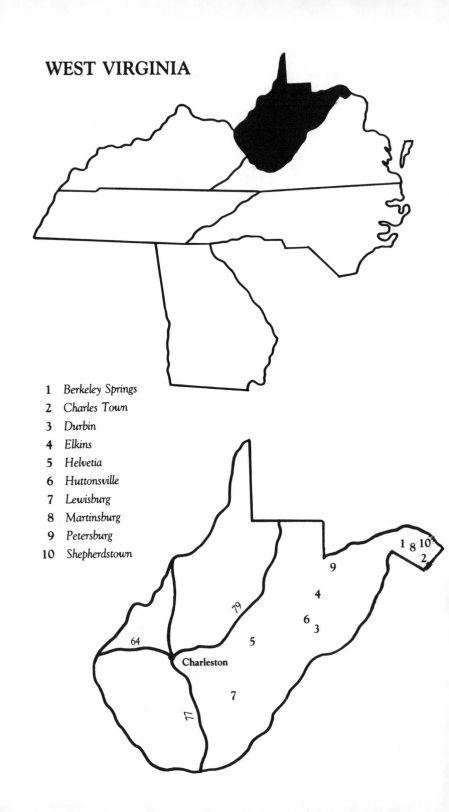

1   *Berkeley Springs*
2   *Charles Town*
3   *Durbin*
4   *Elkins*
5   *Helvetia*
6   *Huttonsville*
7   *Lewisburg*
8   *Martinsburg*
9   *Petersburg*
10 *Shepherdstown*

brass or cast-iron beds. The newer Country Inn West offers over-size luxury rooms with two queen-sized beds and elevator service.

The Wayfarer Lounge, a cozy bar off the lobby is a good spot for socializing. The Gallery, a pleasant room for reading and musical events, is decorated with colorful prints and paintings that can be purchased. The Assembly Room offers a comfortable setting for conferences of up to 50 people.

Although there are opportunities for hiking and other outdoor activities in the area, most guests come to the inn for the rejuvenating warm spring baths and the pampering services available at the spa and salon. Here guests luxuriate in whirlpool baths and choose from a variety of massage techniques. Salon services such as European facials, manicures and pedicures complete the opportunities for self-indulgence that top off a relaxing weekend.

Both the main dining room and Garden Room (where live music and dancing take place on Saturday nights) have full dining facilities featuring entrees prepared tableside. Evenings end early in Berkeley Springs, and most dining rooms—the inn's included—close around 9:30.

Make reservations well in advance for lodging and spa service.

Location	*Take I-81 or I-70 to Hancock, Maryland; then Rt. 522 south for six miles to the center of Bath. Country Inn is next to the village green*
Season	*All year*
Dining	*All meals*
Children	*Yes*
Pets	*No*
Payment	*Cash, check, Visa, MasterCard, AmEx, Diner's Club, Discover*
Rates	*From $35 to $80 per room per night; suites are available from $85–$145*

"The inn with a hilltop view"

HIGHLAWN INN

304 Market St.
Berkeley Springs, WV 25411
Sandra M. Kauffman
(304) 258-5700

Built in 1897 by Algernon Unger as a wedding present to his bride, Highlawn perches on a hill with a view of the town and surrounding country so compelling it was chosen for the cover of the official state map of West Virginia. Originally a summer house, the Victorian-style, white wood structure welcomes weary travelers with an irresistible wraparound porch. One is drawn to a rocker or swing and, when the leaves are gone, to the spectacle of Berkeley Castle—lit by floodlights at night.

Inside, owner Sandra Kauffman has kept the original color scheme of Victorian maroon and dark green but has lightened the shades to dusty rose and soft green. These tones are repeated throughout the house from the rugs and wallpaper to the ribbons on the wreaths and other accessories. Other attractive features are the handsome walnut railing, the brass beds, the cooler of famous Berkeley Springs water for thirsty hikers, Jackie the Puss, who arrived unannounced at the door one Christmas, and Sandra's homemade breakfast pastries. The location is excellent for walking to all Berkeley Springs tourist attractions—antique shops, warm spring baths, hiking and restaurants.

Special multi-course feasts in Highlawn's Victorian dining room are presented for Thanksgiving and New Year's Eve. During December, the entire inn is decorated in Victorian period ornaments and greenery.

There are four new guest rooms in another Victorian home that adjoins the inn. Known as Aunt Pearl's of Highlawn, the rooms have queen-sized beds, private baths, air conditioning and color televisions. Also new are six-course Saturday night dinner parties served from May through October.

Location	*Coming from the north, exit 1-B off I-70 at Hancock, MD; follow signs to 522 south; turn left onto Market St. at Citizens Bank in center of town. Highlawn sits three blocks up on left at top of hill. From south take Rt. 522 north into Berkeley Springs. Turn right onto Market St. at bank*
Season	*All year*
Dining	*Full breakfast buffet with lodging. Dinners are available on holidays and Saturday nights from May–October for $35.00 per person*
Children	*No*
Pets	*No*
Payment	*Personal checks, Visa, MasterCard*
Rates	*$70–$105 per room per night*

An inn near the springs

MANOR INN

415 Fairfax Street
Berkeley Springs, WV 25411

Donald and Dorothy Trask
(304) 258-1552

The Manor Inn bed-and-breakfast was opened in 1988 by the Trasks, who moved to Berkeley Springs after raising a family and selling a business in Vienna, Virginia. Originally a summer house for the mayor, the manor was built in 1878 in a style called second empire Victorian, with mansard roof and cedar shingles. One of only a few its kind in the eastern panhandle of West Virginia, it is on the National Register of Historic Places. The large entry porch gives onto a main street that leads to the center of town only a few blocks away and the famous spas that date from George Washington's visits.

Manor Inn. *Berkeley Springs, West Virginia*

photo by Suzanne K. Lord

Inside, 12-foot ceilings add splendor and help keep the house cool in summer months. The parlor and dining room are graciously appointed and the bedrooms cheerful and spotlessly clean.

The Trasks are quilters and collectors. Many of their stunning antique quilts and those made by Dorothy herself adorn the walls and beds. A memorial quilt dating from 1894 tells the sad story of Mattie Lester who died in childbirth and whose sister reared her children. In the dining room hangs a crazy quilt from 1901. Antique dolls and furniture throughout the house reflect a tasteful mix in style from Civil War days to various British periods. The hand stenciling on the stairs is whimsical.

Don Trask manages the inn and says his intent is to provide an "atmosphere of elegance." Because of the value of the antique furniture and quilts, this is not an inn for young children. There are no showers in two bathrooms at the present time—only old fashioned claw-foot tubs—but they are planned for the future.

Location	*From Washington, DC, take 495 to Rt. 270. Take 270 to 70 West and then 70 West to Rt. 522 at Hancock, MD. Follow 522 South to Berkeley Springs. Turn left at the first traffic light—Fairfax Street. The Manor Inn is the sixth home on the right*
Season	*All year*
Dining	*Complete breakfast*
Children	*12 years and older*
Pets	*No*
Payment	*MasterCard, Visa, AmEx, personal checks, cash*
Rates	*$50–$70 Monday–Thursday; $75–$95 Weekends; $140 for 2-bedroom suite*
Other Considerations	*No smoking*

The best pasta in town

MARIA'S GARDEN & INN

201 Independence St.
Berkeley Springs, WV 25411
Peg Perry
304-258-2021 or 5915

Due to Peg Perry's charisma and the conviviality of family members who help her, there is a very special feeling of welcome and warmth at Maria's. She radiates happiness, an inner joy she attributes to her spiritual devotion to the Virgin Mary. Peg takes great pleasure in sharing with her guests her collection of paintings and statues of Mary displayed throughout the restaurant and garden area. She is particularly proud of the new shrine in the dining room honoring Our Lady of Lourdes. Regardless of one's religion, the listener is impressed by Peg's conviction and inner confidence. Many of her dramatic paintings commemorate Mary's appearances to her followers throughout the world at various times in history. Peg recalls how, through the guidance of Mary, she was led to her vocation as innkeeper; thus the name "Maria's."

After remodeling a 1921 brick colonial, Peg purchased an adjacent house and connected the two structures with a two-story dining room, which leads into the garden grotto devoted to our Lady of Fatima.

Peg, her son Curtis and daughter Alesa make the visitor feel part of the lively family operation. One or more of the Perrys make a point of stopping at each table and chatting with customers. Peg's pasta dishes are probably the best and most popular dining in town. With a little prompting, she will share the secret to her scrumptious tomato sauce.

Inn business is so successful that the family has opened another B&B at Cacacapon State Park about 20 miles down the road. Rooms at Maria's are spacious and simply furnished.

Some visitors return to Berkeley Springs for the famed mineral springs or the mountain air; pasta devotees come back just for Peg Perry's lasagne and her concern for customer satisfaction.

Location	*Downtown Berkley Springs, an easy two-hour drive from the Washington-Baltimore area, six miles south of I-70*
Season	*All year*
Dining	*Full breakfast with lodging. Open for lunch and dinner daily. Entrees between $6.95–$8.95*
Children	*Allowed with attentive parental supervision*
Pets	*No, but pet-sitting is available*
Payment	*Cash, MasterCard, Visa, Diners, AmEx*
Rates	*$39.95–$49.95 per night for single; $49.95–$59.95 for double; two-bedroom suite available: $65 for double, $75 for three, $85 for four*

Charles Town

Pre-Civil War civility

THE CARRIAGE INN

417 E. Washington Street
Charles Town, WV 25414

Robert and Virginia Kaetzel
(304) 728-8003

This historic colonial home dating from 1836 has retained its classic lines and timeless appeal. The front porch with proportioned columns and period rockers recalls the genteel lifestyle of past inhabitants. Sitting off a main street, its American flag waving to passersby, the house is framed by stately old trees and a handsome wrought iron gate. Here in the East Parlor in September 1864, Generals Ulysses S. Grant and Philip Sheridan met to discuss their strategy for the ongoing Civil War. A print commemorating the occasion hangs in the sitting room.

Five bedrooms each with private bath are furnished with period pieces and are named for their color schemes. All the beds, handsome four-posters, were handmade in Charles Town, and four of them are topped by hand-knotted canopies. The Porch Room has a private small porch overlooking the lawn. Most of the bedrooms have working fireplaces.

There are three floors in all, spacious, polished, meticulously maintained. The inviting sitting areas on the first floor are for guests' use.

Before setting out to explore the historic attractions or attend the horse races, guests are fortified with such house specialties as French toast and rasperry muffins. White-water rafting, golf and tennis facilities are nearby.

Location	*From Washington, take Rt. 270 N towards Frederick, MD. Pick up Rt. 340 W to the center of Charles Town*
Dining	*Breakfast and tea*
Season	*All year*
Pets	*No*
Children	*Not under 10 years old*
Payment	*Cash, check, Visa, MasterCard, Discover*
Rates	*Sunday through Thursday $50 per single, $65 per double: Friday or Saturday, $95 per couple*

Country class

HILLBROOK INN

Route 2, Box 152
Charles Town, WV 25414

Gretchen Carroll
(304) 725-4223

It comes as no surprise to anyone who has stayed at Hillbrook Inn and been pampered by innkeeper Gretchen Carroll, that the inn was selected by an independent panel of industry experts for the 1990 "Best Inn of the Year" award. The honor was based on high quality of decor, amenities, ambiance, personalized service and menu served.

Hillbrook Inn centers around a handsome Tudor style mansion set in a secluded wooded area near Charles Town. The rock garden around the front door, bursting in season with brilliant perennials, and the sloping lawns leading to a duck pond and Bullskin Run complete the impression of the English countryside. This pastoral property once belonged to George Washington, and the original springhouse still provides water to the inn.

Inside, six luxurious guestrooms and several sitting areas are furnished with antiques and objets d'art from all over the world. Gretchen acquired most of the art pieces during her many years of living abroad, and she has arranged them with impeccable taste and imagination. Oriental rugs, worn just enough to perfect the patina, suggest old, refined affluence. Sunlight streaming through the large windows floods the interior, emphasizing the unusual angles and hidden niches of the architecture. Despite its decor, Hillbrook is not a stuffy, formal inn. Not infrequently, Gretchen greets her guests shoeless, with a glass of sherry and bouquet of fresh flowers, setting a refreshingly casual style.

All guestrooms have sitting areas and are exquisitely decorated. More tempting books fill the shelves than one could peruse in months. The Bamford suite has a fireplace and porch. The Cottage is very private with a separate entrance and a small balcony overlooking the duck pond. The room named the Point, tucked under the eaves, is accessible only through a tunnel-like passageway. Its paisley prints and high double bed add to the allure of the secret room.

Gretchen serves dinner (by reservation only) in the cozy candlelit dining room. Her special seven-course feast includes wine and features fresh produce from her garden and her neighbors'. A bargain at $68 per person, it is an excellent choice for a memorable birthday or anniversary celebration. She is willing to accommodate special requests, such as lunches, conferences for private companies or receptions for embassies, and will even organize and cater wedding receptions. Breakfast, served on the sunny porch, may include pecan pancakes or French Toast Tatiana with homemade syrup, as well as traditional eggs and sausage.

Hillbrook's storybook charm and private setting invite the visitor to shed city stress and renew the spirit among treasures both natural and man-made.

Location	*From Charles Town take Rt.51 west to Rt. 13, a left turn. Go 4.8 miles to inn on left. (Look for a stone wall.)*
Season	*All year*
Dining	*Breakfast and dinner with wine included with the room rate*
Children	*No*
Pets	*No*
Payment	*MasterCard, Visa, Discover, checks*
Rates	*$330–$380 (MAP) per couple plus tax and service. Special reduced rates offered during some months*

Victorian Renovation

WASHINGTON HOUSE INN

216 South George Street
Charles Town, WV 25414

Ed and Marsha Oot
(304) 725-7923

When Ed and Marsha Oot came to Charles Town looking to buy a bed-and-breakfast establishment, the home that is now the Washington House Inn was not for sale. From the outside, though, the Oots saw promise. The house, built in 1899, was of late-Victorian brick style with a three-story turret, a columned wraparound porch and a shady front yard just near the heart of town. They knocked on the door and inquired about buying it from the family who lived there. The fact that the house had only one bathroom and had been centrally heated for only about a decade did not dim their vision.

After the sale, the Oots created an inn that is true to its Classic Victorian roots. Distinctive floral wallpapers and trim, ceiling fans and airy curtains lend distinct character to each of the Washington House Inn's six guest rooms. The house is filled with comfortable Victorian furniture from auctions and estate sales. During renovations, walls were reconfigured, giving each room a sense of seclusion from the others. Private baths and central air-conditioning further guarantee guests' comfort.

Attention to detail shows in more than just the decor. The second-floor foyer contains a refrigerator stocked with soft drinks and ice. Fresh fruit baskets with crackers and cheese await guests in their rooms. Breakfast is buffet style and might included peach French toast, quiche, mock souffle and homemade muffins.

The Washington House Inn has direct links to George Washington. Colonel Richard Blackburn Washington, George's great-nephew, was in his seventies when he built the house after losing his pervious estate during the Civil War. Local legend says that afternoons often found the colonel in a rocking chair on the porch, sipping on a toddy. The toddy, the rocker and the fact that the porch had no railing may have contributed to the colonel's reputation for occasionally rocking himself into the garden.

The Washington House Inn is near some of West Virginia's famed historical and recreational sites. The Civil War battlefield at Antietam and Harpers Ferry National Historical Park are less than a half-hour away. You can hike on the Appalachian Trail, bike or walk the C & O Canal towpath and raft on the Potomac or Shenandoah. The Charles Town Racetrack and outlet shopping at Martinsburg are other popular destinations. Of course, a weekend retreat does not require planned activities. The Oots say that a walk through Charles Town itself, with its lovely old homes and tree-lined streets, is enough to soothe the souls of city dwellers.

Location *From Washington, D.C. take Rt. 270 to Rt. 340 South, or Rt. 7 to Rt. 9 West. In Charles Town, turn left onto George Street at the Jefferson County Courthouse*

Season	*Year round*
Dining	*Full breakfast included*
Children	*Ages 6 and over. One room has a double and a single bed. An additional room would be required to accommodate a larger family*
Pets	*No*
Payment	*Visa, MasterCard, Discover, AmEx, cash, checks*
Rates	*$70.00 weekdays, $85.00 weekends. Business rates available during the week*

Durbin

Rustic riverside exclusivity

CHEAT MOUNTAIN CLUB

P.O. Box 28
Durbin, WV 26264

Debbie and Norm Strouse
(304) 456-4627

To reach this hidden hideaway, one must traverse 1.5 miles of a gravel country road passing through part of the Monongahela National Forest (900,000 acres), which completely surrounds the 200-acre grounds of the Club. Beautiful Shavers Fork River flows just a few yards outside, offering guests breathtaking views, fresh trout (river is stocked and is considered one of the best in the state), canoeing, tubing and rafting.

On entering the large two-storied living room one is likely to smell freshly baked corn bread. Guests congregate before lunch, which may well include a freshly caught trout, by a roaring fire in the large stone fireplace. Three meals a day are served on monogrammed china from the old days when such luminaries as

Thomas Edison, Henry Ford and Harvey Firestone vacationed here after the Great War.

Built over a hundred years ago as a hewn-log and wood-sided hunting lodge, the club was purchased by a private group in 1988 and is managed by a resident couple, the Strouses. Debbie is the cook (judging from her homemade bread, a very good one), and Norman is in charge of the outdoor activities and guides guests on a variety of excursions (cross-country skiing, hiking, biking, canoeing, rafting). Bedrooms are simply furnished and most have large shared baths. The Spartan style in no way detracts from the "rustic elegance" the Strouses strive to maintain. Crystal, silverware and candles are de rigueur in the large dining room where meals are served family-style. Despite the spaciousness of the high-ceilinged common room, the lodge exudes homey warmth. What makes this inn unique is the unspoiled character of the building, the homecooking, the variety of outdoor opportunities, especially fishing, and above all the paradisal setting of river, sky and woods.

Smoking is permitted in the main lounge and outside porch. No TV. Equipment needed for cross-country skiing, canoeing, mountain biking, rafting and fishing are available at no cost. Because of the secluded setting and aura of aristocratic informality one feels "in" on a delicious secret, only a select few share— perfect for a family vacation, business meeting or honeymoon.

Location	*From Washington DC, take I-66 West to I-81. Exit at Harrisonburg, VA. Go west on Rt. 33 for 57 miles to Judy Gap. Take Rt. 28 south for 22 miles. At the junction of Rt. 250/92, proceed 12.5 miles north to CMC entrance*
Season	*All year*
Dining	*Breakfast, lunch, dinner*
Children	*Yes. Cribs, high chairs and infant play facilities are provided*
Pets	*No*
Payment	*Check or cash*

Rates *From $69 to $99 per person depending on day of week. This includes meals*

Elkins

Hot-tub fishing allowed

CHEAT RIVER LODGE

Rt. 1, Box 115
Elkins, WV 26241

Roxye and Joe Marshall
(304) 636-2301

In one of the most beautiful areas of West Virginia, Cheat River Lodge is really a complex of several structures on a postcard-pretty site where the mountains of the Monongehela National Forest meet the Cheat River. The oldest building, recently renovated, is a cozy lodge with six spacious rooms furnished with private bath, a coffee-making facility and TV (two units have a kitchen). The new screened porch is an irresistible spot for rocking, reading or watching the trout jump in the river. These rooms are year-round favorites of fishermen, hunters, skiers and hikers who prize the location and the laid-back hospitality of owners Roxye and Joe Marshall.

Six private cabins, each with its special appeal, are nestled by the river or in the woods; four of them are right on the Shavers Fork and all have an outside jacuzzi. The cabin called Rhododendron has a porch and jacuzzi so close to the river that you can fish from the hot tub. Roxye recalls one man landing a trout into the lap of his bathing—and dismayed—wife. Walkers Run, a cabin with four bedrooms, sits two miles off the main road in a picturesque setting where bear and deer are common visitors.

The Marshalls are most willing to share tips on the extraordinary opportun̈̇ s for canoeing, skiing, fishing and hiking in

Cheat River Lodge. *Elkins, West Virginia*

the nearby mountains, rivers and the adjacent Monongahela National Forest. Less athletic vacationers can shop, hunt for antiques, or attend cultural events in Elkins just four miles away. Here Davis and Elkins College hosts several arts and music festivals annually.

Another good reason for staying at the Cheat River Inn Lodge is a gourmet restaurant right on the grounds, owned and managed by Rickie and Nancy Krogh. The restaurant has a faithful following of locals as well as appreciative repeats who come just for the shrimp and sausage appetizers, smoked trout, grilled swordfish and salmon. Sitting on the new deck overhanging the river, sipping West Virginia white wine and savoring one of Nancy's secret sauces is the reward of a hard day's fun outdoors.

Location	*Four miles east of Elkins on Rt. 33. Take Stuarts Recreation Park Exit and proceed 1½ miles to the inn, located at a blue bridge spanning Shaver's Fork*
Season	*All year*
Dining	*Meals can be taken at the restaurant or prepared in the cabins or efficiencies*
Children	*Yes*
Pets	*Yes*
Payment	*Cash, Mastercard, Visa*
Rates	*$43–$48 double occupancy per night in the lodge, $4 for each additional person; cabins $124 weekdays, $144 weekend and holiday nights double occupancy with $7 for each additional. Weekly rates from $739. Extended stay discounts and special packages available*

Helvetia

A Swiss Brigadoon

BEEKEEPER INN

Box 42
Helvetia, WV 26224

Eleanor F. Mailloux
(304) 924-6435

Called Helvetia after the original name for Switzerland, this tiny village is a Swiss version of Brigadoon—a magical spot, frozen in time, unspoiled and enchanted. Upon arriving, romantics can easily imagine that a fog has suddenly lifted revealing a town that has been sealed off from the world in another century. The first impression is enhanced by inhaling the air—the sweetest and purest this side of the Alps.

Although Helvetia has a current population of only around 20 (at its peak the population reached about 500), it has a library open nearly every day, a post office, store, museum, sparkling white church, and lovely green common. The newcomer expects Heidi and her goats to appear and stop for a drink at the gentle stream that cuts through the center of town.

Founded by a group of Swiss immigrants in 1869 and later the center of a substantial farming community, the town nestles in a remote forest of the Allegheny Mountains known for its fishing and hunting opportunities, cross-country skiing and scenic beauty. Most of the inhabitants are descendants of the original settlers and continue to celebrate their heritage with annual Swiss festivals featuring ethnic food and dancing. Because of its unique and colorful history, and through the efforts of proud residents, the entire town is on the National Register of Historic Places.

The unofficial hostess of the town, Eleanor Mailloux, seized the chance to fulfill a life-long wish. "I dreamed of doing this—restoring, developing and opening an inn in Helvetia—all my life. I came back 25 years ago and did it."

Born and educated here (her father came in 1873), Eleanor raised her own children in Helvetia, left to live in the Orient

The Cardinal Inn. *Huttonsville, West Virginia*

for 15 years, returned, and for the last 23 years has been the owner-manager of the Swiss Hutte (restaurant) and of the Bee-keeper Inn (named for a resident beekeeper) for the last six. Don't be put off by adjectives like "quaint," "adorable,", "cute" that are commonly used to describe the inn. It is all of these without that saccharine-sweetness of calculated reproductions. The three bedrooms with private baths and cozy sitting areas are furnished with antiques and memorabilia from the early Swiss settlement; in keeping with authenticity, no phones or TV are here. Breakfast is served in the kitchen around a pot-bellied stove. The Hutte restaurant is decorated with typical Swiss mo-tifs—blue and white tablecloths, bouquets of wild flowers—and offers a Helvetian menu specializing in dishes made with local cheese, homemade sausage, sauerbraten, homemade bread and a delicious sauerkraut dish whose recipe remains Eleanor's secret. A steaming, delicious "Stout Soup" filled with meat and vege-tables is hardy enough to serve as a main course. Above the restaurant is an Alpine Penthouse, a separate self-contained apartment with ten beds, and furnished with Swiss antiques and wooden furniture some of which was made by the local wood carver.

It takes an effort to get here. Traversing the 20 miles from Huttonsville up a winding logging road can taken an hour even in the best weather. On the way y ou may surprise a deer, a hawk or a fox, or you may even catch a glimpse of the resident bear that runs through the Hutte parking lot.

Eleanor and her fellow Helvetians take care to preserve the special character of their village. What little development takes place is monitored so that it fits the style and character of the early buildings. (A local cookbook even offers personal advice for escaping the ravages of time: a recipe for wrinkle-remover cream that calls for local honey.) Helvetia is an adventure ex-perience for lovers, skiers, peace seekers, nostalgia enthusiasts—one hour away and 150 years ago.

Location   *From Elkins, WV take Rt. 250 south; turn right at Mill Creek onto Rt. 46 to Helvetia*

Season   *All year*

Dining	*Breakfast is included with lodging at the Beekeeper Inn. The Hutte serves lunch and dinner and a special brunch on Sundays*
Children	*Well-behaved, properly supervised children welcomed*
Pets	*No*
Payment	*Cash or personal check*
Rates	*$45 single; $65 double*

Huttonsville

Labor of love

THE CARDINAL INN

Rt. 1, Box 1 Rt. 219
Huttonsville, WV 26273

Eunice R. Kwasniewski
(304) 335-6149

"It took one year, two people, and 438 gallons of varnish remover to strip and then re-varnish every piece of woodwork in the house. I bought toothbrushes, rubber gloves and steel wool by the carton." Thus innkeeper Eunice Kwasniewski describes how she restored the carved solid oak banisters, walls, door and window casings, paneling and floors in the Cardinal Inn. She also used just under a mile of conduit wiring in replacing the old electrical system. Her gigantean efforts resulted in the complete restoration of a 1901 Queen Anne Victorian mansion now named after the state bird. The sandstone and yellow-brick structure sits regally on a high spot of 75 farm acres in the pretty town of Huttonsville. The view from the front of the wraparound porch—a magnificent sweep of the Tygart River valley below, and beyond, of the Cheat Mountains—challenges the outdoor enthusiast to explore the closest trails and forests.

"I'm a transplant from the Adirondacks," says Eunice, an energetic grandmother and mother of five whose husband bought the house as a surprise (sight unseen by her) in 1983. Shortly afterwards he died from a heart attack. "I was so angry, (about his sudden death) I worked non-stop for five years to get the Cardinal Inn back to its former glory." This included modernizing a huge kitchen, getting the five fireplaces working, and restoring and furnishing nine bedrooms and baths. She has nearly completed restoration of the other buildings on the property—barns, granary and a log cabin—some of which date back to 1800.

Eunice is a lively, informative, helpful hostess who specializes in catering special dinners, and in accommodating weekend skiers and other special groups, many of whom are repeat guests. Her house reflects her warmth and grace. The sun-lit downstairs sitting area, furnished with period antiques, is decorated in soft shades of light rose and green. Eunice herself hung the rolls and rolls of cheerful flowered wallpaper that cover the large areas connecting the three spacious floors. Bedrooms are bright, airy and immaculately clean. Prices at the inn would be a bargain even if the full breakfast of hot casserole, homemade bread and muffins were not included in the room rate.

Eunice claims that the Cardinal Inn is for sale, at the right price. After all those years of stripping varnish, hanging paper, and gracious innkeeping Eunice is unlikely to give up this labor of love easily.

Directions	*From Elkins take Rt. 219 south. Cardinal Inn is ¼ mile from Rt. 250/219 intersection at Huttonsville*
Season	*All year*
Dining	*Full breakfast with lodging; special lunch and dinner for six or more by reservation.*
Children	*Yes*
Pets	*No*
Payment	*Cash, MasterCard, Visa*
Rates	*$50 double occupancy; $38 single occupancy; $12 for extra person in same room, plus tax.*

Other
Considerations *No smoking*

Lewisburg

Meeting history head on

THE GENERAL LEWIS INN

301 E. Washington St.
Lewisburg, WV 24901

Janine Zanecki
(304) 645-2600 or (800) 628-4454

When you come to Lewisburg, WV, and stay at The General Lewis Inn, you can get an excellent look at well-preserved history dating back to the town's origin in the mid 1700s. Or you can come here to enjoy numerous recreation activities against a backdrop of beautiful Greenbrier Valley. Whatever your choice, you are in for a treat.

On a slight rise overlooking a tree-shaded street in the middle of town, the inn, with gable-roofed wings and half-round windows at the top, has a plantation style front porch. Beyond the six two-story white columns, you enter the lobby with its shiny hardwood floors, elegant rugs, antiques and thick, hand-hewn beams taken from slaves' quarters once on-site. The handmade walnut and pine front desk was used to register such notables as Patrick Henry and Thomas Jefferson when it stood in the now defunct Sweet Chalybeate Springs Hotel.

The inn also boasts a Memory Hall with a marvelous collection of tools, guns, household utensils, musical instruments and an old nickelodeon that still works. If that memorabilia isn't enough, you can enjoy a head-on experience with the past when you go to sleep at night. All of the inn's bedsteads are more than 100 years old!

The inn's east wing was built in 1834 as a private home. Today it houses two guest rooms and two, two-bedroom suites all of which have their original mantels. The dining room is also part of the 1834 home and its doorways to the lobby are not in the place once occupied by windows. Guests enjoy all three meals here. Specialties range from country ham, chicken, steaks and mountain trout to homemade pecan pie and fruit cobblers. The home's original front door serves as the inn's main entrance. The lobby and the rest of the inn are a 1929 addition built by the inn's founder, Randolph K. Hock, whose daughter, Mary Noel Morgan, is the current owner.

A total of 26 antique-filled guest rooms are available. All have private baths. Cable TV and central heat and air conditioning make guests feel right at home in this museum-like setting. In fact, the most frequent comment the innkeeper hears is: "It's like going away from home to home."

Stop by the visitors center for a free, self-guided walking tour book of Historic Lewisburg, a town which is on the National Register of Historic Places. You can walk past 50 antebellum residences; the Old Stone Church, the oldest church in continuous use west of the Alleghenies; the North House; the museum of the Greenbrier Historical Society; the 1834 Greenbrier County Library; the Lewis Spring, discovered and named by the town's namesake Andrew Lewis in 1750; and the Confederate Cemetery where the remains of 95 unknown Confederate soldiers from the 1862 Civil War battle of Lewisburg are buried in a mass grave.

Also available at the visitors center is information on numerous nearby state and national parks, hunting and fishing, spelunking in two commercial caves (Organ Cave and Lost World Caverns), as well as other limestone caverns, white-water rafting, golfing, bird-watching and specialty shops.

Location	*From Washington, DC take Rt. 66 west to 81 south. Take I-64 exit and turn on Rt. 219 south. At first traffic light (Washington Street) go left two blocks*
Season	*All year*
Dining	*Breakfast, lunch, dinner Monday–Saturday; breakfast and dinner on Sunday*
Children	*Yes*

Pets   Yes

Payment   MasterCard, Visa, AmEx, cash, personal check

Rates   Suites $80; rooms $55–$80

Martinsburg

Memories and surprises

ASPEN HALL INN

405 Boyd Avenue
Martinsburg, WV 25401

Gordon and Lou Anne Claucherty
(403) 263-4385

Guests often ask for, and are gladly given, a tour of Aspen Hall Inn upon their arrival. While leading the way through this pre-Revolutionary War limestone mansion, owner Lou Anne Claucherty will likely mention the surprises that she and her husband Gordon found during restoration. They discovered a space that formerly held a secret stairway and may have been used for the Underground Railroad. Another secret room had a window, but no door. When a third-floor wall was removed, names and a date—December, 1788—were found written behind in the plaster, probably a final flourish from a group of workers. The Clauchertys left the wall on display so that guests can savor the history that permeates the home. (They are still looking for a rumored tunnel.)

Aspen Hall reflects several architectural styles of the past 250 years. The Beeson family built the original Georgian section of the house, a small stone structure that reflected their Quaker background. Subsequent owners built Federal and, later, Edwardian-style additions. In 1756, George Washington attended a wedding there. It's possible that the house served as a hospital during the Civil War.

These days, Aspen Hall is a comfortable respite, set under towering locust trees and between a stream and a circular driveway. The first floor holds two matching parlors, with fireplaces and eight-foot windows. There is a formal dining room and an intimate breakfast nook for two. The five guest rooms are large and furnished with canopy or four-poster beds. Several of the private bathrooms are retreats unto themselves: one holds a claw-foot tub, which Lou Anne says is often bathed in moonlight; another has a window seat, perfect for bird-watching. The Clauchertys have even supplied the binoculars.

Lou Anne prides herself on serving full breakfasts in which "calories are ignored." Quiche, eggs and meat dishes are accompanied by fruit and special homemade juices and breads. Afternoon teas include tarts and dainty sandwiches. All meals are served with a special flourish of Lou Anne's china and lace. On weekends, Gordon will be your waiter.

The Clauchertys' plans include continued renovations at Aspen Hall, especially when Gordon retires and can devote even more time to the inn. They have cleared the yards in the back of the house for gardens and built a walk bridge over the stream. Guests can wander through the property or linger in the backyard gazebo.

There is more history in the area around Aspen Hall Inn than even serious buffs can absorb in a weekend. Martinsburg is located about halfway between Harpers Ferry and Berkeley Springs. The Clauchertys recommend historic Fort Frederick and charming Shepherdstown as particularly worthwhile destinations. In addition, the area offers antiquing with surprisingly good prices. Local discount outlet shopping is another draw. Guests who prefer the outdoors can choose from hiking, biking and rafting, canoeing or simply admiring the West Virginia mountains.

Location	*From southbound I-81, take the King Street Exit east toward Martinsburg. Turn left at the fourth traffic light (Raleigh St.). Turn right on Race Street, then left on Boyd Avenue. Go to the far end of the boulevard and bear right onto the circle drive.*
Season	*Closed January to Valentine's Day*
Dining	*Full breakfast and afternoon tea*

Children	*Under 12 allowed only in mid-week if no other guests are in residence.*
Pets	*No*
Payment	*Visa, MasterCard, cash, checks*
Rates	*$95.00 per night*

A priceless survivor

BOYDVILLE, THE INN AT MARTINSBURG

601 S. Queen St.
Martinsburg, WV 25401

La Rue Frye
(304) 263-1448 or (202) 626-2896

The sensation of retreating into a less hectic world comes only moments after turning into the driveway of Boydville, a stone plantation mansion located off the main street of Martinsburg. Century-old boxwoods, oak and maples trees shade the mansions's great front porch. Rocking chairs, original to the house, beckon.

Boydville was built by General Elisha Boyd, a hero of the War of 1812. During the Civil War, Union General David S. Hunter ordered that Boydville be burned as retaliation for the Confederate sympathies of Elisha Boyd's son-in-law, Charles Faulkner. Only an hour before the destruction, President Lincoln revoked the order after he received a telegrammed plea from Mrs. Charles Faulkner. The magnitude of the possible loss of Boydville can only be appreciated by a visit to this inn.

Many architectural details of the original Boydville remain intact. Delicate Federal fan windows of hand-rolled glass grace the first floor's interior doors. The doorways are further framed by intricate hand-carved molding of grains, nuts and fruit. Decorative mantels surround the fireplaces, which warm guests on chilly evenings. The foyer walls, which at first look like fine wooden moldings, are actually covered by hand-painted wallpaper made expressly for Boydville in 1812.

Upstairs there are six bedrooms, two of which share a bath, and a foyer for guests' use. Guests may also retreat to a light-filled garden room that overlooks the backyard and historic outbuildings.

Among the choices of things to do nearby on a weekend stay are: a visit to Antietam Battlefield or Harpers Ferry National Park; a pampering session at the Berkeley Springs Roman baths; discount shopping at the Blue Ridge Outlet Mall, only two blocks away; browsing through the charming shops in Shepherdstown; biking the C & O Canal towpath; attending an auction or cheering the thoroughbreds at the races in the Charles Town.

Location	*From the Washington area take I-495 to 270 N and 70 west. Take Charles Town exit (U.S. 340) and follow west to Rt. 9 to Martinsburg. Rt. 9 becomes Queen St. Look for historic marker just past high school on left.*
Season	*Closed during August*
Dining	*Continental breakfast included in room rate*
Children	*No*
Pets	*No*
Payment	*Cash, checks, MasterCard, Visa*
Rates	*$100–$125*

Petersburg

Holy smokes, what a hole!

SMOKE HOLE LODGE

P.O. Box 953
Petersburg, WV 26847
Edward W. Stifel III
(no phone)

Sheer cliff faces, forested slopes of redbud, a bounty of wildlife, a river that meanders through it all; that's the Smoke Hole. At night the stars tumble down into a pure, undisturbed blackness.

By design, Smoke Hole Lodge is for those who want a complete, unchaperoned escape with few modern conveniences and lots of rugged mountain scenery. There is no electricity, and no telephone, either. Owner-innkeeper Ed Stifel calls the Smoke Hole a "spiritual place." Many of his guests think of it that way, too.

It's no cinch getting here. The five-mile access route makes a logging road seem like a freeway by comparison. Ed doesn't expect a passenger car to make the trip, so he carries guests in and out by heavy duty truck or Suburban. Each jolt over a rock or pothole helps shake off the tensions new arrivals have come to lose, and by the time the vehicle lands at the lodge, a few steps from the cool rushes of the upstream Potomac River, everyone is relaxed and invigorated.

Ed Stifel's grandfather discovered the serene beauty of Smoke Hole gorge in 1916 and returned often for its superb bass fishing. Over the years he and some friends bought up available land in the area, eventually acquiring 1,500 acres of pristine wilderness. Ed grew up loving every square inch of it. The property extends for three miles along both sides of the river, gorgeous ridge top views in abundance. Guests are welcome to explore it all. (Bring your hiking boots. There are few worn paths to follow, and the terrain above the river is challenging.)

In early November 1985 heavy rains soaked this region for more than a week, until the water table could hold no more. The usually tranquil Potomac rose up one night, and as Ed stood helpless on the slope above, the rain coming in sheets, the original Smoke Hole Lodge was carried away. It had stood for more than a century.

With the encouragement of old guests and friends, Stifel designed and built a new lodge, three feet above the 1985 highwater mark (of a 2000-year flood) and 20 feet into the mountain so it can't wash away. More than 120 feet long and only 26 feet wide, the new lodge resembles a fanny pack strapped to the back of the mountain. It was opened for business in October 1987, less than two years after the flood.

Constructed of western red cedar from British Columbia, the building has a bright interior, owing to an offset main floor and judicious use of skylights. Even the narrow upstairs hall, only three feet wide and 18 feet high, needs no lights, except at night when a kerosene lantern is set at the foot of every door. The outside lower level is a long patio covered by the extended roof. It has a fireplace (where steaks are grilled), a hammock and rocking chairs. Swallows chatter and soar near their nests in the eaves.

The main room runs most of the building's length. It has a large stone hearth at one end, with lots of space to sit by the fire, read or play games. A wood-burning stove separates this area from the dining room and its long table lined with ladder-backed chairs. At the opposite end is the kitchen with its silent, non-electric refrigerators. (If you think they're nifty Ed can tell you where to get one.) The illumination is all by clean gas lamps and is certainly comparable to anything General Electric could provide.

The five guest rooms are spare but comfortable, and all have private baths. In addition, there are two dormitories. Most rooms have windows that face the river. Open one and your room is suddenly filled with sound, the soothing gurgles of moving water. Ed leaves a lantern by your bed at night; leave the window open just a crack and you're in business for a great night's rest.

When Ed was planning the new lodge, he considered adding some conveniences. He asked his regular guests if he should take this opportunity to install electricity for the first time. To a person, the response was a resounding "No!"

All meals are included in the room rate. Served family style, with Ed presiding at one end of the table, they are home-cooked, hearty and wholesome. Dinnertime is great fun; the inevitable storytelling can move from raucous to reverent in moments.

Although guests could spend all their time watching the river flow by, few seem to want that. Even before breakfast one or two slip out to explore the gorge, fish, watch birds or catch the sunrise. Children love to help Ed tend his Angus cattle, and he is happy to explain the purpose behind his various chores. Talking to Ed is refreshing; he is a quietly resourceful person who can still think independently in a world of imitation. He considers himself a cattleman first and an innkeeper only to the extent that he invites people, in limited numbers, to enjoy his home and its surroundings. He also believes living simply provides great riches and clarifies one's thinking about the importance of land and its preservation.

"Everyone needs time to reflect," says Ed. Smoke Hole Lodge is a fine place for doing it.

Location	*Twelve bumpy miles outside Petersburg, West Virginia. Meet Ed at Alt's Grocery on the south end of town*
Season	*Early May through October*
Dining	*All meals included*
Children	*Yes. No crib*
Pets	*Yes, but not allowed in lodge; two outside dog houses. Must be restrained if they start running the stock*
Payment	*Cash, check*
Rates	*$85 first person in room, $70 each additional. Two days minimum stay*

Shepherdstown

Award-winning comfort

THE BAVARIAN INN & LODGE

Rt. 1, Box 30
Shepherdstown, WV 25443

Erwin and Carol Asam
304-876-2551

The views from the grounds of the Bavarian Inn are as breathtaking as any in West Virginia's panhandle. Here at Shepherdstown the Potomac River roars through rocky cliffs on its way to meet the Shendandoah at Harpers Ferry. Four chalets built in the alpine motif—the latest addition to this reproduction of a Bavarian resort—boast private balconies overlooking the river and the C&O towpath, a recreation area for naturalists and sports enthusiasts throughout the year. These luxury accommodations have whirlpool baths, hand-painted phones and fireplaces.

At the Bavarian Inn, every detail of the entire operation—kitchen, dining room and guest rooms—is carefully monitored by resident owners/managers Erwin and Carol Asam. Born in Munich, Bavaria, they came sixteen years ago when the inn was a four-person operation; Erwin was the chef and Carol was the hostess. Today, the inn has 86 employees.

Now the inn has 42 rooms, tennis courts, a swimming pool and a restaurant that can accommodate over 300 people. Due to their relentless hard work and diligent supervision, the inn is now one of only two establishments in West Virginia rating four diamonds from AAA and four stars from Mobil Travel Guide.

The menu in the dining room changes with the seasons—game, venison, boar and pheasant in the fall; asparagus specials in the spring; fresh fruits in summer. Vegetarian and special diet requests can be fulfilled. A color theme of Bavarian blue and white is repeated in the details throughout the inn, especially in the check tablecloths in the dining area. The house specialties are traditional German cuisine: Wiener schnitzel, sauerbraten,

The Bavarian Inn & Lodge. *Shepherdstown, West Virginia*

photo by Suzanne K. Lord

Black Forest cake and apple strudel. The cozy rathskeller—the hub of evening activity—has a large selection of beer and wines.

Following a European tradition of family-owned inns, Asam is dedicated to his profession and is a gracious, proud host. He rarely takes a vacation and, with Carol, is rearing his two sons on the premises. Their painstaking efforts to maintain the highest standards of hostelry show up in the efficient service and spotless rooms. In sum, the Bavarian Inn offers Old World charm with all modern conveniences.

Location	*From Washington, DC take I-270 to Frederick bypass, then I-70 to Exit 49. Turn left on 40 Alt. to Braddock Hts-Boonsboro. Turn left in Boonsboro on MD 34 to Shepherdstown*
Season	*All year*
Dining	*Breakfast, lunch, dinner served seven days a week*
Children	*Yes*
Pets	*No*
Payment	*Visa, MasterCard, AmEx, Carte Blanche, Diners Club; personal checks are accepted for advance reservations only*
Rates	*$85–$135*

Civility since the Civil War

THOMAS SHEPHERD INN

Corner of German and Duke Street
P.O. Box 1162
Shepherdstown, WV 25443

Margaret Perry
(304) 876-3715

Built in the mid-19th century just after the Civil War, the Thomas Shepherd Inn was orginally used as a parsonage. The spacious white brick house, an early example of American architecture, sits on a busy intersection in the middle of the town. On entering the hall, however, one has a sense of stepping into another world and time, one of privacy and privilege.

The furnishings are a mix of American antiques, old family portraits, colorful Oriental carpets, and unusual ornaments from exotic lands. The immaculate bedrooms on the upper stories are imaginatively decorated with arts and crafts collected from all over the world. All of these rooms have private baths and central air-conditioning. The polished banisters and antique furniture shine. High ceilings add grace to the library and dining rooms. A welcoming fire is lit in the parlour for early risers.

A sample gourmet breakfast begins with homemade pastries like apple pecan muffins and poppy seed muffins, and progresses to apple soup with creme fraiche, poached pears and bananas Veronica. Hearty appetites can tackle the choice of entrees: sour cream pancakes with strawberry sauce, eggs Benedict garnished with caviar, or bacon and egg casserole with shiitake mushrooms. Owner and cook Margaret Perry uses edible flowers and herbs grown in her garden for flavoring and garnishing her dishes—nasturtium and squash blossoms, sage, tarragon, lavender and dill. Her personal warmth and interest in her guests' comfort inspired one visitor to record that an overnight here was "like staying with a congenial relative."

The attractions of historic Shepherdstown are literally a few steps outside the front door. A few minutes drive will take the visitor to the Antietam battlefield, the Potomac River and C&O towpath; Harpers Ferry is only 15 minutes away, and Skyline Drive, a half hour farther.

The fall foliage is unforgetable throughout the area. The Thomas Shepherd Inn is a good choice for honeymooners and other romantics who enjoy the charm of the past and the comfort of the present.

Location   *From Washington take 495 to I-270 West to I-70. If you wish to go via scenic Harpers Ferry take Rt. 340 to Rt. 230 to the center of town. If you wish to go via Boonsboro and Sharpsburg, take Alt. 40 from I-70, then pick up Rt. 34 West over the Potomac River to* *center of town and first stop sign. Inn is on the far right*

Dining	*Breakfast included in room rate*
Season	*All year*
Children	*Over 12 years of age only*
Pets	*No*
Payment	*Mastercard, Visa, AmEx, Discover and personal check*
Rates	*From $85 to $105, double occupancy. Special weekday business rates available.*

Boone Tavern Hotel of Berea College. *Berea, Kentucky*

photo by O'Neil Arnold

KENTUCKY

Berea

Steeped in Southern Appalachiana

BOONE TAVERN HOTEL OF BEREA COLLEGE

U.S. 25 and I-75
CPO 2346, Main and Prospect
Berea, KY 40404

Robert Stewart, General Manager
(606) 986-9358 or (606) 986-9359

The large, three-story, white-columned Boone Tavern Hotel is on the campus of Berea College, a four-year liberal arts college. Located in the foothills of the Cumberland Mountains and founded in 1855, the college is unique for many reasons. It charges no tuition and admits only students from low-income families. All 1,500 students, 80 percent of whom come from the Southern Appalachian area and Kentucky, are required to work at a college job in order to earn back a portion of their educational expenses. The rest of each student's bill is paid out of the college's endowment income and through gifts from friends and alumni. Students can choose work from 138 different departments ranging from computer programming to furniture making. Many hotel management majors gain practical experience working at Boone Tavern Hotel as servers, bellpersons and reservation clerks and later by serving in student management positions.

Named in honor of Daniel Boone and owned by the college, the hotel first opened as a guest house in 1909. Mostly student

KENTUCKY

1   Berea

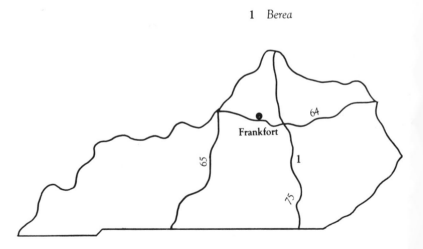

staffed, it has 59 guest rooms all with private bath, carpet, air conditioning, color TV and handmade furniture.

All three meals are served to hotel guests and the public daily in the handsome dining room with broad white free-standing columns and linen tablecloths. The hotel has earned a reputation of preparing delightful regional specialties including Chicken Flakes in a Bird's Nest, spoonbread and Jefferson Davis Pie. You are asked not to tip. Should you wish to express appreciation, you may contribute to the Student Fund. Another policy at the hotel is a dress code for the noon meal on Sunday and all evening meals: coats for men and dresses or dress pants for women.

A visit to Berea offers an especially good look at Southern Appalachian heritage—something Berea College is dedicated to preserving and nurturing. Guided hour-long walking tours of the 140-acre college grounds leave every day except Sunday from the hotel lobby. Not to be missed is the Appalachian Museum featuring a slide show, musical instruments and other past and present mountain folk exhibits, the Hutchins Library with its extensive Appalachian collection, and the Student Craft Industries which produce furniture, pottery, weavings and other handcrafts. Works are displayed and sold at the Boone Tavern Gift Shop and the Log House Sales Room. Also of note are the Weatherford Planetarium and the college's Art Building galleries.

Several craft and music festivals bring out the best work of local artists. During the Christmas season there are open houses, concerts, dances and a parade.

College activities are open to hotel guests. Hiking trails, swimming, tennis and cycling are available.

Location	*40 miles south of Lexington on I-75. Take Exit 76 or 77 at Berea*
Dining	*Breakfast, lunch, dinner seven days a week*
Season	*All year*
Children	*Yes*
Pets	*No*
Payment	*MasterCard, Visa, AmEx, Diners Club, Discover, cash and personal checks*
Rates	*From $47 (single) to $89 (three persons)*

Blue Mountain Mist Country Inn. *Sevierville, Tennessee*

TENNESSEE

Gatlinburg

A dignified old shirt

BUCKHORN INN

2140 Tudor Mountain Rd.
Gatlinburg, TN 37738

John and Connie Burns
(615) 436-4668

For innkeeper John Burns, family ties at the Buckhorn Inn go way back. "It feels so right," he says, "like putting on an old shirt."

Burns's great-grandmother had the idea to build the inn and his great-grandfather financed it. His grandfather was the designer and his granduncle, Douglas Bebb, built the place. That was in 1938.

Bebb was a jack-of-all-trades. "He was a woodworker, and cut the inn's wood paneling himself," says Burns. "He contributed sculptures that are still here. He was the groundskeeper, and he cooked, too." Bebb was granted a patent for cross-breeding dogwoods (there is a specimen on the grounds), and he and his brother created a novel three-hole golf course on part of the inn's 40 acres. "No one plays anymore," says Burns. "It's a strange course—the PGA would never have sanctioned it," he grins. At one point on the course golfers had to pick up their ball and carry it through the woods before continuing.

TENNESSEE

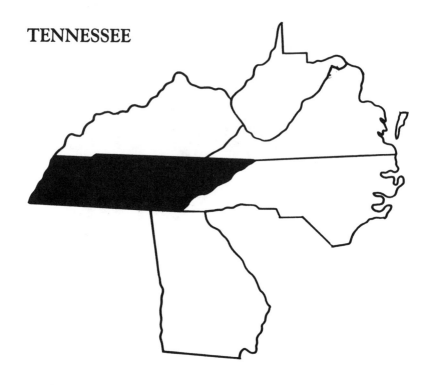

1   *Gatlinburg*
2   *Pigeon Forge*
3   *Rogersville*
4   *Rugby*
5   *Sevierville*
6   *Walland*

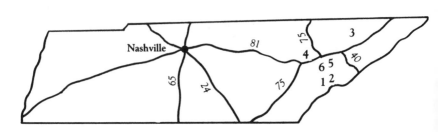

Until 1978, when he retired, multi-talented Douglass Bebb was the inn's only keeper. New owners came along, and in February 1989, they hired Burns and his wife, Connie, to run the inn. The old shirt fits them just fine.

You'll share that feeling when you visit the serenity of this lovely setting six miles from the clatter of Gatlinburg, and only a mile and a half from Great Smoky Mountains National Park. The inn's portal, with its two-story white columns, offers a terrific view of Mount LeConte. The wooded grounds and open fields are beautifully maintained and ideal for a stroll. Bring your fishing pole, if you like, and cast for bass and bream in the pond.

The main house has five upstairs rooms, all with private bath and furnished with spindle beds and antiques. Four guest cottages with rustic furnishings nestle in the woods. Each has a sitting porch, living room with fireplace (and ample firewood) and bedroom with private bath. The conference center, a contemporary one-story building with hardwood floors and large stone fireplace, offers two guest rooms when it isn't reserved for meetings.

At an inn built by Douglass Bebb it's no surprise that there is a guest room in the old water tower. Although it's small, the room is private, and fun. It's got running water, of course.

Bookcases line a wall of the large living room, where a grand piano awaits the talented, across the gleaming wooden floor from the stone hearth. Antiques and contemporary pieces around the room give off a quiet, stimulating atmosphere.

Breakfast and a fixed evening menu, prepared by a professional chef, are served in the dining room. Tables decked with linens, fresh wildflowers and candles suggest a semi-formal tone.

Location	*From Hwy 441 in Gatlinburg, go north on Hwy 321 for approximately five miles, then turn left on Buckhorn Road. Within a mile, turn right to the inn on Tudor Mountain Road*
Season	*Year round, except Christmas*
Dining	*Breakfast, included in room rate; prix-fixe six-course dinner is $26 per person*
Children	*Over six in inn; over ten for dinner*

Pets   No

Payment   *Cash, checks, MasterCard, Visa*

Rates   *$95–$250; $105–$250 in October, double occupancy. Rates include sales tax*

Pigeon Forge

Something new in the mountains

HILTON'S BLUFF INN

2654 Valley Heights Drive
Pigeon Forge, TN 37863

Jack and Norma Hilton
(615) 428-9765 or (800) 441-4188

Not every inn needs to be 100 years old and loaded with antiques to offer a quiet mountain respite. At Hilton's Bluff Inn, a brand new B&B outside Pigeon Forge, guests can get away from it all in a modern environment that represents the latest trend in mountain guest houses.

The two-story cedar building is tucked among tall trees high on a two-acre hilltop. Under the calming breeze of ceiling fans on the inn's covered porches, guests can ease back in one of the oak rocking chairs and be reminded of porches years older. The feeling is just as good. Inside there are ten guest rooms, five on each side of a hallway, each with private bath, carpet and a king- or queen-size bed. An interior decorator by trade, Norma Hilton furnished all the rooms with traditional and antique pieces, which she describes as a romantic mingling of the old and new. Cozy country rooms feature quilts made by Norma's mother. Special occasion rooms are lavished with luxurious taffeta, eyelet and lace. Each room has its own color scheme, ranging from soft pastels to bold primaries. Half the rooms have small private balconies as well as large whirlpool tubs enclosed with paneled

Hilton's Bluff Inn. *Pigeon Forge, Tennessee*

or mirrored partitions. Three of the rooms with heart-shaped tubs are honeymoon/special occasion rooms. One room, called "Wild Rose," has a king-size waterbed with an illuminated headboard! (Honeymoon packages are available, of course.) On the other, somewhat less passionate, side of the hallway, rooms open onto the porch through sliding glass doors.

Beneath a 22-foot cathedral ceiling, large windows in the common areas take advantage of superb views in nearly every direction. The den's big stone fireplace conjures images of gathering with friends before a crackling blaze on a cool night, hot chocolate in hand. The inn has a small library and an upstairs recreation room with bumper pool, darts, card and game tables. The recreation room is easily converted into a conference room for executive meetings and retreats.

A Southern gourmet breakfast is served every day in the dining room and consists of such delightful eye-openers as glazed bacon, apple puffed pancakes, stuffed French toast and breakfast casseroles in puffed pastries. Breakfast in bed (or tub), picnic baskets, lunch, dinner and special events can all be arranged.

It's hard to believe touristy Pigeon Forge is only half a mile away. Travelers seeking a comfortable and imaginative alternative to the run-of-the-mill lodgings there will be glad to know Hilton's Bluff is so near. If the Pigeon Forge attractions aren't what you're after, don't miss the natural beauty of Cades Cove in nearby Great Smoky Mountains National Park.

Location	*In Pigeon Forge, take US 321 south (Wears Valley Road) half a mile to Valley Heights Drive and turn left to Inn*
Season	*Year round*
Dining	*Full breakfast (included with room rate) and refreshments served daily; lunch and dinner by requ for groups*
Children	*Adults preferred, however, limited accommodations for children*
Pets	*No*
Payment	*Cash, check, MasterCard, Visa, AmEx*

Rates	$69–$89 per couple, January through March; $79–$104 per couple, April through December
Other Considerations	BYOB (dry county)

Rogersville

Echoes of the wild frontier

HALE SPRINGS INN

110 West Main Street
Rogersville, TN 37857

Carl Netherland Brown and Edwin S. Pace, Jr.
(615) 272-5171 or (800) 272-5171

Bring an appetite for history and your walking shoes when you come to the Hale Springs Inn, the oldest continuously operating hostelry in Tennessee. A beautiful tribute to our past and practically a museum, the inn is part of a veritable course on antebellum life in Rogersville. With the help of an informative tour pamphlet, you can walk through the history that has been preserved here.

Built in 1824 by John McKinney, a prominent attorney, the large three-story brick building was first known as McKinney's Tavern. Andrew Jackson was a guest during his journey home from Washington to Nashville in 1832; later presidential visitors were James K. Polk and Andrew Johnson. During the Civil War the inn was favored by Union officers, serving as their headquarters whenever they were in control of the town (Confederates preferred Kyle House across the street). By 1884 the name had been changed to Hale Springs Hotel, and many of the guests were tourists stopping over on the way to Hale Springs Resort, a mineral springs 15 miles to the north. Some changes were made

Hale Springs Inn. *Rogersville, Tennessee*

in the early part of this century so the inn could better compete with newer establishments.

The present owner, Captain Carl Netherland-Brown, former master of the liner *S.S. Bahama Star* and a direct descendant of the Netherland family of nearby Kingsport, purchased the inn in 1982 and completed a meticulous restoration in 1985. Now you, like Jackson, Polk, Johnson and others, can enjoy the full grandeur of the inn and its historic surroundings.

Much of what you see here is original, including the heart-of-pine flooring, the long second- and third-story staircases, the wainscoting and chair rails, the third-story dormer window and the paneling and doors to the ten large guest rooms. The rooms are named either in honor of people important to Rogersville or for illustrious former guests. Some have walls angled curiously out of square, with nooks and crannies and high ceilings, and contain actual family pieces of their namesake. All of the furnishings proudly reflect the past: an actual guest register from 1889, large canvases by Samuel Moore Shaver, one of Tennessee's best known early portraitists, antique clocks, photo collections, steamer trunks, a piano dating from 1842, pre-1850 wardrobes and canopy and rope beds with massive headboards. Most rooms have workable fireplaces. Each room has its own bath and a tastefully concealed television.

The Colonial Dining room, located in the original tavern area, has two fireplaces with antique mantels. The room still gives the feeling that Andrew Jackson could walk in at any moment and request a pint of his favorite brew. (You are reminded to bring your own, however.) A small glassed-in porch, with three tables, offers an ideal setting for romantic, candle-lit dining. Prime rib is a house specialty.

The Rogersville Heritage Association has produced an excellent self-guided walking tour of their historic town, which was founded in 1786. Many of the buildings are of the same period as Hale Springs Inn, and some are older. A visit to Rogers Cemetery will remind you that the Tennessee frontier was "tamed" not so very long ago. Davy Crockett's grandparents, massacred by Cherokee Indians, are buried there. Heritage Days, a celebration reminiscent of a harvest festival, is held every year on the second weekend in October.

Location	*Rogersville, 60 miles northeast of Knoxville, TN, and Smoky Mountain resort areas*
Season	*All year*
Dining	*Continental breakfast included in room rate. Dinner for two approximately $30. Bring your own wine.*
Children	*Yes*
Pets	*No*
Payment	*Cash, MasterCard, Visa, AmEx*
Rates	*$45 to $65 for two persons*

Rugby

English village on Tennessee's Cumberland Plateau

NEWBURY HOUSE INN & PIONEER COTTAGE

Highway 52, P.O. Box 8
Rugby, TN 37733

Pearl Nestor
(615) 628-2430

Newbury House and Pioneer Cottage are the names of the lodgings, but your destination is the east Tennessee village of Rugby. Why this unique village was founded is a strange and fascinating story. Thanks to the inspired efforts of a teenager, it exists today as a valuable restoration.

In the late 1870s, English author and reformer Thomas Hughes led a group that bought 75,000 acres of Tennessee wilderness in order to establish a colony. The colonists were to be younger sons of England's upper class, boys who had no inheritance to expect (estates traditionally went to the eldest son) and few socially acceptable professions to pursue. Though well educated, they had only limited career choices.

Hughes, author of the widely read *Tom Brown's School Days*, felt the British gentry "would rather see their sons starve like gentlemen than strive in a trade or profession that is beneath them." He hoped the new community in America, founded in 1880 and called Rugby, would offer an alternative. But his belief that the colonists would eagerly embrace manual and agricultural trades was extremely optimistic, if not fanciful.

The community was carefully planned and laid out, the young men came, and by the mid-1880s Rugby was the largest town in three counties. At its peak it had 450 residents and more than 70 buildings, many with the high peaked roofs, gabled windows and decorative millwork typical of the Victorian period. There were gardens, hiking trails and grounds set aside for lawn tennis. The Tabard Inn, a hotel and social center that drew visitors from around the world, unfortunately was destroyed by fire in 1884.

Instead of rolling up their sleeves and doing the practical work necessary to make a success of Rugby, many colonists busied themselves with cultural activities they had enjoyed in England, to the occasional dismay of their native Tennessee neighbors. They formed social, musical, dramatic, tennis, football and baseball clubs, dressed for tea in the afternoon and held balls and other entertainments. Meanwhile, their business ventures usually failed. It seemed possible to take the boy out of the gentry, but nearly impossible to take the gentry out of the boy.

By the early 1900s a series of problems had taken its toll and most of the original colonists had moved away, leaving Rugby a remote farming town of about 125 people. The population continued to dwindle over the next half century.

In the mid-1960s, a student named Brian Stagg happened upon Rugby's story while researching another project. Although only 15, he became charged with the idea of restoring the village. Before long he was directing the Rugby Restoration Association (now Historic Rugby, Inc.), compiling information to have the town listed on the National Register of Historic Places (accomplished in 1972) and doing anything else he could to attract support. By 1985 Rugby looked much as it had a century earlier.

Newbury House and Pioneer Cottage, two of Rugby's oldest buildings, were restored for use as guest lodgings. Pioneer Cottage was the first frame house built on the town site in 1880. Thomas Hughes stayed here on his first visit to Rugby, and many incoming colonists used it as a temporary home. The two-story cottage rents as a separate unit for up to ten people, offering one bedroom downstairs and two on the upper floor. There are 1½ baths, a fully equipped kitchen, a screened porch and a full house fan. The pine board walls and worn wooden floors are charming reminders of Rugby in the 1880s.

Newbury House was the colony's first boarding house, in use as early as 1880. There are five upstairs guest rooms; two share a bath and the others have their own. Beautiful borders, painted wood floors and Victorian furnishings, including some early Rugby pieces, dominate the rooms. Tea and coffee are served in the parlor, which has a small library.

The Harrow Road Cafe, built in 1985 to blend architecturally with its historic surroundings, serves Cumberland Plateau home cooking and British specialties. Breakfast and lunch are served daily, dinner Friday through Saturday.

A visitors center, housed in the restored schoolhouse, has excellent historic exhibits. Guided tours are available daily from February 1 through December 31. Most of the colony's 17 restored buildings are open to the public during the annual Rugby Pilgrimage, which is held the first weekend in October. The Spring Music and Crafts Festival takes place in May.

Just to the north of Rugby is the recently established Big South Fork National River and Recreation Area, with 100,000 acres of hiking, camping, fishing, canoeing and other river sports.

Location	*Rugby, about 17 miles southeast of Jamestown on Highway 52*
Season	*Year round*
Dining	*Breakfast, lunch, dinner (at Harrow Road Cafe)*
Children	*All ages at Pioneer Cottage only (crib available); over 12 at Newbury House*
Pets	*No*
Payment	*Cash, check, MasterCard, Visa*
Rates	*Newbury House: $50–$60, single; $60–$70, double, breakfast included. Pioneer Cottage: $58, double occupancy; $8 each additional person*

Sevierville

Like blue smoke

BLUE MOUNTAIN MIST COUNTRY INN

1811 Pullen Rd.
Sevierville, TN 37862

Norman and Sarah Ball
(615) 428-2335 or (800) 497-2335

While relaxing in a rocking chair on the wraparound porch here, you can gaze out to the Smoky Mountains and see how Blue Mountain Mist Country Inn got its name. A smokey blue mist rises from the abundant vegetation. The Cherokee name for the Smokies meant "like blue smoke."

Spurred by a desire to do something new, innkeepers Norman and Sarah Ball decided to share the beauty of their home surroundings with others by building this inn on part of the family farm. (Sarah grew up in the house across the road, where her parents still live.) Using his architectural and drafting experience, Norman drew up plans for the inn. "And then I re-did them," laughs Sarah. "I wanted it to feel like a home."

Completed in 1987, the large inn looks Victorian with its cone turret, front gable and lattice underpinning. It sits on 60 acres of rolling countryside, only minutes from the Great Smoky Mountains National Park. A small pond and horseshoe pit are visible from the front porch, where a hammock, rockers and checker boards, in addition to the fine view, create a peaceful feeling. Just inside the entrance shiny hardwood floors, old photographs, local crafts and paintings continue the country flavor.

Five quaint, romantic cottages are tucked into the woods behind the inn, each one with a jacuzzi, TV with VCR, fireplace, kitchenette and a front porch with a swing. In the morning, cottage guests can join the other guests in the inn for a country breakfast.

There are lace tablecloths in the dining room, where biscuits and gravy or stuffed French toast are part of the hearty breakfast that comes with your lodging. Numerous sitting areas, both downstairs and up, give guests a choice of mingling or seeking privacy. A conference room and television room are downstairs.

The 12 guest rooms, all with private bath and a combination of carpeted and hardwood floors, are named for nearby areas or communities such as "Greenbrier," where Sarah's father lived before the Park Service bought up his land for the Great Smokies Park, and "Elkmont," where Norman's family lived before their land was similarly acquired.

Handmade quilts are important here. In addition to those in the guest rooms, quilts decorate many of the walls of the inn, including a friendship quilt with local family names and a maple leaf design quilted by Sarah's grandmother. In one guest room is an old school desk from the Smoky Mountain Academy, one of the first public schools in the county (Sevier), and the one from which Sarah's parents graduated. Another room features furniture from Sarah's grandmother's family, one of the first to settle here. Modern amenities include jacuzzies in two of the rooms and one in the back yard; those who like old fashioned touches can get a room with a claw-footed tub. There are three deluxe rooms, each opening onto an upper level porch.

For Sarah and Norman, the hard work and long hours they devote to the inn pay off when they get to meet their guests. Says Sarah, "We get a lot of enjoyment out of providing a pleasant place and experience for people."

Location	*From north on Rt. 441 through Pigeon Forge turn right at the 2nd traffic light on Lower Middle Creek Road. From south turn left at the 7th traffic light. Continue 2.5 miles and turn right onto Jay Ell Road. Go 1.5 miles to inn on left*
Season	*Year round*
Dining	*Breakfast*
Children	*Yes (no cribs)*
Pets	*No*
Payment	*Cash, check, MasterCard, Visa*
Rates	*$79 to $125*
Other Considerations	*Ramp for handicapped*

In the trees, a place to hide

MILK & HONEY COUNTRY HIDEAWAY

2803 Old Country Way
Sevierville, TN 37862

Cathey and Gary McFarland
(615) 428-4858

The road that leads to Milk & Honey Country Hideaway is just right for a mountain retreat. Winding gently uphill, it helps put whatever you're hiding from (busy world, kids, parents. . .) a little farther behind with each passing curve. Even better, when you pull into the parking area and see the bed-and-breakfast nestled among tall trees above you—almost like a tree house— you are likely to think no one could find you here. Best of all, you don't need a password to get into this hideout, just a reservation. A short path takes you to the steps to the covered porch, where innkeepers Cathey and Gary offer a warm welcome.

As native East Tennesseans, Cathey and Gary McFarland have lived most of their lives within sight of the Great Smoky Mountains, and operating the Milk & Honey has afforded them the opportunity to fulfill their dream of living in the mountains that they have held so dear. In addition to her culinary expertise, Cathey is talented in a variety of handcrafts including needlepoint and crocheting, and Gary is a part-time photographer who loves to share his knowledge of the nearby Great Smoky Mountain National Park with guests. The fruits of their labors can be seen throughout the inn.

Peace and quiet prevail here. In the living room, a stone fireplace, ash and pine ceiling, flowered wallpaper, comfortable furniture and country knick-knacks suggest the charm of a cozy 100-year-old home rather than a new building.

Antiques, lace curtains and quilts handmade or picked up at local yard sales and auctions reinforce this feeling in the six guest rooms. Each room has its own sink; two have a private bath, two share an adjoining bath and two share one in the hall. The rooms all have names hinting at their furnishings. For example,

"Jennie's Ruffles and Lace" has lace curtains and ruffled bed covers and is home to the beautifully restored oak bedroom suite that was Gary's great-grandmother's. "Irene's Morning Mist" looks like morning if ever a room could and has morning glories in the wallpapers. "Speck of Heaven" is another room, but to see what that means you'll have to come visit. Modern touches, such as air conditioning, rose carpeting on the stairway and a jacuzzi in one room, mix well with the overall turn-of-the-century tone.

A hearty Southern-style breakfast will get you off on a full stomach in the morning, and there are always fresh cakes and other goodies for a midnight snack.

There are dozens of sites and activities in the area. If you want to come out of hiding, Pigeon Forge is only a five-minute drive. There you'll find restaurants, Dollywood, outlet malls, craft shops and miniature golf, among other things. If you've come to enjoy the mountains, Cades Cove, a beautiful wilderness valley, is nearby in Great Smoky Mountains National Park.

Location	*From Pigeon Forge, take Hwy 321 to a right turn on Walden Creek Road. Go one mile and turn left onto Little Valley Road, then 1.3 miles to Milk & Honey on left*
Season	*All year*
Dining	*Full breakfast, snacks*
Children	*10 and older*
Pets	*No*
Payment	*Cash, check, Visa, MasterCard*
Rates	*$60–$90 in season, April–December; $49–$75 off season, January–March*

High in the sky

VON-BRYAN INN

2402 Hatcher Mountain Road
Sevierville, TN 37862

D.J. and Jo Ann Vaughn
(615) 453-9832 or (800) 633-1459

You might come for what you can see from the Von-Bryan Inn, but chances are you'll stay for the rocker and the hammock and the quiet and relaxation that go with them.

The view from all sides of the Von-Bryan Inn is not to be missed, especially at sunset. The inn commands a panoramic look at the Smoky Mountains, including Cove Mountain and Mount Leconte in the distance and Wears Valley at your feet. Situated on a 2,100-foot mountaintop known as Hatcher Mountain, it seems much higher. "People who live in the valley like to come up here to spot their homes and farms," say owner-innkeepers D.J. and Jo Ann Vaughn. "It's much like looking out from an airplane."

The inn itself is well-suited for what the Vaughns want to offer their guests: "a private, relaxed atmosphere of quiet seclusion and old-fashioned hospitality." Built in 1986 and purchased by the Vaughns two years later, the log and board and batten home tastefully combines an old-time feeling, thanks largely to the wood and stone work, with traditional American furnishings. The living room, with its huge, stacked stone fireplace, has a cathedral ceiling supported by cedar beams. The paneling is a mixture of woods, including western red cedar, spruce and white oak, installed at contrasting angles to produce a unique, vaulted effect that guides the eye gently up to the tongue and groove ceiling. Large windows throughout the building accent the overall spaciousness and insure that guests are never very far from the surrounding views.

All of the six guest rooms in the main house have private baths and two have whirlpools. Named for trees, the rooms are carpeted and very large. The Red Bud Room, complete with cherry-red whirlpool, is popular with honeymooners.

Von-Bryan Inn. *Sevierville, Tennessee*

Antiques, Jo Ann's childhood dolls and handmade quilts contributed by the family grandmothers are among many personal touches at the Von-Bryan Inn. Also on display are paintings by Nadine Vaughn, an artist who also happens to be D.J.'s sister. D.J. himself is no slouch; the clocks, bookcases and china and corner cabinets are all examples of his craftsmanship.

The garden room with many plants has a reading loft, queen-size bed and steam shower surrounded by windows and skylights. There is also a large outdoor pool.

A common area upstairs can serve as a meeting room for business gatherings; it is equipped with a television and VCR.

A separate cottage, the Log Chalet, is built on a slope and offers additional privacy and views from its wraparound porch and balcony. It has two bedrooms with private bath, a living room with fireplace, fully equipped kitchen, television and whirl-pool. A two-night minimum stay is required.

Rice and asparagus casserole is a specialty of the full breakfast. Picnic baskets and other special services can be arranged, including pickup and delivery to the inn by helicopter. Now, that would be a view.

Location	*Between Knoxville and Great Smokies National Park, about seven miles south of Pigeon Forge and eight miles north of Townsend, TN. From Pigeon Forge go 7.2 miles south on Hwy 321 to Hatcher Mountain Road and inn sign; turn right and go 2.4 miles to inn. From Townsend go eight miles to Hatcher Mountain Road and sign; turn left*
Season	*Year round*
Dining	*Full breakfast*
Children	*Log Chalet only*
Pets	*No*
Payment	*Cash, check, Visa, MasterCard, AmEx, Discover*
Rates	*Main House $80–$125; Log Chalet $160; 10% discount for any stays of two or more nights weekdays*

Walland

A ridgetop rambler

INN AT BLACKBERRY FARM

1471 West Millers Cove Road
Walland, TN 37886

Gary Doyle
(615) 984-8166 or (800) 862-7610

Before our visit, innkeepers Gary and Bernadette Doyle had described their country-house hotel and mountain estate to us like this: "Blackberry Farm was built 50 years ago of mountain stone, shingles and slate to ramble over a ridgetop almost as though it grew there. It is the dream of two people who loved the Smokies and were determined to create a retreat where others of their mind could find rest, fun and contentment."

The dream lives on beautifully, we are happy to report. Located on 1,100 secluded acres outside of Walland—and, surprisingly, only 20 minutes from Knoxville Metropolitan Airport—Blackberry Farm is elegantly designed for comfort and relaxation, truly a place where visitors can leave the rest of the world behind.

Within the two-story Main House and several additions—the Cardinal Suite, the Guest House and the Gate House Cottage—there are 25 guest rooms. The matching fieldstone rock and mortar used on all the buildings gives them a tasteful unity. The Main House's flagstone entryway takes visitors to a large handsome living room with gleaming hardwood floors, Oriental rugs, fireplace and a picture window with a view of West Millers Cove. The dining room, where guests enjoy unhurried delightful meals planned by Bernadette and prepared by an expert chef, extends from the living room. Dinner is served by candlelight. The steep slate roof of the Main House, together with its dormer windows, creates wonderfully interesting angles, closets, nooks and crannies in its upper-level guest rooms. Well-chosen carpet, wallpaper, English and American antiques, flowered quilts and down comforters combine to make these rooms especially cozy and appealing.

Just as attractive as the hotel's interior are its surroundings. The two-mile jogging/walking trail that leads from the Main House down a steep terraced hill and passes a smoke house, barn and gentle creek is among the most beautiful we have visited. Other nature walks, including one three miles long to the Great Smoky Mountains National Park boundary, are available as well. Fishing tackle is available for those who wish to wet a line in either of the two stocked ponds or in Hesse Creek, and trips can be arranged with hotel's Orvis fly-fishing guide. Mountain bicycles are provided for cyclists to explore winding country roads. Other activities provided for include tennis, swimming (either in the pool or the creek), croquet, shuffleboard, horse-shoes, volleyball, basketball, softball, putting on a green and non-stop rocking on the hotel's front terrace.

With such a range of activities, it is no wonder that Blackberry Farm caters successfully to business meetings, strategy planning sessions, executive retreats, weddings and family reunions. Should any guests want to venture farther afield, Cades Cove (the reconstructed primitive settlement in the Park), Gatlinburg, Pigeon Forge, Lambert Acres and Laurel Valley Golf Courses, Clingmans Dome (the observation tower at the highest point in the Smokies), Little River and Abrahms Creek Watershed and Knoxville are all nearby.

Location	*3 miles off U.S. 321 in Walland, TN*
Dining	*Breakfast, lunch, dinner included in rate*
Season	*All year*
Children	*Holidays*
Pets	*No*
Payment	*Personal check, MasterCard, Visa, AmEx*
Rates	*$595–$795 per couple for 2-night weekend package; $350–$470 per couple daily*

Grandview Lodge. *Waynesville, North Carolina*

NORTH CAROLINA

Asheville

Apples, apples, apples: a triple A rating

APPLEWOOD MANOR

62 Cumberland Circle
Asheville, NC 28801

Susan Poole and Maryanne Young
(704) 254-2244

You don't need a map to Applewood Manor. Just follow your nose. Innkeepers Susan and Maryanne keep their inn smelling like fresh apples all year-round (apple-scented air freshener)—mouth-watering good. Nearly hidden from the street among large trees and flower beds, their gracious 1912 manor was designed in a Colonial Revival style: (symmetrical plan, turned banisters, wide foyers, and Federal pediment on the porch) with a shingled exterior reminiscent of New England. Two acres of tree-shaded grounds provide privacy for reading on the porches and ample space for croquet and badminton. More athletic guests can explore Asheville on the inn's bikes or use complementary passes to aerobics classes or a workout at a nearby fitness club.

Four spacious, sparkling rooms in the main house, all with queen-size beds, private baths and some with fireplace, and a separate cottage with kitchen facilities are named after different kinds of apples. Hence the York Imperial Room with separate sitting area and veranda overlooking the garden; the cheerful, blue Mackintosh Room trimmed with wallpaper of bright red

NORTH CAROLINA

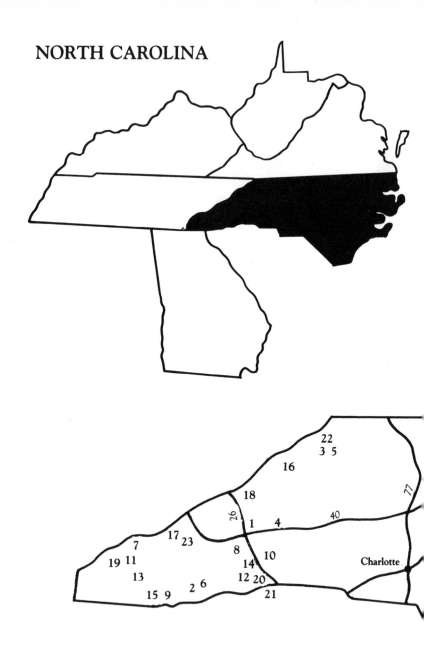

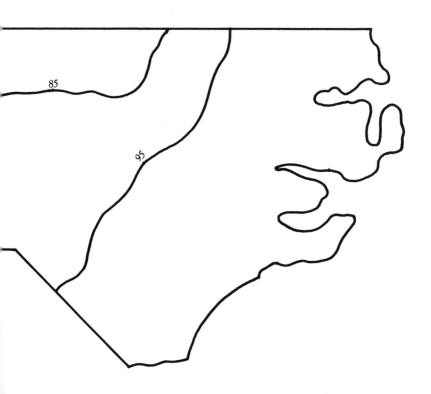

Applewood Manor. *Asheville, North Carolina*

apples; the peach-hued Granny Smith Room decorated with country hats, and the Northern Spy Room. The common rooms are gracious but not intimidating, welcoming readers, card players and good conversation; here guest peruse brochures on local activities and menus from local restaurants. An added convenience is being able to buy tickets at Applewood to the biggest attraction in town, the Biltmore Estate, thus saving a wait at the entrance.

A meticulously prepared breakfast is served on the porch in season or in the cozy dining room. Before tackling Asheville's many attractions or hiking in the Smoky Mountains, your day may start with such fine fare as fresh fruit, baked spiced peaches, pineapple muffins, herb egg bake with Swiss cheese, basil and tomatoes, oven-roasted potatoes, orange pecan waffles, raspberry and cream cheese-filled French toast. Tea and/or sherry are served in the afternoon.

The manor, run by the present owners for only two years, enjoys a three-diamond rating from AAA and the reputation for a high number of repeat guests—the best proof of a successful inn.

Location	*From I-240 take exit 4C. Go north on Montford Ave., east on West Chesnut, north on Cumberland Ave. and bear right on Cumberland Circle.*
Season	*Year round*
Dining	*Breakfast and tea*
Children	*12 and older*
Pets	*No*
Payment	*MasterCard, Visa, Discover, personal checks*
Rates	*$75–$100 (for private cottage that sleeps four)*
Other Considerations	*No smoking inside*

Opulence and elegance, oh my!

CEDAR CREST VICTORIAN INN

674 Biltmore Avenue
Asheville, NC 28803

Jack and Barbara McEwan
(704) 252-1389

In 1983, Jack and Barbara McEwan traded a 200-room hotel in Wisconsin for what was then an old, run-down mansion in Asheville. Improving their own quality of life was one reason for the move. Quality of restoration is what guests can admire when they see the results of the McEwan's painstaking seven-month refurbishment. All the lavish touches are here.

Now on the National Register of Historic Places, the three-story Queen Anne style home was built in 1891 for prominent Asheville businessman William E. Breese. A confederate veteran, Breese had moved to Asheville during the town's boom period as a summer retreat. His home, with its sharply peaked gables, stained-glass windows, second-floor porch and large veranda, became a part of Asheville's high society. When growth slowed in the 1920s, the mansion changed hands, becoming a sanitarium and later a boarding house.

Answering an ad in *Preservation News*, the magazine of the National Trust for Historic Preservation, the McEwans rescued Cedar Crest from years of neglect. In some rooms, as many as 13 layers of wallpaper had to be removed and replaced with period reproductions. New wiring was installed, and new plumbing was a necessity. Decades of grime had to be cleaned from the incredible interior woodwork, matched in the region only by that in nearby Biltmore House.

A glimpse at the spectacular solid oak trim work is reason enough for a visit to Cedar Crest. The dream of a lover of fine craftsmanship, it complements the fully paneled entryway, the parlor's intricate mantels and the massive carved staircase leading to the second level. "Guests come to indulge their Victorian fantasies," says Barbara.

The ten guest rooms are furnished with Victorian finds, including canopied or brass beds, large claw-footed tubs, lace and replica drapes. Every guest room is air-conditioned and has a telephone. Several guest rooms have working fireplaces. Each of the two upper levels has a sitting area.

The Guest Cottage, a 1915 bungalow, offers two suites ideal for families or those wishing extra privacy. Dogwoods and rhododendron line the grounds between the main house and the cottage. The property's four acres have a variety of flower gardens, planned for continuous bloom. There is also a Croquet Pitch for anyone who favors an authentic Victorian challenge.

Breakfast is served buffet style, either in the dining room or on the veranda. For a special treat, "breakfast in bed" is offered at no additional charge. Favorites include hot compotes of fruit, muffins, sweet breads and preserves, all homemade.

Location	*Asheville*
Season	*Year round*
Dining	*Deluxe Continental breakfast. Afternoon and evening beverages to suit the season*
Children	*Over 12*
Pets	*No (state law)*

Cedar Crest Victorian Inn. *Asheville, North Carolina*

Payment   *Check, travelers' check, MasterCard, Visa, AmEx, Discover*

Rates   *$75–$130 for two persons*

Two choices in the heart of town

FLINT STREET INNS

100 & 116 Flint Street
Asheville, NC 28801

Rick, Lynne and Marion Vogel
(704) 253-6723

When Lynne and Rick Vogel moved from New Orleans to Asheville in 1980, they intended to take a year off to renovate the house they had found at 116 Flint Street. They had just become the second owners of the tree-shaded 1915 home in the peaceful Montford historic district, Asheville's oldest neighborhood. The idea of an inn came up after they got here and, as Rick points out, "There was not another similar inn" in town at the time.

A few years later the home next door, at 100 Flint Street, became available. Once a quiet boarding house renting exclusively to elderly—"No married couples and no 'fooling around' were permitted," smiles Rick—it is now the second part of the Flint Street inns, kept by Rick's mother, Marion.

The inns are convenient to the Civic Convention Center, restaurants and shops. A driveway between the two houses leads to a private, lighted parking area where big trees, shrubs, flowers and mountain laurel make for a pleasant welcome. Any of six friendly cats are likely to greet you before the innkeepers have a chance. Once inside, the sensation is as if you've arrived at your best friend's house to spend the night.

Comfortably and tastefully furnished throughout with period pieces, the houses offer a total of eight double guest rooms, each with private bath and air conditioning. Some have fireplaces. Personal touches, like knickknacks from the 20s and 30s and silly hats, give each room a little spice.

A complete Southern style breakfast is served to guests each morning from 7:00 to 9:00 A.M. Many visitors will be pleased to know it includes a morning paper.

Location	*Asheville*
Season	*Year round*
Dining	*Breakfast*
Children	*14 and older*
Pets	*No*
Payment	*Cash, check, Discover, MasterCard, Visa, AmEx*
Rates	*$80 double; $65 single; $20 each additional person*

Another winner the second time around

THE INN ON MONTFORD

296 Montford Avenue
Asheville, NC 28801

Ripley Hotch and Owen Sullivan
(704) 254-9569

Ripley Hotch, in his book *How to Start and Run Your Own Bed and Breakfast Inn*, quotes Maureen Magee in telling potential innkeepers to "Look to what you love; let your inn be a stage for who you are."

Fortunately for their guests, Hotch and Owen Sullivan took this advice themselves when establishing their second successful venture, the lovely Inn on Montford. They bring with them not only their years of experience at making guests happy, but their enviable good taste, antiques and graciousness that marked their Inn at Boydville in Martinsburg, WV. They have again created an inn of distinction without pomp, comfort without excessive frills, warmth without intrusiveness. Here are the little comforts that make one feel at home—or at least in the kind of home one dreams of. Each side of the bed has a good reading lamp, and there are several common rooms for guests' privacy (for reading, for talking, for listening to music or, as in the garden room, for just watching the sun stream through the maples). The paintings, photographs and accent pieces are personal statements with histories guests enjoy, like Ripley's ship collection inherited from five generations of sea captains and the stunning bed quilts made by his mother.

Located in the historic, tree-shaded section of Montford, the 1900 house is an English cottage interpretation of the Arts and Crafts style; hence the shingles, natural materials, large windows and wide porches. All four bedrooms have private baths (three with whirlpool tubs) and queen-size beds and are named for famous writers associated with Asheville: Thomas Wolfe, O. Henry, F. Scott Fitzgerald and Edith Wharton.

Over breakfast, guests get helpful hints on where to go and what to see, while relishing morning marvels like croissants stuffed with cream cheese and raspberry, baked Caribbean pears, Tex-Mex souffles with sour cream, quiche, frittatas, Bavarian pancakes, apple bread, cranberry muffins. Tea is served in the afternoon with pound cake and chocolate chip cookies. For walking off these scrumptious offerings, downtown is just seven blocks away; the Civic Center, a mile. But in spirit and setting, you're far removed from modern madness; unlike Wolfe, you can go home again—to the Inn on Montford.

Location	*Take I-40 to I-240 to the Montford Ave. exit (4C), go north about 3/4 of a mile and the inn is on the left.*
Season	*Year round*
Dining	*Breakfast and tea*
Children	*At adult rates and with parental supervision*
Pets	*No*
Payment	*MasterCard, Visa, Discover, AmEx, check, cash*
Rates	*$90–$110 double occupancy*

Like Wind in the Willows, *a classic revived*

OLD REYNOLDS MANSION

100 Reynolds Heights
Asheville, NC 28804

Fred and Helen Faber
(704) 254-0496

If an award were given for an energetic, resourceful couple fru-
gally tackling a seemingly impossible restoration job, Fred and
Helen Faber would surely deserve to win. You will no doubt agree
when you visit their very impressive Old Reynolds Mansion.

One of the few antebellum brick houses remaining in Asheville, and the only one in a semi-rural setting, the three-story
home sits on four acres of a ridge leading up Reynolds Mountain.
Built in 1855 by Colonel Daniel Reynolds, it was renovated in
the early 1900s by his son, Nathaniel Augustus Reynolds. Nathaniel added a finished third floor with a dormered mansard
roof, Colonial woodwork inside and out and, sometime before
1914, a covered wraparound porch with large white columns and
a second-story tier.

When the Fabers bought the 17-room mansion in 1977 it was
in terrible disrepair and known locally as Toad Hall. The porches
were rotting, the plumbing leaked, the plaster was peeling, the
wiring was bad. But the foundation was solid. Nonetheless, building "experts" told the Fabers restoration was either impossible
or outrageously expensive. One recommended bulldozing the
place.

Such talk only hardened the Fabers' will to bring the building
back to life. Fred kept his job in Minnesota, and for the next
three years he and Helen planned their attack.

To the chagrin of those who said it couldn't be done, the
mansion did get restored—and also listed on the National Register of Historic Places. The Fabers spent more than two years
working full-time, seven days a week on the rejuvenation, completing the work within $1,000 of their original budget estimate,
a fraction of what they were told it would cost.

The mansion has ten guest rooms filled with antiques. Eight

Old Reynolds Mansion. *Asheville, North Carolina*

have a private bath and a few have fireplaces. One bath has a four-poster *tub*. An open stringer stairway, with elegantly crafted railings and balusters, leads from the large entryway to the upper levels. All of the rooms are bright and the first two floors have at least 12-foot ceilings. Some details remain, like the original doorknobs.

There is a large swimming pool on the grounds, and the story of how Fred cleaned it out is perhaps the best illustration of how much work the Fabers have done. Like so much here, it's hard to believe. He first had to *mow* it. Then he dug it out with a shovel and wheelbarrow before he finally could fix it.

One thing you can believe, they don't call it Toad Hall anymore!

Location	*Ten minutes north of downtown Asheville. Take Merrimon Avenue (Rt. 25) north of town past Beaver Lake. Turn right just past stop light onto Beaver Drive, then left up gravel lane*
Season	*Year round (weekends only January and February)*
Dining	*Expanded continental breakfast*

Children	Six and older, except weekends when they must be at least 12
Pets	No
Payment	Cash, checks, travelers' checks
Rates	$45–$85 double occupancy

A national standout

RICHMOND HILL INN

87 Richmond Hill Drive
Asheville, NC 28806

Susan Michel
(704) 252-7313
(800) 545-9238

When its three-year-long, massive renovation was complete in 1989, the Richmond Hill Inn was a natural to be chosen one of the Ten Outstanding New Inns in America by *Inn Review Newsletter*. Those that make it to the top ten must offer "that special something that sets them apart from others—abundance of charm both architecturally and in decor, distinctive amenities above and beyond the norm, and perhaps most important, conveying all-around comfort to the guests." These criteria, we found, are generously met in the western Asheville inn and signal what you can expect on a visit here.

Designed by James Hill, the supervising architect of the United States Treasury buildings, and built in 1889 of native North Carolina materials including granite for the foundation, slate for the steep pitched roof, poplar for the exterior siding and oak, walnut and cherry for the interior paneling, the 30-room mansion was the private home of Asheville Congressman and diplomat Richmond Pearson and his wife, Gabrielle.

Unique for its time with running water, its own communication system, a gas-lighting system and a pulley-operated elevator, the three-story Queen Anne home stayed in the Pearson family until the early 1970s. It sat empty, though, for many years

Richmond Hill Inn. *Asheville, North Carolina*

in the 30s and 40s before the Pearson children returned to open the home as a museum. It was sold to North Carolina Baptist Homes, Inc. in 1972 who agreed to preserve it for ten years. The Preservation Society of Asheville and Buncombe County also worked to maintain the mansion by getting it listed on the National Register of Historic Places in 1977 and then by purchasing seven acres of adjacent land in 1981 so that the home could be moved if necessary. The Society's foresight paid off when they got the opportunity to purchase the mansion for $1, provided it be moved from its original site.

In November 1984, with the necessary funds raised, the mansion was carefully moved 600 feet to the east. The moving company, Mitch Construction, was presented a national award for moving the largest structure in the United States that year.

Finally, in 1987, the Society sold Richmond Hill to The Education Center, Inc., a Greensboro, NC, company whose president, Albert Michel, and his wife, Margaret, had an interest in historic preservation. They spent three years restoring the estate to its original grandeur. In addition, The Education Center, Inc. purchased 40 acres of land once part of the original estate, added at the rear of the inn a 900-square-foot octagonal ballroom for meetings and receptions, enclosed part of the wraparound porch in glass to serve as a restaurant and added five guest rooms on the inn's third floor. High on a hill overlooking the French Broad River, the inn has reclaimed its distinctive prominence, proudly wearing its original colors of yellow with dark green and burgundy trim.

The Michel's daughter, Susan, is the innkeeper who welcomes visitors to the inn's luxurious surroundings. The inviting entry hall with its warm, raised oak paneling, exposed beams and 12-foot-high ceiling, boasts a portrait of Gabrielle Pearson hanging in a foot-wide, hand-carved, gilded frame over the mantel. The handsome library contains over 200 books from Richmond Pearson's original library in addition to many titles about western North Carolina and others written by western North Carolina authors. Two well-appointed parlors and two conference rooms are also available on the ground floor for use of guests.

Visitors climb the inn's grand staircase with its hand-turned oak spool balusters to reach the second- and third-story guest rooms. Each of the 12 rooms has hardwood floors with rich rugs, period antiques, private bath, TV and telephone and is complemented with fresh flowers and down pillows. Most of the seven second-story rooms are named for well-known historic persons who were connected to the Pearson family. Many of these rooms have fireplaces and claw-footed bath tubs. The canopy beds in the Gabrielle Pearson Room and the Colonel Pearson Room are especially beautiful. The five third-story rooms are named for writers who were either Asheville natives or who had Asheville connections. Somewhat smaller, these rooms have skylights built into the ceiling, cozy angled nooks and crannies, window seats, fan windows and a copy of each author's biography.

Cottages on the west side of the mansion complement the inn's Victorian architecture while offering an attractive addition to the original accommodations. Each of the nine cottage rooms have been named for trees found in western North Carolina. The rooms feature a fireplace, pencil-post bed, spacious bathroom, porch with rocking chairs, television, telephone and refrigerator with complimentary drinks. Each front porch overlooks a neatly manicured croquet courtyard.

The inn has a fine restaurant named for the home's first hostess, Gabrielle. Guests may choose to dine in either the formal cherry-paneled dining room or in the glassed-in porch with wicker chairs and tables and an inspiring mountain view. The meals are gourmet and center on American and nouvelle showpieces such as sauteed breast of maple leaf duckling, grilled scallopini of venison and veal rib eye.

Location	*I-240 in Asheville; take the 19/23 North Weaverville exit. Continue on 19/23 and turn at Exit 251 (UNC-Asheville). At the bottom of the ramp, turn left. At the first stoplight, turn left again on Riverside Dr., turn right on Pearson Bridge Road and cross the bridge. At the sharp curve, turn right on Richmond Hill Drive. The mansion is at the top of the hill*
Dining	*Breakfast included in room rate; Dinner and Sunday brunch available in restaurant; gourmet picnic lunch available*
Season	*All year*
Children	*Yes*
Pets	*No*
Payment	*Cash, check, Visa, MasterCard, AmEx*
Rates	*$125–$295*

Balsam

Past treasure, today's pleasure

BALSAM MOUNTAIN INN

Box 40
Balsam, NC 28707

Merrily Teasley
(704) 456-9498

This imposing, three-story structure sits on a mountainside, 3,400 feet high, like an aging empress on her throne, confident and classy. A few character lines belie a romantic and glamorous past: a lifestyle of wealth, servants and country leisure. One longs to share her memories, if only for a weekend.

The good news is you can. With impeccable taste, sensitivity and considerable resources, owner Merrily Teasley is completing a remarkable renovation of this turn-of-the-century mountain marvel. She's recreating the era when well-to-do city dwellers packed up maids and children, boarded the Southern Railway and disembarked at the highest railway station east of the Rockies, just a few steps below the Balsam Mountain Inn. Some unpacked their trunks and stayed all summer, climbing the area's impressive mountains, picnicking at waterfalls and partaking of the inn's seven springs, known for their therapeutic properties.

From the moment you cross the front veranda (100 feet long and lined with rockers) and push open the double screen doors you'll recognize a special place. The lobby—bright, open, filled with ferns and cheerful chintz-covered wicker—is at once homey and grand. Next to the reception desk—an old fashioned charmer itself—is a blackboard listing the day's fare. Most days of the week three meals are served in the large, formal dining room. At each end of the lobby, the library and game room, furnished with more wicker and colorful rugs, have enough books, games and puzzles to keep you busy for weeks. Large fireplaces remind that even a summer evening at this altitude requires a cozy fire.

On the two floors where renovation is complete, extra-wide hallways, designed for holding steamer trunks, lead to 34 spacious

The Balsam Mountain Inn. *Balsam, North Carolina*

bedrooms, some with sitting areas, all with private bath (some with claw-foot tubs) and beautiful linens, including six luxurious pillows per bed. All beds are double or king size; some have down comforters. Each room has a different color, motif and personality—evidence of Merrily's talent and previous innkeeping experience. With bold flair she has coordinated florals, checks, stripes, paisleys, prints and pastels with unusual accent pieces and gaily painted walls. Toiletries and extra-thick towels complete guests pampering.

In all, it took over 800 gallons to refresh the walls and exterior. Merrily's sensitive renovation successfully preserves the character and dignity of a century-old classic while providing all the comforts for a contemporary clientele. No TV or phone breaks the spell here. You can read on the veranda or keep fit exploring the grounds' 26 acres of trails, ponds and woods.

Location	*Close to milepost 443 of the Blue Ridge Parkway, near the crossing of U.S. 74/23 and 13 miles from I-40. From the parkway take the exit for 74/23 and turn towards Sylva (south). Turn off 74/23 about 1/4 mile south of the parkway overpass at a small sign marking the village of Balsam. Make a right up a hill, cross the railroad tracks, and continue straight for another 1/3 mile*
Season	*Year round*
Dining	*Full country breakfast included. The lunch and dinner menu, available Tuesday through Sunday, emphasizes healthful, low-fat fare. You are welcome to BYOB*
Children	*Over two years*
Pets	*No*
Payment	*MasterCard, Visa, checks and cash*
Rates	*From $75 double occupancy (for off season weekday) to $150 (in season) for two-room suite; $15 each extra person*

Beech Mountain

Round-the-calendar sociability

ARCHERS MOUNTAIN INN

Rt. 2 Box 56-A
Beech Mountain, NC 28604

Bill and Toni Coleman
(704) 898-9004

Archers Mountain Inn is a popular destination in any season of the year. At its height, three-quarters of the way up Beech Mountain, spring and summer visitors enjoy temperatures as lovely as the views of the mountains and Elk River Valley. Lovers-of-fall visitors come to warm their hearts at the glow of the burnished foliage. And in winter when so many other inns close down, Archers stays open. It matters not if you come to ski the nearby slopes and cross-country trails or just to sit in front of the fireplace, the welcome mat is out.

Friendly and down-to-earth innkeepers have combined three buildings into an inn that reflects their personalities. The lodge, built as a private residence about 25 years ago with large stone pillars and a small fountain, now has six guest rooms each with private bath and all with fireplaces. No TVs or phones in these rooms, but a pay phone is available and cable TV can be watched in the big living room where guests gather near the impressive field stone fireplace. One lodge room has a large, outdoor hot tub.

The Annex, completed at Archers in December 1984, offers eight more guest rooms with exposed beams and knotty pine paneling and doors. Each room has two queen-size beds, stone fireplace, private bath, microwave, small refrigerator, cable TV and glass doors that open onto a porch complete with rockers.

Once a fudge and gift shop, the Wobbly now houses the inn's office and dining room. Full country breakfasts are served year round. The entire inn is available for special occasions such as family reunions, weddings, etc. Special menus available.

Location	*On state highway 184 between Banner Elk and Beech Mountain. From Boone take Rt. 105 south to Rt. 184 north*
Dining	*Breakfast included*
Season	*All year*
Children	*Yes*
Pets	*No*
Payment	*Cash, travelers' checks, MasterCard, Visa*
Rates	*$45 to $95 per room in the spring and summer; $45 to $115 in the color season; $55 to $125 during ski season; rates based on single or double occupancy. Extra charge for additional persons*

Black Mountain

Built for the farmer's daughter

RED ROCKER INN

136 North Dougherty Street
Black Mountain, NC 28711

Pat and Fred Eshleman
(704) 669-5991

An innkeeper's life is a busy one, often requiring the juggling of many chores and responsibilities. This is certainly true of Pat and Fred Eshleman of the Red Rocker Inn. Allowing time for our interview shortly before lunch, Fred ushered us in, smiling "Follow me—I'm making mud pies in the kitchen."

Up to his elbows in a vat of ice cream and confections—not mud—Fred told background stories about the inn. He seemed accustomed to doing two things at once. Though tending an inn "looks glamorous," he says, "it's a very strenuous pace."

The Eshlemans looked at 35 different properties before settling on the Red Rocker Inn in 1982. Built by Silas Dougherty, a farmer, as a wedding gift for his daughter, the country home with wraparound porch and hipped roof became a boarding house known as Dougherty Heights in 1927 when a wing was added. In 1964 the name was changed to Red Rocker Inn. Situated in a quiet residential section of Black Mountain, the inn is within easy driving distance of more than 30 antique dealers and the region's major sights. Asheville, Biltmore Mansion, Blue Ridge Parkway, hiking, tennis and golf are all nearby. And, should you decide to go no farther than the inn's front porch, yes, there are red rockers.

The inn's 18 guest rooms, each with private bath, are pleasantly decorated and conducive to relaxation. The Eshlemans try to keep it that way and, to that end, have installed no televisions or phones. They want this to be "a comfortable oasis to get off the world and find inner peace." The rooms have names that suggest pathways to that peace. The walls of the Music bedroom are papered with a piano score (it's Chopin, according to Fred, who used to teach music). The Preacher's bedroom has stained glass, and the Three Mountaineers room has wonderful wood carvings.

A line begins to form at the dining room door as meal time approaches, with good reason: food is a Red Rocker strong suit. The menu changes daily, and is served family style. Guests may choose from such dinner entrees as Southern style baked chicken with pecans and orange sauce, roast pork loin to country ham and mountain trout with almond butter. That's the easy part. Then it gets tough: there are soups and chowders, homemade breads, biscuits and muffins, vegetables, casseroles, salads and relishes (sauerkraut salad, Amish chow-chow and marinated cucumbers). For dessert, you can try Fred's "Black Mountain Mud," or something called "Sawdust." If those don't tempt, perhaps warm blackberry cobbler topped with ice cream will, or a slice of "X-rated" chocolate cake. Before the meal begins, the innkeeper extends a welcome to all guests and asks a blessing, a nice pause in a hurried world.

Red Rocker Inn is popular among country-inn hoppers, and it's no wonder. The Eshlemans' hard work proves they care about their guests.

Location	*In the town of Black Mountain, 17 miles east of Asheville, just off I-40*
Season	*May 1 to November 1*
Dining	*Breakfast, lunch, dinner (not included in room rate)*
Children	*Well behaved; no crib*
Pets	*No*
Payment	*Check, travelers' checks*
Rates	*$45–$75 double occupancy*

Blowing Rock

Unique setting, food, lodging, views and entertainment

THE FARM HOUSE INN

P.O. Box 126
Blowing Rock, NC 28605
The E.J. Blackwell Family
(704) 295-7361

Blowing Rock's Farm House Inn is known for its large restaurant and lively entertainment and—as if that weren't enough—its incredible panoramic view and antiques. Once called the Skyland Inn, it was built by the Stewart family in 1893 and has been in continuous operation ever since. The E.J. Blackwells, longtime innkeepers, whose family have been in the area for more than 450 years, are only the second owners of this summer retreat.

A nice, bustling air about it, upbeat and theatrical, welcomes you. All of the singing waiters and waitresses and dancers and instrumentalists who entertain every night in the dining room and the adjacent auditorium called the "parlour" are college students from universities all over the United States. You can enjoy their performances, ranging from excerpts from Broadway shows to light opera to country music, while you dine as well as after dinner. The favorite table fare is fresh Carolina Mountain Trout, Roast Turkey and Stuffing, New York Strip Steaks, Fresh Baked Chicken and fresh summer vegetables plus a great assortment of desserts including fresh fruit cobblers in season.

The three-story rambling farm house with angled additions commands one of the most beautiful views in the area. John's River Gorge, Grandfather Mountain and Hawk's Bill are all part of the panorama. On a clear day, the Mount Mitchell Range, which boasts the highest peak (6,684 feet) east of the Mississippi, can be seen in the distance.

The inn has an especially wonderful collection of antiques acquired by the senior Blackwells during their sixty years of marriage and found throughout the house and in the guest rooms where the various period pieces complement brass beds. All 12 inn rooms have private baths. Lodging is also available in cottages and in a motel-like structure.

A sidewalk cafe and lounge at the inn offers a pleasant spot from which to enjoy the spectacular views and sunsets. And, the inn's shops have items priced so that there is something for everyone.

Location	*Above business 321 on South Main Street, two miles off Blue Ridge Parkway, 90 miles northeast of Asheville, 90 miles northwest of Charlotte, 90 miles west of Winston-Salem*
Dining	*Continental breakfast for inn guests; lunch and dinner for two, $27 to $37, served to the public*
Season	*The musical program runs from the first week of June to Labor Day, but facilities are available spring and fall, also*

Children	*Welcome! All ages*
Pets	*Provisions for pets*
Payment	*No credit cards, but personal checks are accepted*
Rates	*$50–$75, double occupancy*

Deluxe gentility and privacy

GIDEON RIDGE INN

P.O. Box 1929
Blowing Rock, NC 28605

Cobb and Jane Milner
(704) 295-3644

Just south of Blowing Rock on a secluded five-acre wooded rise overlooking both the Blackberry and John's River gorges, sits an especially fine inn. The Gideon Ridge Inn, built during the years 1939–42 of red stone that was quarried from nearby Grandfather Mountain, was a private summer home. Today's innkeepers, Cobb and Jane Milner, have transformed the large, two-story dwelling into a romantic retreat.

The center room of the inn is its library where chairs and tables are grouped near the gigantic stone fireplace, Oriental rugs below and heavy beams above. Guests often get together here to play games and converse. They also gather on the inn's impressive terrace to drink in the view of the mountains as well as the gardens and trails in the foreground.

All eight guest rooms have private baths. The three terrace rooms and the Carriage Room have fireplaces with gas logs. Most rooms are furnished with fabulous family antiques.

A full country breakfast ranging from cornmeal pancakes and omelettes to scrambled eggs and sausage is included in the room rate. It is served in the newly expanded dining room with large windows that take advantage of the view. Groggy guests who like a little private time at breakfast to wake up, will appreciate that the dining room has individual tables, not family-styled seating. No forced conversation. Other meals can be arranged in advance, and often are, for small business meetings, wedding parties, private lunches.

Location	*From 1½ south of Blowing Rock turn right on Rock Road; go 200 yards, take left fork; proceed up the ridge; road dead ends at the inn*
Dining	*Full breakfast included in room rate; afternoon tea is included in rate for inn guests*
Season	*All year*
Children	*Over 12 years old*
Pets	*No*
Payment	*Personal and travelers' checks, Visa, MasterCard and AmEx*
Rates	*$100–$130 per night, double occupancy*

Old-fashioned smiles and parlors

MAPLE LODGE

Sunset Drive
P.O. Box 1236
Blowing Rock, NC 28605

Marilyn Bateman
(704) 295-3331

The sunny disposition of Maple Lodge makes it a popular spot to stay in the resort town of Blowing Rock. Located a half block off Main Street within easy walking to arts, crafts and curio shops and excellent restaurants, the lodge extends the comforts of home—thanks to friendly innkeeper Marilyn Bateman.

This unpretentious 1946 two-story frame house draws distinction, as well as its name, from a large maple tree in its front yard. Inside, two parlors, one with fireplace and the other with an old fashioned pump organ, are shared by guests. Homemade muffins and breads are part of a full buffet breakfast served from 8:00 to 10:00 A.M. in the stone-floored Garden Room. Choose a cozy table warmed by the woodstove, or overlooking the wild-flower garden. Pull up a rocking chair later for reading, games, television, or just relaxing by the fire.

Twelve guest rooms, all have private baths and are furnished with antiques, handmade quilts and family heirlooms. The choice of beds varies from twin, double, queen and king, some with canopies, so ask ahead of time if you have a preference. A two bedroom, two bath cottage can also be rented.

Summer stock theatre, antique shopping, numerous hiking and horseback riding trails, golf courses, white-water rafting, fishing and, in winter months, many skiing resorts, are near at hand. Tennis and swimming can be enjoyed only half a block away from the Lodge at the municipal park.

Location	*A half a block off Main Street on Sunset Drive, next to summer stock theater*
Dining	*Full breakfast included in room rate*
Season	*Closed during March*
Children	*Over 12 years of age*
Pets	*No*
Payment	*Visa, MasterCard, check or cash*
Rates	*$65 full, $74 queen, $83 king, $100 for two room suite, $150 cottage*

Best of two worlds

RAGGED GARDEN INN

Box 1927, Sunset Drive
Blowing Rock, NC 28605

Joe and Joyce Villani
(704) 295-9703

You get the flavor of both the Old World and contemporary America when you visit the Ragged Garden Inn in Blowing Rock.

In the inn's ambiance it is only fitting to find continental cuisine, mostly Northern Italian. Homemade pasta and veal dishes are the specialties. But only a block away, on this mountain village's main street, you can stroll from one craft and curio shop to another. You can also walk to a tennis game in the park or take in a show at the summer theatre.

Chef Joseph Villani, who has shared the innkeeping duties with his wife, Joyce, since they purchased and renovated the inn in 1983, has a strong background in the restaurant business. His years of experience date back to work at New York's famous Sardi's Restaurant and includes long-time ownership of other establishments in Greenwich, CT, and Winter Park and Vero Beach, FL. Running the Ragged Garden agrees with the Villanis; for them it's "a dream come true."

Shaded by big trees, the large two-story, stone and chestnut bark home was built in 1900. Chestnut paneling, cut from trees before the blight, enriches the interior forming a warm backdrop for the antique and country style furniture. All of the five guest rooms have private baths and several rooms open onto a balcony that overlooks a garden, rhododendron and roses. Guests are also welcome to stay in a two-bedroom cottage/efficiency that rents either as one or two units.

Blowing Rock serves well as a base to many area attractions including Tweetsie Railroad, Mystery Hill, the Linn Cove Viaduct, the Ashe County Fresco Churches, Linville Falls and Linville Caverns. And, not to be forgotten: horseback riding, golf, white-water rafting, canoeing and fishing to boot.

Location	*From Charlotte, NC airport (Douglas): Take 77 North to Statesville; I-40 West to Hickory; 321 to Blowing Rock. At light with Scotchman on right, take left turn. This is Sunset Drive; Ragged Garden is on the right, opposite the school*
Dining	*Full breakfast is included in room rate; Prearranged in-house catering only*
Season	*April through January 1*
Children	*Children under 12 in Cottage only*
Pets	*No (kennel nearby)*

Payment *Visa, MasterCard, personal check, cash*

Rates $50–$90

Where sun and hosts smile on children

SUNSHINE INN

Box 528, Sunset Drive
Blowing Rock, NC 28695

Jim and Sue Byrne
(704) 295-3487

Located one mile off the Blue Ridge Parkway in Blowing Rock, the Sunshine Inn is known primarily for its homey atmosphere, good home-cooked breakfasts, and attention to young 'uns. Innkeepers Jim and Sue Byrne, with five children of their own, gladly welcome yours.

Jim left the corporate world in 1980 to spend more time with his family and start the guest house. The inn's accommodations, unlike most others, were planned with little ones in mind.

One guest room with bunk beds has a crawl space that kids love to play in. There are dolls, marbles, train sets—you name it—even a bathroom decorated in a baseball motif. Another room joins with a nursery. Seven guest rooms, which combine as needed, are available in all, including a two-bedroom cottage. The rooms are furnished comfortably with many hand-made family items.

The Byrnes encourage their guests to make themselves at home. The coffee pot is always on so you feel free to stroll back to the kitchen for a cup anytime. Your hosts like to tell you about the many things to do in the area. Blowing Rock's central park lies just one block away, and half a mile down the road, beckoning bikers and horseback riders, are 28 miles of trails. Parents who want to be alone for a bit, will be glad to know that babysitters are usually available.

Location *At main light in front of park in the center of town, turn onto Sunset Drive, one and one-half blocks to the* *elementary school. Inn is across the street from the school*

Dining	*Breakfast included in room rate*
Season	*Year round*
Children	*Yes*
Pets	*No*
Payment	*MasterCard, Visa, cash, personal check*
Rates	*Double occupancy $60–$95 per night*

Brevard

In the hills, the sound of music

THE INN AT BREVARD

410 East Main Street
Brevard, NC 28712

Eileen and Bertrand Bourget
(704) 884-2105

In 1911, Confederate troops who had served under Stonewall Jackson gathered here in the valley of the French Broad River. They met for a reunion at this large mansion with its stately white columns and front balcony. The event, with Mrs. Jackson present, was hosted by the home's owner, William E. Breese, a well-known attorney and mayor of Brevard.

The soldiers are a memory now, but the mansion that had been transformed into an inn in the 1940s when it became known as the Colonial Inn remains an ideal spot for any type of reunion, honeymoon or quiet getaway. Music lovers are especially drawn to the Inn at Brevard because in summer they can attend outstanding classical concerts at the nationally acclaimed Brevard Music Center.

Now hosted by Eileen and Bertrand Bourget and listed on the National Register of Historic Places, the inn consists of two buildings, the grand main house, which dates back to 1885 and, behind it, an air-conditioned lodge. Ten guest rooms with private showers are available in the lodge. The main house has five non-smoking rooms. Three (including the Woodbridge Suite) have private baths. All rooms are attractively furnished with antiques.

Overnight guests enjoy a full breakfast (included in the room rate) in the inn's dining room. Patio dining daily from 2:00–8:00 P.M. Fresh mountain trout highlights the inn's evening meals, served on Friday and Saturday evenings.

Location	*Take Interstate 26 East from Ashville; exit on Route 280 at Brevard. Continue on to 64 West and then take Route 276 south to center of town. Inn is five blocks from center of town on the left*
Dining	*Full breakfast included in room rate; dining room open to public for dinner and Sunday Brunch; Dinners: $12.95–$18.95; brunch (table service): $6.95–$11.95*
Season	*Closed January*
Children	*In lodge only*
Pets	*No*
Payment	*Cash, travelers' checks, Visa, MasterCard*
Rates	*$59 to $75 double occupancy; suite $125*

Checkered past, genteel present

THE RED HOUSE INN

412 W. Probart St.
Brevard, NC 28712

Lynne and Peter Ong
(704) 884-9349

Part of the charm of a stay at an old, restored mountain inn is being able to relive its past in your mind's eye, especially if it saw service in many ways. At Brevard's Red House Inn your mind can wander endlessly, starting in 1851, before either Brevard or Transylvania County was established, when the structure was built—as a trading post. Weathering Civil War damages and years of neglect, the house in time became Brevard's railroad station. It went on to become the county's first court house, Brevard's first post office, a private school and the beginning of Brevard College.

Peter and Lynne Ong have once again restored the large, venerable house and now offer it as a B&B for, as their brochure reads, "ladies and gentlemen." Its hipped roof with eyebrow window, two-story veranda and expansive sunroom combine with turn-of-the-century antiques to create a genteel Southern look. In contrast to its postwar years, the house today shows the results of tender, loving care. Each of the six guest rooms has a distinct personality. Single or double bedrooms are available; three rooms have a private bath. All other guest rooms share a bath.

There is no shortage of outstanding cultural events near the B&B. The house sits on the road to Brevard's Music Center where excellent summer classical music concerts have become a tradition. At the well-known Flat Rock Playhouse, summer stock theatre is enjoyed by many visitors. The B&B is also within easy walking distance of downtown curio shops and restaurants. For nature enthusiasts, a trip to Brevard is not complete without an outing to at least one of the area's 120 waterfalls.

Location   *One block north of Main Street, four blocks from the*
center of Brevard

Season	*April–November*
Dining	*Breakfast, full, large*
Children	*Over 7*
Pets	*No*
Payment	*Cash or check, MasterCard, Visa*
Rates	*$47–$65, double occupancy*

Bryson City

Preserving special moments

FOLKESTONE INN

101 Folkestone Rd.
Bryson City, NC 28713

Norma and Peter Joyce
(704) 488-2730

Norma and Peter Joyce have done a masterful job preserving, restoring and adding on to this 1926 farmhouse. In an astonishingly short period of time since acquiring the inn in June, 1988, they now offer guests the ultimate in a mountain bed and breakfast experience.

Before coming to Bryson City, Peter, an Englishman, worked in corporate finance in Jacksonville, Florida, while Norma taught elementary school. Fond of entertaining as well as the outdoors, they carefully planned their switch from city dwellers to mountain innkeepers, inspired by the European B&Bs they had often stayed in while traveling.

"We do it all," says Peter of their new career, but he is quick to point out that they have had some help. The building, formerly known as Folkestone Lodge, was mostly empty when the Joyces arrived. "During our first week here," he recalls, "the Chamber

Folkestone Inn. *Bryson City, North Carolina*

of Commerce called, hoping we could accommodate Fourth of July visitors. I said yes, but that we would need help getting ready." They were full their first weekend and "hit the ground running," says Peter with a grin.

In their first off-season, which lasted about ten weeks, the Joyces raised the roof and added four rooms, three of which have private balconies. One room, with a tub big enough for two, is designated the honeymoon suite. The new rooms are tied into the old so beautifully in both construction and decor that one nearly forgets being in a new part of the house. "We finished the new floors ourselves," remembers Norma, "to make sure they would have that 'old look' feeling." Private bathrooms have been painstakingly created for each of the nine guest rooms (exposed brick and original stone work remain in some) using Victorian claw-footed bathtubs with antique washstands. Other room furnishings include a tasteful blend of English family heirlooms, high headboards and pieces made by a craftsman neighbor.

Downstairs, three bedrooms have a decidedly European flavor, with stone floors and pressed tin ceilings. "This·is as close as we come to an English pub," says Peter nostalgically. Of note is an antique double hide-a-bed. A different landscape painting by Tennessee artist Ben Hampton hangs in each room; and each room is identified by the painting in it.

The Joyces cater to their guests. The combination Southern-English full breakfast is served in a relaxed way so late risers can still get fed. The house specialties include blueberry pancakes and, if eggs are on the day's menu, Peter's scrambled eggs, a delicious treat.

The Folkestone Inn is located only minutes from numerous activities: white-water rafting, tubing (a must for the adventuresome), hiking, horseback riding, gem mining, antiquing and craft shopping, train rides and the Cherokee Indian reservation.

One lucky couple had a special moment preserved thanks to the Joyces' thoughtfulness. A young man once asked Norma to suggest a romantic spot where he could take his unsuspecting girlfriend, pop the question and give her a ring. Norma happily told him exactly where to go. Later, at breakfast, she was horror struck to overhear a large group making plans to visit the very same place. "You can't go there!" she blurted. She then had to explain the reason for her outburst. "We waited on pins and needles all day," she says. "What if the young lady had said no?" She didn't and it's hard to imagine she could have, given the aura of the Folkestone Inn.

Location	*Bryson City*
Season	*Open all seasons*
Dining	*Breakfast*
Children	*Limited accommodations for well-behaved children*
Pets	*No*
Payment	*Cash, personal check, travelers' check*
Rates	*$59–$79*

Old-Fashioned, laid-back

FRYEMONT INN

P.O. Box 459
Bryson City, NC 28713

Sue and George Brown
(704) 488-2159 or (800) 845-4879

In 1923 Captain Amos Frye, a timber baron, realized his dream of building a rustic mountain lodge entirely from native lumber and stone. Now, seven decades later, he'd be pleased to see what has happened to his dream: virtually nothing. Innkeeper Sue Brown says Fryemont is much the same as it was in the Captain's day, and she and husband George intend to keep it that way.

Fryemont Inn has a porch full of rocking chairs from which guests can look out over little Bryson City to Great Smoky Mountains National Park just beyond. She describes the town and the inn as "old fashioned" and "laid back." The inn's exterior walls, joined at wide angles to form a building resembling a short, broad "U", are covered with bark from enormous poplar trees.

Fryemont Inn. *Bryson City, North Carolina*

New arrivals entering the big lobby are greeted by glossy hard-wood floors, exposed beams and a tremendous stone fireplace that accommodates eight-foot logs. A gift shop off the one side specializes in local crafts, including pottery.

There are 36 chestnut-paneled guest rooms, each with private bath, wall-to-wall carpeting and multi-paned pocket windows. Rooms on the corners of the building are adapted to the odd angles. A cottage on the grounds, remodeled from a 1940s recreation and dance hall that later also served as a private home, has three two-level suites. Each has air conditioning, loft bedroom with king-size bed, living area with cathedral ceiling, fireplace, television, wet bar or small kitchen.

A large swimming pool, reputedly the first built west of Asheville, and a tennis court are nestled among hemlock, dogwood and poplar trees down the slope from the inn. Watch for Amazing Grace, the resident cat with one eye.

The dining room has a raftered, vaulted ceiling, brass and wood paddle fans, shiny hardwood floors and stone hearth. Wooden tables and chairs are all original from the 1920s; there are also armchairs from the Vanderbilt Hotel in Asheville. Breakfast and dinner are included in the room rate. Pancakes, omelettes and grits, of course, are breakfast features. Dinner entrees range from country and mountain fare to standards such as chicken, ham, steak and prime rib. Vegetables are served family style (pass-the-platter), homemade soups, breads and desserts round out the selection. The mountain trout dishes are house specialties, as are cheese soup, mushroom casserole and the freshly baked cakes, pies and cobblers. There is a full-service bar.

It's hard to believe the Fryemont Inn sat empty during a part of the 50s and 60s. Recent reviews applaud this "architectural masterpiece" and its "remarkable aura of homeyness." There's a sense of fun here, too. To-wit: a British flag decorates a wall in the waitresses' station. "A group of British sailors on leave from Jacksonville, Florida, came to see the Smoky Mountains," remembers Sue. "They stayed here and presented this flag to us after a farewell dinner. The young lady waitresses had a wonderful time while they were here." Sue smiles. "The sailors were well-behaved," she adds.

Location	*Bryson City*
Season	*Lodge open mid-April to November 1. Cottage open all year*
Dining	*Breakfast, dinner included during lodge season*
Children	*Yes, in lodge*
Pets	*No*
Payment	*Cash, check, travelers' check, MasterCard, Visa*
Rates	*$80 to $160 for two people, including two meals*

Rockers for nature's picture show

HEMLOCK INN
Bryson City, NC 28713
Elaine and Morris White
Ella Jo and John Shell
(704) 488-2885

"Our philosophy hasn't ever changed," say Hemlock Inn inn-keepers John and Ella Jo Shell. "We want to give our guests a change of scene and a change of pace. We want to share the beauty and the peace we enjoy here. And we want to know that our guests' holiday has been restful, relaxing and happy." The Shells, originally from Marietta, Georgia, have been living this vision at the inn since they bought it in 1969.

From either the closed-in sun room or the covered side porch, visitors will be drawn to the beautiful, always-changing view of the Great Smokies. Chairs are set up on the porch in rows next to a stone hearth as if the scenery were a big screen in a theatre. (Rockers cannot be reserved for morning coffee at 7:30!). From here most guests begin their day, mingling with others until the 8:30 breakfast bell sounds.

First opened in 1952, the Hemlock Inn is on 65 wooded acres, three miles from Great Smoky Mountains National Park. It has twenty guest rooms in the main building, four cottages and a secluded log cabin (popular with honeymooners) with eat-in kitchen and fireplace. All rooms have a private bath. There are no televisions or phones, except for a pay phone in the library.

Retired naturalist Arthur Stupka, who comes to the inn each season, helps visitors learn about the nearly 1,500 different flowering plants found in the national park. He offers slide shows and wildflower walks during his residency early each season. There are countless other area activities. The Shells have a great affection for the region and are eager to suggest suitable outings for every interest. The Hemlock Inn has intentionally been kept small and simple to retain its friendly, informal atmosphere.

Many hearty food specialties are featured here, contributed through the years by house cooks, as well as neighbors and guests. Meals are served family style on large Lazy Susans in the chestnut-paneled dining room. A highlight of the full breakfast are the hot homemade biscuits, said to induce "euphoria." Dinner, served in one seating at 6:00 P.M. includes such dishes as country-fried steak, a squash souffle, fresh vegetables from local gardens, and a relish called "Something Good." Myrtle's Butternut Pound Cake and Velda's Old Fashioned Lemon Pie typify the desserts.

Frequent requests for house recipes led the Shells to put together a cookbook, *Recipes From Our Front Porch*. Only the recipes for Apple Chips and Pumpkin Chips have been omitted—they remain a house secret. Says Ella Jo, "You'll have to come to the inn to enjoy them."

Location	*Three miles north of Bryson City and seven miles west of Cherokee on US 19. Hemlock Inn sign is at dairy farm; turn west (away from dairy farm) and go one mile to inn*
Season	*Mid-April through October Week-ends only November through mid-December*
Dining	*Full breakfast and dinner included with room rate. Packed lunches available*
Children	*Yes. Cribs, rollaway beds available*
Pets	*No (state law)*

Payment   *No credit cards; cash, travelers' check or personal check only*

Rates   *$114–$156 for two persons*

Other
Considerations   *No tipping policy; no smoking in dining room*

Say Ruth, what's cookin'?

RANDOLPH HOUSE INN

*Fryemont Road, P.O. Box 816
Bryson City, NC 28713*

*Bill and Ruth Randolph Adams
(704) 488-3472*

The Randolph House was built in 1895 "of the finest timber in the Smokies" by Captain Amos Frye, a prominent figure in the western highlands, and his wife, Lillian, the first woman licensed to practice law in North Carolina. Their daughter, Lois Frye, and her husband, John Randolph, opened the house to visitors in 1923, calling it Peaceful Lodge.

At that time, the elder Fryes decided to add on to their inn business, building the larger Fryemont Inn next door. Today the Fryemont Inn is owned by others, but the Peaceful Lodge—now called Randolph House—remains in the family. John Randolph's niece, Ruth, and her husband, Bill Adams, are the innkeepers. They renamed the inn in honor of "Uncle John," who used to say of these mountains, "The Lord finished his handiwork here." John's portrait hangs in the inn's large parlor.

On the National Register of Historic Places, the tree-shaded, white frame house with 12 gables and granite stone work looks much as it did at the turn of the century. The furniture is original, some of it dating back to 1850. There seems to be a spot for everyone to recline. The six guest rooms, three with private bath and three that share, are each coordinated in a different color. Among the various old pieces packed into the rooms are dark walnut beds, mirrored dressers, heavy wood rockers with embroidered pillows, loveseats, white wicker chairs and woven rugs.

Guests inquire of Bill or Ruth as to the evening meal, which is open to the public. Bill is deservedly proud of his wife's cooking, and quick to point out that her culinary talent has become "legendary." Diners have a choice from twelve main courses, such as veal, pan-fried trout or Cornish hen. The rest of the meal is a surprise consisting of Ruth's vegetable, bread and dessert creations. A wine list offers a choice of imported and domestic vintages. Meals are enjoyed in the dining room or on the covered front porch, weather permitting. The porch tables, with their white tablecloths, are nestled between French doors, granite pillars and rockers.

Meeting people from "all over the world" has been a highlight of Bill and Ruth's innkeeping experience. "We've had visitors from Holland, Italy and New Zealand, to name a few," says Bill. It's easy to see why they come: Bryson City is a quaint little town only a stone's throw from the Great Smokies Park, Blue Ridge Parkway and Cherokee Indian Reservation. The streams are some of the nation's best for trout fishing, and the Nantahala River is renowned for rafting, canoeing and kayaking. And, of course, there's Ruth's cooking.

Location	*Follow Highway 74 into Bryson City. Turn right (uphill) at inn sign before reaching first traffic light*
Season	*April through November 1*
Dining	*Breakfast and dinner included in room rate. Public served by reservation*
Children	*Prefer age 8 and older*
Pets	*No (state law)*
Payment	*Cash, check, travelers' check, MasterCard, Visa, AmEx, Discover*
Rates	*$90–$135 per night double occupancy; includes breakfast and dinner*

Candler

Scaling the heights of country hospitality

PISGAH VIEW RANCH

Rt. 1
Candler, NC 28715
Ruby Cogburn
(704) 667-9100

The 2,000 acres of fields and woods of the Pisgah View Ranch have belonged to the same family since the adoption of America's Constitution, in 1789. Now a family-run business with Ruby Cogburn, the innkeeper, and daughter and son-in-law, Phyllis and Sam Parris, the managers, the ranch offers lodging, recreation and entertainment for the entire family in the shadow of picture-perfect Mt. Pisgah.

"You have to love people to be in this business," says Sam. He joined his wife at the ranch after he retired from the army. "We are on to our second generation of guests now," he says, adding with a smile, "many families repeat their visits year after year."

The ranch has a minimum-stay policy of two nights. The average vacation runs one week. "You can't get the feel for the place otherwise," says Sam. Besides, there is so much to do.

Daytime activities include swimming in the large, L-shaped heated pool; playing tennis on the ranch's court, enjoying Ping Pong, volleyball, shuffleboard or lawn games and horseback riding and hiking. The ranch will pack a picnic lunch for you if you want to ride, hike or sightsee a bit farther afield. There are also 17 golf courses in the area. The original log cabin from 1790 has been preserved and now houses an antique shop and a small museum available for your perusal. A gift shop called the "gift stall", because it occupies the space that used to be the horse stall, obliges the ever-present love of shopping.

Nightly entertainment features country western or bluegrass music, a magician, and talent night with the innkeeper's son, Max, as emcee. The ranch sponsors a square-dancing team that has won numerous competitions. The team performs regularly at the ranch and invites guests to join in the fun.

Forty-nine guest rooms, each with private bath, fill the cabins and cottages that spread across the rolling, well-maintained grounds. Country-style cooking, featuring locally grown fruits and vegetables, are served family style to ranch guests (and to the public by reservation) three times a day in the large, bright, white-beamed dining room. As Sam puts simply, "Everything is included in the room rate except horseback riding."

If you had any question about the family nature of the ranch, you wouldn't after you'd had a look at the wonderful collection of photographs displayed outside the dining room.

Location	*18 miles southwest of Asheville, NC. Go past Asheville on I-40. Take Exit 44. Turn right and go to fourth stoplight. Turn left on NC-151. Follow Pisgah View Ranch signs (eight miles)*
Dining	*Breakfast, lunch, dinner*
Season	*May 1 to November 1*
Children	*Yes*
Pets	*No*
Payment	*No credit cards. Cash, personal checks and travelers' checks*
Rates	*$45 to $78 per person per day, double occupancy*

Cashiers

Mountain view with breakfast

MILLSTONE INN

Hwy. 64 West, P.O. Box 949
Cashiers, NC 28717

Heinz Haibach
(704) 743-2737

With an innkeeper's name like Heinz Haibach, it comes as little surprise that German is spoken at the Millstone Inn. There is Old World charm at this western North Carolina mountain inn, just outside of Cashiers. The inn is a delight for those seeking a retreat, for honeymooners or travelers simply passing through.

Built as a private home in the early 1930s, the two-story inn with two bay wings and large windows sits among towering trees on a seven-acre rise. At an elevation of 3,500 feet, the inn commands a beautiful view of Whiteside Mountain and Devil's Courthouse. The inn's exterior wood shakes, most of which are original, create a rustic yet elegant look, much like the bark of a proud tree that has weathered the test of time.

Inside, the country, rustic feeling continues with exposed-beam ceilings, pine-paneled guest rooms and antiques. Renovated in 1987, the inn offers a total of 11 comfortable guest rooms furnished with a combination of antiques and traditional pieces. All guest rooms have a private bath and color TV. In the main house are two two-room suites, one of which has a kitchen. Four other guest rooms are in an adjacent Garden Apartment. Two of these rooms have kitchens and are available without maid service and the full house breakfast. If you can, do partake in the breakfast because it's hard to imagine a more pleasant spot in which to relish a meal than here in the glass-enclosed porch in full view of Whiteside Mountain.

The short walk through native forests and past rhododendron and mountain laurel to Silver Slip Falls is a favorite pastime here. Visitors can also find golf, tennis, horseback riding and water sports, all near to the inn.

Location	*From 64/107 intersection in Cashiers go one mile west on US 64*
Season	*April–November*
Dining	*Breakfast*
Children	*No*
Pets	*No*
Payment	*Cash, check, Visa, MasterCard*
Rates	*$82–$118*

Chimney Rock

Frankly, my dear, I'll have quail

ESMERALDA INN

P.O. Box 57, Highway 74
Chimney Rock, NC 28720
Ackie and Joanne Okpych
(704) 625-9105

If you come to stay at Esmeralda Inn, pretend you're a movie star seeking relief from the crush of your many, many fans. After all, you'll be following the lead of such former guests as screen giants Clark Gable, Mary Pickford, Douglas Fairbanks and Gloria Swanson. Or pretend you're a writer in search of atmosphere; the inn is named for a novel that was written nearby, and author Lew Wallace finished *Ben Hur* here.

Surrounded by tall trees and located within sight of the "Chimney Rock" for which the town is named, the three-story Esmeralda Inn was built in 1891 by Colonel Tom Turner along the old Pony Express route over the mountains. A fire destroyed the original building, but it was rebuilt on the same foundation in 1917. Floors that sag from wear and age let you know this place has been around awhile.

To own a little inn and restaurant had been a long-held dream of Ackie and Joanne Okpych—a dream that came true in early 1990 when they purchased the Esmeralda Inn. Their backgrounds have helped them adjust quickly to the challenge of innkeeping: carpentry and running a small home cleaning business. Son Michael, who has a degree in culinary arts, is the chef; his siblings, Amy and Jimmy, also work at the inn, so it is truly a family affair.

The lobby might make you feel that you have stepped into an old lodge at a national park. Constructed of peeled logs and sturdy timbers, it has a wraparound balcony made of large scaffold branches with many smaller branches still attached, sort of like random deer antlers. Deer heads, owls, hawks, beehives adorn the room, the focus of which is a huge stone fireplace. The inn features two levels of long, covered porches with overhead paddle fans, rockers and game tables.

The irregular flooring adds charm to the 13 upstairs guest rooms, seven of which have a private bath. Quilts hang on the paneled walls.

The Esmeralda Inn is regionally famous for its "country gourmet" dining. Folks have come 100 miles just for dinner. Fresh seafood is a big draw: salmon, sole, scallops and oysters. Quail, frog's legs, trout, steaks and wiener schnitzel are some of the mouth-watering selections.

Location	*Chimney Rock, 22 miles east of Asheville via US 74*
Season	*Closed mid-December to mid-March*
Dining	*Continental breakfast daily with room rate; Lunch available six days a week; dinner available everyday*
Children	*Over 12*
Pets	*No*
Payment	*Cash, MasterCard, Visa, Discover*
Rates	*$40–$60 per night, double occupancy*

Dillsboro

Doing nothing and resting afterward

THE JARRETT HOUSE

P.O. Box 219
Haywood and Hill Streets
Dillsboro, NC 28725

Jim and Jean Hartbarger
(704) 586-0265 or (800) 972-5623

You can easily find your way to the Jarrett House. It is "downtown," next to interesting shops on the main street of the small town of Dillsboro, 47 miles west of Asheville.

For the first visitors who came to this mountain dining and lodging spot, built by the town's founder William Allen Dills in 1884 and known then as the Mount Beulah Hotel, the journey must have been more adventuresome. They came on the Western North Carolina Railway passenger train, established only two years earlier. For years it was a common custom for travelers to telegraph ahead their reservations for lunch at the hotel. Summer visitors came for lodging as well, and the town thus got its start as a tourist spot, hosting "comers and stayers." Of course, there was no telling what the train might bring to town. Story has it that two cigarette-smoking women came from Edenton. They were the first to be seen puffing like that here.

The three-story wood frame hotel with wrought-iron balustrades, has passed through many owners including R. Frank Jarrett. In 1894 he changed the name to the Jarrett Springs Hotel and made available a sulphur spring at the rear of the hotel for guests seeking new vigor. He also cured hams and served quantities so huge and so good men wept because they couldn't eat as much as they wanted. After "Mister" Frank died in 1950 new owners named the hotel The Jarrett House out of respect.

The current owners, Jim and Jean Hartbarger, acquired the property in 1975. Jim had coached basketball at Western Carolina University for 18 years and Jean had taught school for 16 years. "I wanted out of coaching," says Jim. The family-oriented nature of The Jarrett House business has turned out to be just right for him and Jean and their two sons, Buzz and Scott.

The emphasis today remains on good food with an extra accent on relaxation. You can still order country ham with red-eye gravy and hot biscuits or other traditional fare in any of the three dining rooms. As for unwinding, Jim and Jean make a point of "real loafing." "How beautiful it is to do nothing," they write in their brochure, "and then to rest afterward."

This is a good place to do just that. Now designated a National Historic Place, the house has a front porch and two upper balconies that run three-quarters of the length of the building all lined with rockers for some serious lollygagging. For resting, 18 guest rooms have been renovated and all have private bath and are nicely furnished with antiques. "We worked room by room," says Jim. "It took us ten years."

A marble might be set in motion on some of the gently out-of-plumb floors, but the TLC the Jarrett House has received from the Hartbargers is obvious and adds to the genuineness of the mountain hospitality felt here. An enclosed porch at the back of the building is used for special meetings, rehearsal dinners, banquets and tour-bus groups.

Location	*47 miles west of Asheville, NC. Take Rt. 40W to Exit 27/23-74 Great Smoky Mountain Expressway to Dillsboro*
Dining	*Breakfast, lunch, dinner; price of dinner for two, from $25–$30*
Season	*Third weekend in April till October 31*
Children	*Over 12*
Pets	*No*
Payment	*Cash, check, travelers' checks*
Rates	*$40.00 for one, $3 each additional person*

Flat Rock

In Carl Sandburg's neighborhood

WOODFIELD INN

P.O. Box 98 - Greenville Highway
Flat Rock, NC 28731
Jeane Smith
(704) 693-6016; (800) 533-6016

Formerly a stop on the stagecoach route south of Asheville, The Woodfield Inn has been entertaining guests in fine fashion since it opened its doors in 1852. Built by slaves under the supervision of hotelier/contractor Henry Tudor Farmer, it was known then as The Farmer Hotel. The large three-story building is set on a hand-hewn log foundation held together with wooden pegs and rests on 25 manicured acres only a short walk from Carl Sandburg's beloved Connemara estate.

Rather than buy furniture for his new hostelry, "Squire" Farmer started a factory to make his own. In the process he developed the popular "Flat Rock" rocker, a walnut rocking chair that stays put no matter how vigorous the rocking. He also cultivated lemon trees successfully here in the mountains and celebrated by creating a lemon julep. Farmer ran the inn until his death in 1883, and the property stayed in the family until 1917, when it was purchased and renamed Woodfield Inn.

In stagecoach days passengers were asked to get out and walk the steeper mountain grades along the route, a lousy request, but evidently necessary to get the coach up. For his part, Farmer tried to make his hotel "worth climbing mountains for." Confederate soldiers were lodged in the hotel at the end of the Civil War to help prevent plundering of the community by renegades. Gold and other valuables were kept in a secret compartment under the floorboards of a second-story bedroom. In the later years of the 19th century, high society of Charleston, South Carolina, frequented the hotel, so much so that it became known as "Little Charleston." If you're suffering from a case of Victorian vapors or a broken heart, a recuperative stay here will help perpetuate a tradition begun by Southern ladies a century ago.

A careful restoration of the inn was undertaken by Stephen Levin, the present owner, in the early 1980s. The original paint colors were reproduced with help from experts from the University of Pennsylvania. Shaded by tall evergreens, the yellow inn with wide porches, lattice work and green shutters offers 18 beautiful guest rooms. Half the rooms have private baths; most of the hall baths are shared by only three or four people. Some rooms have fireplaces and French doors opening onto wide verandas.

Three dining rooms offer an assortment of critically acclaimed meals. Catering is available for special occasions at the inn; and the garden gazebo and outdoor pavilion are ideal for weddings.

In addition to Connemara, the town of Flat Rock is within walking distance. You can get to this designated National Historic Place also by riding in a carriage available at the inn. Wednesday through Saturday during the warm months one of the nation's best summer stock theatres, the Flat Rock Playhouse, stages hit shows from Broadway and London. Three signers of the Declaration of Independence are buried in the cemetery of historic St. John's Church. Many other points of interest are only minutes away, and challenging golf courses are among them.

Woodfield Inn bills itself as "North Carolina's Original Country Inn," which suggests the state had no rural inns across its 600 miles until 1852. This makes us wonder where those signers of the Declaration took up lodging in their travels more than 75 years before Henry Farmer broke ground for his hotel.

Nonetheless, when you enter the front parlor and see the crown molding, antiques, grand piano, lavish carpets and wallpaper and carved wood seats, you're likely to forgive this apparent concession to the language of modern marketing. Farmer's phrase, "worth climbing mountains for," may be the one that comes most readily to mind.

Location	About 23 miles south of Asheville, and 2½ miles south of Hendersonville, on US 25
Season	Year round
Dining	Continental breakfast with room rate; lunch, dinner
Children	Yes

Pets *No*

Payment *Cash, travelers' checks, MasterCard, Visa*

Rates *$60–$115; Special week-day package rate available*

Franklin

Right on the greens

BUTTONWOOD INN

190 Georgia Road
Franklin, NC
Liz Oehser
(704) 369-8985

This small western North Carolina B&B, 75 miles southwest of Asheville, is tucked away among tall pines, dogwoods and rhododendron between the 5th and 7th greens on the Franklin Golf Course. Innkeeper Liz Oehser says guests come "because the inn has a comfortable home-away-from-home feeling and a good breakfast." No doubt the likes of delicious, energizing treats such as Strawberry Omelets, Apple Sausage Rings, Dutch Babies with Baked Peaches and Sausage and Scones with Homemade Lemon Butter will tempt you and add yards to your tee shots—if not inches to your waistline.

The original part of Buttonwood was built as a summer cottage in the late 1920s. A wing was added in 1957 and now, after renovations in 1981 when the cottage was transformed to a B&B, this extension houses the four guest rooms. Quiet and unpretentious, the B&B has a batten board exterior and white pine, tongue-and-groove interior. Country style furniture, including a few handmade pieces, lend simple, rustic charm. At an altitude of 2,050 feet, air conditioning isn't needed; numerous ceiling fans supply a pleasant breeze.

Gem mining, hiking, water rafting, horseback riding and fishing are among the favorite amusements of guests here. The Nantahala National Forest, nearby and full of a wide range of wildlife, is frequented by many.

Location   *76 miles southwest of Asheville. I-40W to south on 19-23. South on 441 and 23. Exit on 441 Bus.*

Season   *April–December*

Dining   *Full breakfast*

Children   *Yes (prefer over 10)*

Pets   *No*

Payment   *Check or cash*

Rates   *$55–$70, double occupancy; $10 extra person*

Hendersonville

An Irish ring to it!

CLADDAGH INN

755 North Main Street
Hendersonville, NC 28792

Vickie and Dennis Pacilio
(704) 697-7778 or (800) 225-4700 Reservations

This downtown Hendersonville bed-and-breakfast takes its name from a traditional Gaelic engagement ring known as a "Claddagh." Symbolizing loyalty, love and friendship, the ring originated about 400 years ago. According to custom, it doubles as a wedding ring, although it is most frequently given as a friendship ring today.

The three-story Classical Revival turn-of-the-century home has operated as a guest house ever since it was built. Before becoming a bed-and-breakfast inn in 1985, it was known as the Hotel McCurry, when it was home to many of Hendersonville's oldtimers. Now on the National Register of Historic Places, the yellow inn with green trim sits on a pretty, tree-lined street just one block from Hendersonville's hub of antique, gift shops and fine restaurants. The 14 guest rooms, very clean and peaceful, retain their original louvered doors and each has a private bath, phone, TV and air conditioning. Business travelers will also appreciate the availability of the inn's fax machine.

The innkeepers want every guest's day to start out right, so they offer a big, all-you-can-eat breakfast. Fill up on pancakes, muffins, coffee cakes, French toast, bread pudding, or biscuits and gravy. Later on, savor a complimentary afternoon glass of sherry while you make plans for the evening. The Carl Sandburg Home (Connemara) and Flat Rock Playhouse are only five miles away.

Location	*Downtown Hendersonville*
Season	*Year round*
Dining	*Breakfast*
Children	*Yes*
Pets	*No*
Payment	*Cash, check, MasterCard, Visa, Discover, AmEx*
Rates	*Double, $63 to $89; single, $55 to $79*

An Englishman's country retreat

HAVENSHIRE INN

Rt. 13, Box 366
Cummings Road
Hendersonville, NC 28739

Cindy Findley
(704) 692-4097
FAX (704) 696-8450

The Havenshire Inn rests on Bowman's Bluff eight miles outside of Hendersonville in the small, secluded community of Horse Shoe. On the French Broad River, its 40 acres of rolling pastures, well-maintained trees and shrubs and lush, green lawns create a tranquil backdrop for rest and relaxation.

Built in 1882 by English settler George Holmes, the large two-story redwood and cedar structure, now painted brown, was a country retreat for numerous owners before Cindy Findley purchased it and began operating it as a B&B in 1981.

The inn has a wonderful, big screened-in porch, complemented in season by vases of fresh cut flowers, that is an ideal spot for quiet moments any time of the day. From here, guests pass through a grand entryway to large living rooms, with ceilings 12 feet high. Gracefully furnished with antiques, this space also houses a TV and VCR giving evidence that the space is used, not just admired. Near the stairway to the upper level visitors pass by a fabulous English tapestry of horses and dogs on their way to a hunt. Upstairs, antique bookcases line a wall of the long hall from which four guest rooms open. Two rooms have a private bath while the others share a bath. The attic has been transformed into a spa area, complete with massage room. Lodging is also available in a three-room cottage where a two-night minimum stay is required.

Those who like a bit of activity can paddle the canoe and fish for bass in the inn's pond. Or they can play golf at the nearby Cummings Cove Golf Club. A do-it-yourself bar awaits them back at the inn where guests gather to shoot the breeze.

Location   *From Hendersonville, take 64 West to the small community of "Horse Shoe" which is so small that one can pass it without knowing it. However, the railroad track crosses 64 West in Horse Shoe. From the point of crossing the track, it is 1½ miles to Cummings Road. Turn left onto Cummings Road, and the inn is then two miles on the right. It is the only dwelling on the right and is an English country manor that sets back off the road with a driveway between two stone columns. Drive down and around the inn to the front—you have arrived!*

Dining	*Breakfast included in room rate*
Season	*All year*
Children	*Yes*
Pets	*No*
Payment	*Cash, personal checks, travelers' checks*
Rates	*Cottage $85 per night; rooms $65–$75, double occupancy*

The best of small-town charm

THE WAVERLY INN

783 N. Main Street
Hendersonville, NC 28792

John and Diane Sheiry
(704) 693-9193
(800) 537-8195

Ask about special weekends such as "murder mysteries" or wine-lover's weekend when you call to plan your stay at the Waverly Inn, the oldest operating inn in Hendersonville. The inn is open all year and makes an ideal stopover should you be in the area for any of numerous other attractions including the Apple Festival or the Home for the Holidays Festival, the Biltmore House (19 miles away in Asheville), the Flat Rock Playhouse, Carl Sandburg's home or Mt. Pisgah National Forest. Wherever else you may go, a friendly welcome awaits you here from innkeepers John and Diane Sheiry and Darla Olmstead (Diane's sister).

Built in 1898 as a guest house and now on the National Register of Historic Places, their tree-shaded inn is only two blocks from the downtown historic district. Three-stories high with a hipped roof and inviting covered front porch and second-story veranda, it was previously known as The Waverly when it hosted many of the town's retirees.

John had a background in the hotel and convention business

before coming here and, says Diane, "His fantasy was to one day run an inn. So we did it," she smiles. They purchased the property in 1988.

The couple began fixing up the inn in January 1989. "We sat around and thought about what people wanted," says Diane. The couple worked with a hotel renovation contractor from Atlanta and as many local contractors as possible adding private baths for each of the 16 large, bright and airy, high-ceilinged guest rooms. Diane says that despite the building's years, it is in great shape, so most of their work after the additions was cosmetic. All rooms now have telephones. Nothing seems out of place. Tasteful choices for wallpaper, curtains, furnishings and bed covers complement the charm and grace of this old building, which includes a rare "East Lake" style stairway to the third floor. The original louvered doors to each guest room are great for ventilation and the terrific canopy and four-poster beds are finds of Diane's from Hendersonville.

Fill up on blueberry pancakes (when blueberries are in season) or French toast or Moravian sugarcake before starting your day in Hendersonville. Diane describes her town aptly. "This town is great for me," she says, "It's large enough to have the things I need, but it still feels like a small town."

Location	*From I-26, take Exit 18B. Drive on US 64 west for two miles. Turn right on Main St. The inn is located one block up on the left*
Dining	*Full breakfast, cooked to order, included in room rate; social hour from 5:00–6:00 P.M. with complimentary beverages and hors d'oeuvres*
Season	*All year*
Pets	*No*
Children	*Yes*
Payment	*Cash, check, AmEx, Visa, MasterCard, Discover*
Rates	*$79–$99 double occupancy*

Highlands

Highlands' best

THE OLD EDWARDS INN

4th and Main Street (PO Box 1778)
Highlands, NC 28741

Rip and Pat Benton
(704) 526-5036

HIGHLANDS INN

4th and Main Street (PO Box 1030)
Highlands, NC 28741

Rip and Pat Benton
(704) 526-9380

Not only does Highlands, NC, have the highest elevation (4,100 feet) of any incorporated town in the Eastern United States, but the friendly town also boasts two fine inns on its main street, The Old Edwards Inn and The Highlands Inn. Built directly across from each other within two years of the town's founding in 1876, both inns are now owned by the indefatigable couple, Rip and Pat Benton. The Bentons have a flair for authentic restoration and fans of the old will appreciate their careful work.

The Bentons began first on the three-story **Old Edwards Inn**. Built by David Norton and his family in 1878, the frame inn was acquired by Mr. and Mrs. James G. Edwards in 1913. The Edwards expanded the operation in 1933, building a three-story brick addition. Highlights of the inn's heyday included Mrs. Edwards' popular cooking and the addition's "real steam heat," which was a rarity for both the time and area. The inn remained in the Edwards' family until the late 1960s when its lower level was used for a short time for curio shops. The rest sat empty, suffering wind and water damage until the Bentons came to the rescue in 1981. Before starting work, they queried surviving Edwards family members and Highlanders about such details as the inn's paint colors, wall coverings and furnishings in order to

Highlands Inn. *Highlands, North Carolina*

restore the inn as close as possible to its original prime. They also added baths on the third floor where there had previously been only one and enlisted the services of top-notch stenciler Brenda Kellum for final-touch wall decorations.

Nineteen guest rooms, each with private bath and most with balcony, are now available. The rooms have an elegant, country feeling and are furnished with antiques, some from as far away as New Orleans. The original wooden part of the inn houses the highly respected Central House Restaurant where seafood entrees garner top honors. No phones, few TVs, large tubs and very good beds are also noteworthy at this quiet inn.

Highlands Inn, across the street was constructed from virgin lumber and handmade nails by Joseph Halleck in 1880. Its 30 guest rooms, each with private bath, were completely renovated in 1983 and a new wing added in 1984 by one of its former owners. Acquired by the Bentons in 1989, it has been re-done by them too and, like Old Edwards Inn, now features antiques and hand-stenciled wall decorations. Because the Bentons feel conversation in front of a crackling fire is a far better way to pass time than watching television, it will surprise no one to find few TV sets around but many long-staying guests, who love to talk about the inn's colorful past and share local yarns. Be sure to ask about the circus elephants who visited and the whiskey traders involved in the Moccasin War.

The inns are not far from hundreds of waterfalls including one, Dry Falls, that has a path visitors can use to walk behind the falling water—and still stay dry. Tennis courts and a pool, auction galleries and antique shops, a nature center and hiking trails, horseback riding and golf are also nearby.

Location	*Two hours north of Atlanta and 60 miles south of Asheville on downtown Highlands' Main Street*
Season	*Both inns are open April 1–November 30*
Dining	*An abundant continental breakfast is included in the room rate. Lunch and dinner are served at the central house with an average lunch for two at $15, and dinner for two at $30. The Highlands Inn has food service on a limited basis during periods of heavy guest travel*

Children *Due to room configurations The Old Edwards Inn has no way to accommodate extra guests in any room. The Highlands Inn does have a limited number of rooms to accommodate children*

Pets *No*

Payment *Cash, checks, MasterCard, Visa, AmEx*

Rates *Range from $69 to $89 for the Old Edwards Inn and from $79 to $99 for Highlands Inn*

Linville

Where the well-heeled play

ESEEOLA LODGE

Box 98, Hwy. 221
Linville, NC 28646

John Blackburn
(704) 733-4311

If you are one who wants recreation to be a main part of a getaway, then set your sights on Eseeola Lodge, located in a pristine setting at the foot of Grandfather Mountain in Linville, NC. On some 2,000 acres 70 miles northeast of Asheville, the lodge has both the amenities and feel of a country club.

It has its own Donald Ross-designed 18-hole golf course with bent greens (golf instruction is available), clay tennis courts, heated swimming pool, croquet court and clubhouse where lunch is served. Hiking trails, trout fishing, manicured gardens and a children's playground are here too. Each July and August the Lodge offers a recreation program especially for children.

The Lodge itself is striking. Built in the 20s and 30s, it has unusual chestnut siding that is likely one of a kind. Inside, wood paneling creates a warm rustic feeling. A large main room with high-beamed ceiling, fireplace, books and game tables is available for all guests as is the Lodge's dining room where both breakfast and dinner, included in the room price, are served. Gentlemen are asked to wear coat and tie for dinner, which includes such mouth-watering specialties as Poached Carolina Flounder Stuffed with Spinach, Salmon and Crab Mousse with Red and Yellow Pepper Sauce, and Grilled Loin of Veal Chop with Sundried Tomatoes and Black Truffles Sauce Armagnac.

Most of the 29 guest rooms have private porches. The rooms are small, nicely furnished. The idea here is to get outside, enjoy your favorite pastime and relax. Many repeat guests, described by innkeeper John Blackburn as "well-heeled Southerners from old families," have been doing just that for years.

Location	*From Boone take Highway 105 to Linville, go through intersection of Route 105 to 221 (there is a traffic light here). Inn is two blocks on left past this intersection. Do not take the 221 Bypass*
Dining	*All meals*
Season	*Mid-May–mid-October*
Children	*Yes*
Pets	*No*
Payment	*Check, Visa, MasterCard*
Rates	*$90–$120 per person for double room; $150–$200 for single room; Modified American plan–breakfast and dinner included in room rate*

Maggie Valley

Saddle up for a complete holiday

CATALOOCHEE RANCH

Route 1, Box 500E
Maggie Valley, NC 28751

Tom and Alice Aumen
(704) 926-1401 or (800) 868-1401

Cataloochee Ranch is a world all its own. Situated on 1,000 mile-high acres of beautiful mountain countryside bordering Great Smoky Mountains National Park, the ranch offers its guests an ideal place to delight in numerous activities throughout the year.

Set your own pace and pick your pleasure:

Ride one of 30 available trail horses; guides will accompany you on full- or half-day outings along some of the finest trails in the eastern U.S. (Avid riders and nature enthusiasts may want

Cataloochee Ranch. *Maggie Valley, North Carolina*

to inquire ahead of time about the schedule of special wilderness adventure trips.)

Fish in a pond stocked with rainbow trout; the kitchen will prepare your catch.

Hike across the rolling landscape.

Swim in the novel swim-spa, a 20-foot heated pool that creates a current to swim against.

Play tennis on the newly resurfaced court. Horseshoes, table tennis and lawn games are also available.

Read a book on the front porch.

In winter, ski at the Cataloochee Ski area, only a mile away.

During any season, use the ranch as a base for visiting the many other attractions nearby.

Innkeepers Tom and Alice Aumen anticipate you'll work up quite an appetite, so "family style feasts," including regional specialties, vegetables from the ranch's garden, homemade jams, breads and desserts are prepared. An outdoor barbecue is held twice a week.

Alice's parents, Tom and "Miss Judy" Alexander, started the ranch in 1939. It has always been a part of Alice's life. "I was raised here," she says. "I went away to school and to pursue other careers, but I always came back in the summers." Tom joined her at the ranch when they married in 1965. "He's an everyman," says Alice. "You have to be—to be in this business." Tom tends to the grounds' considerable upkeep, as well as many ongoing projects. A working ranch with cattle, horses, managed timberlands and evergreen plantations—in addition to serving guests—Cataloochee is more than a mom-and-pop operation.

Accommodations range from rooms in the main ranch house and new Silverbell Lodge to seven cabins, three of which are adapted from an old mountain homestead. The main sitting room in the ranch house has broad, random-length floorboards made from trees on site. Comfortable sofas and hand-carved tables are arranged in front of the stone fireplace. The original front porch has been enclosed to create an additional dining room, and a new stone porch has been added to that. Each of the eight bedrooms in the ranch house has a private bath and is furnished warmly with antiques, quilts and handmade furniture.

The Silverbell Lodge, built in 1986 and named for the flowering shrub that reaches tree-size proportions in this area, has six rooms with private bath. Some can be converted into two-room suites. The rooms are large and bright, with high ceilings and exposed beams. The Balsam Room, which serves as a common room for lodge guests, can be adapted for use as a meeting room for groups of up to 30 people.

The cabins, which vary in size, are quite private and appropriately rustic. They all have baths, all have fireplaces, and three have kitchenettes. The Azalea Cabin is secluded and features a hot tub and deck with a fine view; the Rhododendron overlooks the trout pond.

Bring a sweater or jacket. Even in the warmer months the daytime temperature doesn't hit 80 degrees; nighttime can be brisk and, next to a good fire, perfect for cuddling.

Location	*Above Maggie Valley, North Carolina. From I-40 follow 19S through Maggie Valley to west end to sign for ranch and ski area. Go three miles up paved Fie Top Road to ranch*
Season	*May 1 through October; Christmas to mid-March*
Dining	*Complete dining and bar facilities. Modified American Plan (lunch available but not included in room rate)*
Children	*Six and over*
Pets	*No*
Payment	*Cash, check, MasterCard, Visa, AmEx*
Rates	*$110–$200 for two persons, double occupancy. Four-person suite or cabin, $320–$340; Additional children $45–$50, adults $55–$60*
Other Considerations	*A 15% gratuity is automatically added to room rate; no additional tipping is expected. Interested parties should inquire about proper riding gear. Half-day rides for ranch guests cost $27; all-day rides, with lunch, are $60*

A homey "Shinn-Dig" dream come true

SMOKEY SHADOWS LODGE

P.O. Box 444
Maggie Valley, NC 28751

Bud and Ginger Shinn
(704) 926-0001

Ginger Shinn's childhood dream was to own and operate Smokey Shadows Lodge some day. She and her mother often stayed at the lodge when visiting relatives in Maggie Valley. "I was in love with the place," Ginger recalls. Years later, in 1983, the lodge was sitting empty when she and her husband, Bud, learned it was for sale. They decided to dive in. "We were crazy to do this," says Ginger, "but if you asked if I'd do it again, I'd say yes."

At first Bud continued to work at home in Miami and look after three of the couple's four children while Ginger and daughter Tracy got the lodge off and running. The family is now together and everyone is involved in the lodge. "We don't think of it too much as a business," says Ginger, "it's more like home." For visitors, it's a home away from home.

Built in 1953 of hand-hewn chestnut logs from the Cataloochee Valley, the lodge sits at an elevation of 4,500 feet, on a bluff overlooking Maggie Valley. Its long porch, lined with rocking chairs, offers a breathtaking view. For a closer look at the scenery, guests can swing out over the treetops on a rope that hangs from a large maple tree.

Inside the lodge, exposed beams and wormy chestnut walls dominate. The living room, converted from an old log gristmill, has a large stone fireplace. Each of the 12 guest rooms, small but comfortable, has a private bath. The accent is on "country" in the furnishings, which include handmade quilts and pillows, antique photos and wood and leather door locks. Downstairs is "the stable," a small dormitory ideal for groups of children. Two cabins on the property, the "Shinn Dig" and the "Shadow Shack," are for those who want greater privacy.

Hand-crocheted tablecloths cover the long tables in the large dining room. A continental breakfast comes with the room, but few guests want to miss the home-cooked, everything-from-scratch lunches and dinners also served. During the growing season, the family-style meals feature fresh vegetables from the lodge's garden.

Smokey Shadows Lodge has an apt motto: "Secluded, but five minutes to everything." Sightseeing, outdoor sports (including golf, and skiing in the winter) and nightly entertainment such as clogging, square dancing and country music are all within reach. And it isn't necessary to leave the lodge to have fun either. Something always seems to be going on, whether it's a country wedding, family reunion or an impromptu performance by guests.

"I like doing things for people here," says Ginger. "I like to get involved. It's not like running a hotel—it's more like my home and having company all year round."

Location	*40 minutes west of Ashville; 1.5 miles up Ski Mountain Road from Maggie Valley*
Season	*Year round*
Dining	*Continental breakfast. Lunch and dinner additional. Picnic baskets available*
Children	*Yes (cribs and babysitter available)*
Pets	*No*
Payment	*Check, MasterCard, Visa*
Rates	*June–October: Rooms $60, Cabins $80, Week Special: Rooms $360, Cabins $480. Inquire for group and off-season rates*
Other Considerations	*Wheelchairs can be accommodated (no stairs) No smoking indoors*

Mars Hill

With thanks for loving medical care

BAIRD HOUSE

P.O. Box 749
41 South Main Street
Mars Hill, NC 28754

Yvette K. Wessel
(704) 689-5722

Dr. John Hannibal Baird was a turn-of-the-century medical doctor who tended the sick in the mountains surrounding Mars Hill. In "grateful appreciation" for his services, his patients built Baird House in the early 1890s so that he, his wife and their nine children might live comfortably. When completed, the house was immediately considered the grandest in the area, and it became the center of community life. Dr. Baird continued to live and practice in Mars Hill until his death in the 1920s. As his children came of age, he sent them across the street to attend Mars Hill College.

One son, John W. Baird, was also a physician. He lived in the Baird House with his wife, Lexine Williams, until he died in 1929. Grieving and presumably unable to bear remaining in Mars Hill, Lexine left town and became a nurse-on-horseback in Harlan County, Kentucky. Many years later she returned to run Baird House, renting its rooms to college students. She was called "Ma Baird" or "Aunt Lex" by the appreciative young people.

Today, the house retains the feeling of warmth and hospitality instilled by the Baird family and Aunt Lex. Yvette Wessel, the current owner and innkeeper, says "a house needs to be peopled." One gets the feeling she could have picked up that eloquent phrase from old Aunt Lex herself, except that would be slighting Yvette's own spirit and dedication.

Yvette first came to Baird House as a visitor from Connecticut. She learned the house was for sale and, with all her children grown, thought running a bed and breakfast would be fun. "And it has been," she says. She purchased the house in 1984, completed restoration work and redecorated with outstanding antiques. "As soon as I had any money, I started buying antiques," she recalls, describing her love for old furnishings. Her choices for decor include French pieces as old as the early 18th century, Oriental rugs, a collection of busts, a portrait of George Washington and accessories such as Wellington chests used by British naval officers. Every piece in every room has a story to tell, reflecting Yvette's strong sense of history.

There are five guest rooms, two of which have a private bath and two, working fireplaces. A beautiful marble patio provides a quiet spot for reading, visiting with other guests or enjoying the garden of perennials. A fan light encased in wood hangs proudly on an ivy-covered brick wall near the patio. Yvette saved it from demolition on New York's 58th Street when she lived near there and now says with satisfaction, "I finally found a home for it."

Mars Hill has a population of 2,000, nearly a third of whom are students at Mars Hill College, a four-year Baptist School. There is a wide variety of regional recreational activities and historic sites such as the Biltmore House, Thomas Wolfe's boyhood home, Vance Homestead, Carl Sandburg's home and the Cherokee Indian Reservation. The Southern Appalachian Repertory Theatre is based at the college. And fine dining can be found at many area restaurants.

Location	*18 miles north of Asheville, North Carolina. From Route 19/23, turn at entrance to Mars Hill (stoplight on four-lane), proceed to stoplight at top of hill and turn left. Baird House is third house past Post Office on the left*
Season	*Year round. Closed month of December*
Dining	*Full breakfast*
Children	*Yes, crib available*
Pets	*No*
Payment	*Personal check or AmEx*

Rates $40–$50, double occupancy; suite of two rooms, $50 for two; $70 for four

Robbinsville

Bring pocket knife, just in case

BLUE BOAR LODGE

200 Santeetlah Road
Robbinsville, NC 28771

Roy and Kathy Wilson
(704) 479-8126

If you've been looking for a fishing and hunting retreat, a glance at the fish and game trophies covering the living room walls of the Blue Boar Lodge lets you know this is the place to be. But you don't have to be a trophy hunter to enjoy this small, rustic hideaway.

Innkeepers Roy and Kathy Wilson, natives of Robbinsville, feel "There is something here for everyone." Guests can hike mountain trails into the Joyce Kilmer Memorial Forest, photograph wildflowers, watch birds, boat or swim in clear, deep Lake Santeetlah and raft in the Nantahala Gorge. Maple Springs Observation Point and historic sites, such as an old gold mine, are also suggested. Or visitors can simply unwind.

The Blue Boar was built as a private hunting resort in 1950. Roy first worked here as a hunting guide, taking sportsmen into the woods in search of black bear and Prussian boar (he has been known to kill wild boar with a pocket knife). When he was persuaded to operate the lodge for the owners, Roy then had to convince Kathy, who was working in a Robbinsville mill at the time, to join him. "We never thought we would do anything like this," she admits.

The couple purchased the lodge in 1983. The eight guest rooms, although small, are comfortable, each with private bath. Breakfast and dinner are included in the room rate and are served family style on an eight-foot Lazy Susan. "We serve hearty food in generous portions," says Kathy.

Anglers can test their skill against trout, bass and walleye in Lake Santeetlah, only a long cast away. Guides, rental boats and canoes are available through the lodge. According to Roy, some of the trout streams "haven't been fished more than four times a year." He does note that "It takes some hiking to get there." For the less adventuresome, a large, stocked trout pond is on the site. Guests pay for their catch by the pound. Both fishing and hunting licenses can be purchased at the lodge.

Interested hunters should write for information on fall and winter three-day hunting packages. Roy raises his own "cross-breed" dogs for the hunt. When asked recently how many dogs he has, he had to pause before answering. "Forty-two, I think."

Location   *Two hours west of Asheville and two hours south of Knoxville, Tennessee. In spite of its Santeetlah Road mailing address, Blue Boar Lodge is located on Joyce Kilmer Forest Road, ten miles northwest of Robbinsville. From Robbinsville, take US 129 north to Joyce Kilmer Forest Road and turn left, following the signs to the Lodge*

Season   *April through December*

Dining   *Breakfast, dinner included in room rate. Picnic lunches available by arrangement. Meals are served to non-guests for $8.95 plus tax per person by reservation only. No wine or alcoholic beverages are served as we are a dry county*

Children   *Yes*

Pets   *No (state law)*

Payment   *MasterCard, Visa, cash, personal checks. Hunting trips must be paid for in cash*

Rates $45 per person, double occupancy; $50 single, private
room. Guided fishing trips on Lake Santeetlah are $55
per person, per day, including boat, gas, guide and
bait. Guided stream trips are $55. Three-day fall
hunting packages, including all meals, guides, dogs and
lodging, are $325 per person

Last of the untouched timbers

SNOWBIRD MOUNTAIN LODGE

275 Santeetlah Road
Robbinsville, NC 28771

Eleanor and Jim Burbank
(704) 479-3433

Ten miles outside Robbinsville in the Nantahala National Forest,
and within two miles of Joyce Kilmer Memorial Forest (one of
the few remaining stands of virgin timber in the eastern U.S.),
rests an especially peaceful and picturesque getaway, Snowbird
Mountain Lodge. As you sit on its flagstone terrace, soaking up
inspiring views of the Snowbird Mountains and Lake Santeetlah
in the valley below, it is reassuring to know that such an unspoiled
natural spot for a vacation still exists.

Built in 1940 to accommodate bus tour groups, the lodge and
two nearby cottages offer 21 guest rooms, all with private bath.
Constructed of native stone and local chestnut logs, the lodge
blends well with its surroundings. Inside, stone fireplaces complement the two-story beamed lounge with big picture windows
and the handsome dining room. (Three delicious meals are served
daily; mountain trout, stuffed pork chops, prime rib and homemade desserts are among the many specialties.) Much of the
interior woodword and furniture is made of hardwoods—including wild cherry, butternut, chestnut, maple and silver bell—that
were milled in Robbinsville.

Recreational opportunities rival the scenery for top honors
here. A hike to see the huge trees, rhododendron, mosses, ferns

and wildflowers of the Joyce Kilmer Forest is a must. Birders, hikers, and river runners find the forest a splendid base for their pursuits. Guided wildflower walks and evening slide shows are scheduled in the spring, conducted by veteran naturalists who take up week-long residences. Rafting is popular on the Nantahala River; fishing and swimming can be enjoyed in streams and three lakes, Santeetlah, Cheowa and Fontana.

Informal clothing, good walking shoes and wraps for cool mornings and evenings are the rule in the lodge, although shorts are not allowed at dinner. Shuffleboard, table tennis, croquet, horseshoes, badminton, billiards, skittles and cards are some of the leisure activities available. The library is well stocked.

Innkeepers Eleanor and Jim Burbank avoid planning too many structured activities. In such a beautiful environment, it's enough to let guests choose their own recreation.

This, folks, is a wonderful place to get tangled up in choices.

Location	*From Robbinsville, follow signs for lodge and Joyce Kilmer Memorial Forest. Lodge is ten miles northwest of Robbinsville*
Season	*Late April to early November*
Dining	*Breakfast, lunch, dinner. Pack lunches available*
Children	*Over 12 years old*
Pets	*No*
Payment	*Personal check preferred; MasterCard, Visa, Discover*
Rates	*$112–$130 for two people (includes three meals)*

Saluda

A welcome retreat for mind and palate

ORCHARD INN

P.O. Box 725
U.S. Highway 176
Saluda, NC 28773
Newell and Ronnie Doty

(704) 749-5471 or (800) 581-3800

"When we first saw the Orchard Inn, we knew that this beautiful mountain inn was the *inn* for us," say Newell and Ronnie Doty, the new owners of this quiet, sophisticated country inn. Newell, an early-retired insurance executive, fly fisherman and handyman, and Ronnie, a former counselor and decorator, acquired the inn in early 1993.

Secluded on 12 wooded acres of the Saluda Rise, the two-story inn was originally known as the Clerks Mountain Home. Built in the early 1900s by the Southern Railway Company, it was used as a summer retreat for railway clerks and their families. The building was in severe disrepair when the former owners, Ken and Ann Hough, gutted it and completely rebuilt it.

The Dotys maintain an atmosphere at the inn they consider "conducive to quiet deliberation," which is why many writers and other artists come here to recharge their creativity. In addition, couples find the lovely grounds, the inn's many conversation areas, along with the three separate two-room cottages a perfect spot to celebrate renewing their own relationships.

The large living room is furnished with Oriental rugs, antiques and original art. There is a private bath in each of the 12 guest rooms, which are furnished with an assortment of pieces that, depending on the room, may include iron or brass beds, quilts, baskets and handwoven rag rugs. Although some guests come to this haven to rest and think, others enjoy jaunts through the woods, antiquing, wildflower identifying, bird-watching along with many other area activities. Businesses and small groups take advantage of the inn's air-conditioned meeting facility.

Meals are served in the glassed-in dining porch that commands a magnificent view of the Warrior Mountain Range. A full breakfast for inn guests, which may feature French toast, pancakes and coddled eggs, is offered at 8:30 A.M. Coffee and juice are available for late risers. Jackets are required for gentlemen at the evening meal, which is open to the public by reservation.

The inn has an excellent reputation for elegant dining and the Dotys continue that tradition, offering many of Ken Hough's special dishes. They have secured the talents of a local chef who brings with him many individual specialties, including a wonderful garden potato soup, cold peach soup, marinated pork tenderloin, trout almondine, old-fashioned lemon pie and cobblers made with seasonal fruits.

Directions	*Take I-26 to Exit 28, Saluda. Turn towards Saluda, up the mountain about 1 mile to US 176. Turn left on US 176 for ½ mile, and the inn is on the right*
Season	*Year round*
Dining	*Full breakfast with room; picnics and dinner available at additional cost: dinner, about $30. Saluda is a dry town; BYOB permitted*
Children	*12 and older*
Pets	*No*
Payment	*Cash, check, Visa, MasterCard*
Rates	*$85–$115 single; $95–$130 double*

Sit a spell and watch life ease by

WOODS HOUSE INN

P.O. Drawer E
Saluda, NC 28773
Dorothy Eargle
(704) 749-9562

In the early 1920s the small town of Saluda had more than 20 country inns. Passenger trains brought tourists seeking recreation and relaxation on the eastern slope of the Blue Ridge, only a stone's throw from the South Carolina state line.

At that time, many visitors found their accommodations through magazine advertisements. "The Depression killed all of that activity," says Dorothy Eargle of the Woods House. But in keeping with the style of the old ads, Dorothy calls herself the "proprietress" of her century-old inn. And well she should, because Saluda hasn't changed much over the years. Main Street is still only two blocks long, complete with angle-in parking and vintage storefronts.

As any house in a small town should be, Woods House is only a block away from Main Street. Built in 1892 as a lodge, the large, three-story frame house is named for the Woods family, who owned the property in the early 1900s. Dorothy and her husband Roy revived the original innkeeping intent of the building when they opened it as a bed-and-breakfast in 1983.

Former owners of an Alexandria, VA antiques dealership, the Eargles have filled their six guest rooms with pieces they acquired before opening the inn. Old steamer trunks, restored by Dorothy and Roy, are of particular interest. Five of the guest rooms have private baths. A separate cottage on the grounds is also available.

Breakfasts include fresh fruit, homemade breads and homemade applesauce.

From Woods House, behind City Hall on a steep slope above Main Street, visitors can relax on the large wraparound porch and watch life in Saluda saunter by down below. Rockers and a swing seat invite everyone to sit a spell, and according to Dorothy, just about everyone does.

Location	*Corner of Church and Henderson Streets*
Season	*April 1 through October 31*
Dining	*Breakfast included*
Children	*No*
Pets	*No*
Payment	*Cash or check*
Rates	*Double with private bath $50 per night; shared bath $45 per night. Suite or cottage $55 per night*

Tryon

From Lazarus tomb to Carolina horse country

FOXTROT INN AND GUEST HOUSE

800 Lynn Road (Route 108)
P.O. Box 1561
Tryon, NC 28782

Mimi Colby and Betty Daugherty
(704) 859-9706

"Graciously serving the Tryon community since last Thursday" is the motto of Foxtrot Inn proprietors Betty Daugherty and Mimi Colby. It's an apt introduction to the elegant fun-loving manner in which these two active women run their small lodge in the footholls of the Blue Ridge near the South Carolina border.

Natives of the Northeast and Midwest, respectively, Betty and Mimi met at Lazarus Tomb while both were vacationing in Israel and discovered they shared a love for bringing old houses back to life (Lazarus-like). This led to their first joint venture, an historic restoration business called, appropriately, Lazarus Unlimited.

Both women made their homes in Marblehead, Massachusetts, until their children (Betty has four, Mimi three) were grown. After telling a friend of their interest in buying an inn, they wound up talking to a broker that same afternoon, and things fell quickly into place. They bought the Tryon property in January 1989, and after putting their restoration expertise to use—painting, re-doing floors, installing a new kitchen, adding a pool, landscaping and decorating—they opened for business in April.

Designed by award-winning architect Albert Kahn, the main house was built in 1915 for the black-sheep son of a New York banking family. The house was later owned for many years by the Nelson Jackson family; many local residents still call it the Jackson House. Just inside the town limits of Tryon, it sits on ten acres in the company of 200-year-old hemlocks, oaks and pines, and native rhododendron and mountain laurel. Much of the building's detail work was done by artisans who worked on the famous Biltmore House in Asheville. Betty and Mimi have furnished the house traditionally, including unusual finds from their extensive travels. Wall-to-wall windows, hardwood floors and high ceilings help create an atmosphere of quiet elegance.

The two rooms and two suites in the main house all have private baths, and some are furnished with four-poster or canopy beds. The more modern Guest House, tucked into the woods, has two bedrooms and is well suited to families or to couples who want to be off by themselves. There is a large living room with TV, fully equipped eat-in kitchen and deck facing the sunrise. Both buildings are air conditioned.

Guests are welcome to enjoy their full breakfast either in the formal dining room or on the gray stone patio. Among the house specialties are crepes filled with cheese and apricot butter, sausage apple ring filled with scrambled eggs and cheese, hot fruit compote, chipped beef with mushrooms and hard-cooked eggs and homemade muffins. Late afternoon here is spent sipping wine and nibbling cheeses and light hors d'oeuvres.

Tryon enjoys a long-standing equestrian and cultural tradition as well as a small-town feeling. Numerous horse and hound events are staged in the area. Flat Rock Playhouse, Pearson's Falls,

Chimney Rock Park, Saluda and the productions and ongoing exhibits at the Tryon Fine Arts Center vie for your attention.

Location	*From I-26 Exit 36 (Route 108), go south toward Tryon for about five miles. Inn is within Tryon city limits on Route 108 (Lynn Road), near junction with Route 176*
Season	*All year, except December 15–March 15*
Dining	*Full breakfast and afternoon refreshments*
Children	*Over 12 in the main house; any age in guest house. Playpen and tot-minder on hand*
Pets	*No*
Payment	*No credit cards. Personal checks or cash. 50% deposit required at time of reservation*
Rates	*Rooms in main house $65–$95, double occupancy. Guest house season is May 15–October 30: $450, weekly. Off-season rates on request*

Fine wine in horse country

PINE CREST INN

200 Pine Crest Lane
Tryon, NC 28782

Jennifer and Jeremy Wainwright
(704) 859-9135
(800) 633-3001

Only a half mile from the South Carolina state line and within easy walking distance of Tryon's center, the Pine Crest Inn hosts a variety of mountain travelers. Whether here for a quiet vacation with privileges at Tryon's private golf courses, business meetings (word processors, copiers and fax equipment are on the premises) or receptions, all guests are kept happy by innkeepers Jennifer and Jeremy Wainwright and their attentive staff. Says Jennifer "We've stayed in hotels and inns all round the world and we're very picky. Here we're trying to run the sort of place we'd like to stay in with attention to detail, personal service and first-class food and wine."

Pine Crest Inn is listed on the National Register of Historic Places. Four of the ten buildings that comprise today's inn complex were built in 1906 to serve as a tuberculosis sanitarium. However, the altitude wasn't high enough for effective treatment and the property was sold in 1917 to Carter Brown, who developed it as a seasonal counterpart to a summer retreat he operated on Lake Michigan. He added new cabins that blend into secluded spots on the inn's three wooded acres. An avid horseman, Brown also built stables; he is credited with starting the horse shows, fox hunts and steeplechases for which Tryon is now famous.

The Wainwrights are only the fourth owners of the inn, having bought it in 1990. Since then, they have entertained guests who stayed here as youngsters back when the inn was in its first year.

A total of 28 guest rooms are scattered over the property, each with private bath, air conditioning and heat. There are televisions and phones also, which prompt the Wainwrights to suggest "You may be in the mountains, but you can stay in touch with your world—if you want to." Most rooms have a fireplace, and there are some suites available with a jacuzzi. A conference center can accommodate meetings for 15–60 people.

Meals are served in the dining rooms of the main building. The menu is wide ranging; fresh seafood is a specialty. There is an extensive wine list.

Location	*In Tryon, four miles south of I-26*
Season	*All year*
Dining	*Breakfast, dinner; bar facilities*
Children	*Yes*
Pets	*No*
Payment	*Personal check, MasterCard, Visa*
Rates	*$95–$150 per two persons; includes continental breakfast*

Daydreaming about dinner

STONE HEDGE INN

P.O. Box 366, Howard Gap Rd.
Tyron, NC 28782
Anneliese and Ray Weingartner
(704) 859-9114

Outside Tryon at the base of Tryon Mountain, Stone Hedge Inn offers a quiet, secluded setting ideal for weekend getaways, weddings, honeymoons and small family reunions. Of all of this, innkeeper Anneliese Weingartner says her favorite part is "meeting the people from all over."

Built by an Ohio florist in 1934, Stone Hedge was a private estate until the late 70s. A total of six guest rooms are available in three buildings, all with mountain views. Each has a private bath, a mixture of antiques and traditional furnishings, air conditioning, telephone and television. A one-room "cottage" on the top level of the pool house has a stone fireplace and is especially cozy and private. The main inn, built of stone, has two rooms upstairs. The guest house adjacent to the inn offers three large, carpeted rooms: one pine-paneled with a large stone fireplace and four-poster bed; another with a full kitchen and two entrances; and a third with an antique brass bed, white wicker furniture and a kitchenette. A full breakfast is served to overnight guests.

The Weingartners bought Stone Hedge in 1987. "This business fit my criteria of wanting to work at home," says Anneliese. She gets lots of help from husband Ray, and her two sons, Erik and Kurt, who pitch in after school and on weekends.

The inn is graced with very attractive stone work, including the patio in front, where weddings have often been held, and the walkway leading down the hill to a modern, crystal-clear pool. (The pool was once olympic-size but has been scaled down.) The pool is a delightful spot to dream, dip and tan.

A poolside daydream might include mulling over the dinner menu, which changes two times each week. Fresh seafood (examples: sea scallops in basil cream sauce, broiled yellow-fin tuna and shrimp flambéed in vermouth) and continental cuisine are specialties of the house. German dishes are often featured, owing to Ray's heritage.

Location	*About two miles north of Tryon. From I-26 Exit 36, go 2½ miles toward Tryon on State Route 108. Turn right on Howard Gap Road and go 1½ miles to inn on right*
Season	*All year*
Dining	*Full breakfast with room rate. Dinner served Wednesday through Saturday 6:00 to 9:00 P.M. and Sunday, 12 to 2:30 P.M., BYOB*
Children	*Over age 6*
Pets	*No*
Payment	*Cash, check, MasterCard, Visa*
Rates	*$65–$85 for two people, including breakfast*
Other Considerations	*Restaurant is wheelchair accessible*

Valle Crucis

Sublimely Swiss

THE INN AT THE TAYLOR HOUSE

Highway 194
Box 713
Valle Crucis, NC 28691

Chip and Roland Schwab
(704) 963-5581

A quiet vacation at The Inn at the Taylor House offers what you might expect from a first-rate mountain B&B. But when you consider its other attractions, such as European style duvets on the beds, Swiss cereal for breakfast and hosts with innkeeping in their blood, you will likely find this western North Carolina inn in Valle Crucis so appealing you can't pass it by.

A graduate of the well-known Swiss Hotel Association's Ecole Hoteliere de Lausanne, Roland Schwab is a fifth generation innkeeper. His family owned a 30-room hotel near Bern, Switzerland. His wife, Chip, operated the Truffles Cooking School in Atlanta before opening with Roland and his brother, Heinz, the Hedgerose Heights Inn, one of Atlanta's best restaurants. Tired of the pace of Atlanta, the couple looked for a country inn to operate. Chip was familiar with the Valle Crucis community and The Taylor House from her many years as a summer resident of the Blue Ridge Mountains.

Built in 1911 for the C.D. Taylor family, it has been converted for the Schwabs' B&B needs, but keeps its personality as a farm house—a very fancy one! The couple added baths, improved the wiring, plumbing and heating system, painted inside and out, fitted the kitchen with restaurant grade equipment, refinished the hardwood floors and did some gorgeous landscaping. Shaded by tall trees, the two-story white structure with hipped roof and double chimneys, plus three outstanding hipped roof dormers with double windows and transoms, is in mint condition. A large wraparound porch with wicker furniture, a porch swing, plants and flowers invite immediate use.

Inside, the Schwabs' collection of antiques, Oriental rugs and artwork exudes luxury. There's one guest room downstairs that combines with a sitting room with fireplace and private bath to make a suite. The five other guest rooms, all with private bath and carpeting, are upstairs and range from Oriental to Country in decor. You will be glad to have a down comforter on your bed even in the summer months when evenings are sometimes cool. Summer and winter weight duvets are offered, and if you've never snuggled up under one, you are in for a treat.

Considering their background as chefs, it is a pity Chip and Roland serve only breakfast to guests. There are many fine restaurants in the immediate area. The fare varies from omelettes and blueberry pancakes to French egg casserole with fresh asparagus and grilled tomatoes. Birchermuesli, a Swiss cereal of oats, grated nuts, dates and yogurt, is served every day with fresh fruit and berries in season, grown by the Schwabs' neighbors.

Be sure to visit the historic Mast General Store for unique items. Gardeners must make a stop at Charlotte's Greenhouse in Valle Crucis and the Gardens of the Blue Ridge, a nursery known nationally for its native wildflowers and ferns, in nearby Linville.

Location	*Between Valle Crucis and Banner Elk on Highway 194. From Boone take Rt. 105 south five miles to exit to Valle Crucis on SR 1112. Continue 2.8 miles to Highway 194, turn left and go ⁸/₁₀ mile to Taylor Inn on the right*
Dining	*Breakfast included in room rate*
Season	*April 15–December 15*
Children	*No*
Pets	*No*
Payment	*Visa, MasterCard, cash or personal check*
Rates	*$110–$145, double occupancy*

Legacy from past masts

MAST FARM INN

P.O. Box 704
Valle Crucis, NC 28691

Sibyl and Francis Pressly
(704) 963-5857

Come see an excellent example of a self-contained family homestead by visiting the Mast Farm Inn, seven miles outside of Boone in Valle Crucis. Aunt Josie and Uncle Finley Mast first operated an inn here in the early 1900s, and the place was held by the Mast family until 1980. Today's innkeepers, Sibyl and Francis Pressly, have completed a certified historic renovation of many of the homestead's venerable buildings. New again are the main

18-room house, a two-room log cabin, the spring house, wash house, ice house, large barn, blacksmith shop and gazebo.

The main house, site of today's inn, is the building made famous by Finley's and Josie's hospitality and good, plentiful food—as many as 20 different dishes at a meal. Josie was also known for her expert weaving, some of which found its way to Smithsonian Institution exhibits. She had as many as three looms in the log cabin, the Mast family's first home, built in 1812 by David Mast.

Missionaries gave this community its name in the mid 1800s when they saw from atop the mountains the cross formed by the junction of Clarks Creek and Dutch Creek—thus the Latin "valley of the cross." Roads and farms have since changed the courses of the river and creek so that the cross is no longer visible.

A stroll around the farm's 12 different buildings will conjure up images of a past way of life. But don't think you have to roll up your sleeves and work on this farm; it is here for a wonderful getaway.

On the National Register of Historic Places, the three-story, green frame inn with tin roof and terrific gables has a wraparound porch from which you can view the rolling countryside. Nine cozy guest rooms, seven with private bath and the other two sharing a bath, are available. Named either for Mast family members, a past guest or employee, the rooms are furnished with simple country antiques. Fresh flowers from the inn's garden grace each room, and quilts, many locally made, decorate the white pine-paneled walls. Lodging is also available in the original two-room log cabin called the Loom House. It has a kitchen, fireplace and sleeping loft. The blacksmith and woodwork shops have also been carefully restored for guest accommodations.

Fresh vegetables, many grown here, highlight the popular, family-style dinners served to inn guests and the public in two evening seatings. There are small tables for those who prefer a more intimate setting. It is especially interesting to find a kitchen in the South that does not have a deep fat fryer—a tribute to the Presslys' health consciousness. The fried chicken on the menu is pan fried—and delicious!

You won't want to miss stopping at the Mast General Store. Also on the National Register of Historic Places, it is the real thing, displaying many items not often found anymore.

Location	*From Raleigh take I-40 West to Winston-Salem, then take US 421 to Boone. From here take 105 South to SR 1112. Turn left and follow for three miles to signs*
Dining	*Breakfast (included); dinner Tuesday–Saturday and Sunday lunch. Dinner for two (for guests not staying at inn) $28 plus tax*
Season	*Late Dec.–early March and late April–early Nov.*
Children	*Inn not suitable for small children*
Pets	*No*
Payment	*Visa, MasterCard, personal checks, cash*
Rates	*$90–$155, double occupancy, MAP (two meals included)*

Waynesville

Everything, topped by chocoholic tarts

GRANDVIEW LODGE

809 Valley View Circle Road
Waynesville, NC 28786-5350

Stan and Linda Arnold
(704) 456-5212
(800) 255-7826

Many of the reasons for a stay at Waynesville's quiet Grandview Lodge are the same as for other popular mountain inns. The lodge gives off a home-away-from-home feeling; its innkeepers have a wonderful success story of leaving the confines of the corporate world; it is an ideal setting for a honeymoon, anniversary, reunion or weekend getaway; and, at a 3,000-foot elevation, it is cool in summer. What makes this lodge especially delightful is its creative, mouth-watering food. Served family style in a large dining room, the meals are both healthful and original. And when you add the fact that one of its innkeepers speaks Polish, Russian and German, the Grandview Lodge is quite a place to be.

It is true that Stan Arnold came home from his corporate management job in Chicago and announced to his wife, Linda, that the time had come for them to follow their dream of running an inn. They decided to return to North Carolina where they had previously lived, and bought the Grandview Lodge in May 1986. Within just a few days of closing, they had moved in and begun greeting their first guests. The combination of Stan's management skills and Linda's experience as a home economist specializing in foods and nutrition—she has also studied at New York's Culinary Institute of America—serves the friendly couple and the lodge well.

The main building dates back to the late 1800s when it was part of a large farm and orchard. For the last 50 years it has operated as a lodge. Extensive remodeling and renovation has resulted in the present day, five-building layout with a total of 11 guest rooms and apartments, all with private bath, cable TV and two beds (some of which are king/queen size). The pleasant antique furnishings are unpretentious. Apple trees, grape arbors and a rhubarb patch dot the lodge's rolling 2½ acres.

Golf, hiking, swimming, tennis and white-water rafting are all near at hand as are Asheville's Biltmore House, the Great Smoky Mountains National Park, Ghost Town and Smoky Mountain Railway. Waynesville also holds an international folk festival, Folkmoot, during the last week of July through the first week of August.

You may wish to choose active activities while here because you will have excellent meals to work off. Health conscious diners will be glad to hear that Linda serves food that is low in fat, salt and sugar, high in fiber and boasts many vegetables fresh from a neighbor's garden. She happily accommodates any special dietary requirements. Among the many Southern Gourmet specialties she serves are Whole Grain Pancakes or Apple Oatmeal Muffins for breakfast; Pork Roast, Chicken in Orange Juice and White Wine, Barbecued Beef Ribs, Chicken and Dumplings, Corn Pudding and Grandview Lodge Sweet Potato Casserole for dinner. The breads are by Linda and her desserts range from Open-faced Apple Pie with Cheddar Cheese Crust to Lemon Meringue Pie. Chocolate lovers, who will compromise even the best diet when the chocolate urge hits, won't be able to resist her Chocoholic Tart.

In response to many requests for her recipes, Linda has written a cookbook called *Recipes from Grandview Lodge*. It—and a grand time—are available at the lodge.

Location	*From Asheville: I-40 westbound to Exit 27. U.S. 23-74 to the West Waynesville exit; go left off ramp to stop sign; go left to the first traffic light (Allens Creek Road); turn right and go one mile to the left fork (sign on the left shoulder); turn left and continue 4/10 mile to Grandview Lodge. From Knoxville: I-40 eastbound to Exit 20; follow U.S. 276 south; after passing town of Waynesville city limits get on U.S. 23-74 towards Sylva and follow directions above. Please call if additional directions are needed*
Dining	*Family-style full breakfast and dinner included in room rate; non-resident guests reservations accepted (dinners are $15–$17.50 per person)*
Season	*All year*
Children	*Allowed; cribs may be rented when available at local furniture store*
Pets	*No; arrangements may be made in summer*
Payment	*Personal checks, travelers' checks, cash*
Rates	*$90–$105 per day for two; weekly rates are available*

Listen for the old dinner bell

HALLCREST INN

299 Halltop Circle
Waynesville, NC 28786

Martin and Tesa Burson
David and Catherine Mitchell
(704) 456-6457 or (800) 334-6457

Listen for the old dinner bell when you stay at Hallcrest Inn. It echoes through the woods and hills surrounding the old farmhouse, waking you at 8:00 A.M. Half an hour later it invites you to a full country breakfast, and in the evening it calls you for a Southern home-cooked dinner. Finally, when you end your stay it rings to bid you a safe journey.

Hallcrest Inn, purchased in 1979 by Russell and Margaret Burson, is now managed by their children, Martin and Catherine and their families. "We look forward to maintaining the same home-like atmosphere and award-winning Southern country cooking that our parents offered," says Catherine. "The recipes that Martin and I grew up on will remain staples. We will also introduce new ones that we receive from our guests."

Built around 1880 as a farmhouse for the first commercial apple orchard in western North Carolina, the two-story home with tin roof and dormer windows sits on three wooded acres atop Hall Mountain. From the porch, rocking chair enthusiasts will savor the view of Waynesville and the Balsam Mountains.

There are 12 guest rooms, eight in the house and four in an adjacent modular unit dubbed the "side porch." Each has a private bath. Family pieces, including a medical diploma earned in 1874 by Russell's great-grandfather and quilts made by Margaret's mother and grandmother, furnish the rooms in the main house. The "porch" rooms are simply decorated and have private balconies.

Word has spread about the good cooking at Hallcrest Inn. The dining room can accommodate the overflow patrons who come for treats like homemade ice cream on Saturday nights. (Watch for a gathering of folks in time for the dinner bell.) Meals are served family style on large Lazy Susan tables. Reservations are required.

Nearby Lake Junalaska offers water sports, and there are many other mountain activities to choose from, a few being antiquing, craft shopping, golfing, hiking and horseback riding.

Location	*Thirty miles west of Asheville. From Waynesville, take US 276 north 1.3 miles to left on Mauney Cove Road and follow signs to inn*
Season	*May through November and first two weekends in December*
Dining	*Breakfast, dinner*
Children	*Yes, baby sitter available by arrangement*
Pets	*No*
Payment	*Cash, personal check, MasterCard, Visa*
Rates	*$55–$80 includes breakfast and dinner; double occupancy*

Classic country coziness

HEATH LODGE

900 Dolan Road
Waynesville, NC 28786

Robert and Cindy Zinser
(704) 456-3333, (800) 432-8499

After living in cities from Riyadh, Saudi Arabia, to Vancouver, British Columbia, for 18 years, Robert and Cindy Zinser decided to put their nomadic life behind them and settle down to the peace and serenity of the North Carolina mountains. They found Heath Lodge on a Sunday afternoon in 1991 and bought it within a week.

The main building was constructed from native stone and poplar in 1946 by musician Wendell Furry who, in his nineties, still drops in from time to time. Over the years other buildings, keeping the original rustic charm, have been added resulting in a total of eight on the Zinsers' six acres. Nestled among huge oaks, dogwoods, mountain laurel and rhododendron, the lodge has a cozy country feeling despite its proximity to downtown.

Eighteen rooms and four suites are spread out through the various buildings. All rooms have private baths, color cable TV, porches with rockers; each has its own character enhanced by the handmade quilts, Oriental carpets and art work the Zinsers picked up in their travels. "Returning guests normally request the same room they had during their last visit," says Robert. (Many also stay for a week, for which there are special rates.)

Visitors may want to relax in the lodge's hot tub, read or play cards or the piano in the lounge, or take advantage of golf and tennis nearby. Opportunities abound in the area for fishing, white water rafting, tubing, hiking, horseback riding, shopping and attending annual music and dance festivals.

On most days a roaring fire in the main lodge's stone fireplace takes the chill from crisp mountain mornings. The dining room, which serves up to 75 guests at round tables, with its exposed beams, oak floors and hand-hewn oak tables, boasts Cindy's fine cooking. The dinner menu changes nightly so you may have to plan ahead in order to taste her steak teriyaki or Kentucky pot roast. Following an appetizer and/or a homemade soup, two entrees come with a choice of four vegetables, homemade breads/biscuits and luscious deserts. Emphasis is placed on a low fat, no cholesterol menu, including the angel food cake. The full breakfast is all down home: fresh fruit, muffins, pancakes, French toast, special breakfast pies, poached eggs on a bed of sauteed potatoes, bacon and sausage. "Most guests don't even want to think about eating again until dinner," says Cindy. With both meals included in the room rate, the Heath Lodge is an unbelievable bargain and a popular retreat year-round.

Location   *About 25 miles west of Asheville. From I-40 Exit 27 take Hwy 19/23 six miles to US 276 S and Waynesville exit. Go about ¼ mile to KFC outlet on right and the Pizza Hut on left. Turn right, making almost a U-turn up hill on Love Lane. Take first right* onto *Dolan Road and go down the hill to lodge drive on left*

Season *All year*

Dining *Full breakfast and dinner included. Dinner available by reservation to outside guests; wine/beer service optional*

Children *Yes; no charge for cribs*

Pets *No*

Payment *Cash, check, Visa, MasterCard, Discover*

Rates *$45–$60 per person, double occupancy, daily; $270–360 weekly per person*

On top of Old Smoky

PISGAH INN

P.O. Drawer 749
Waynesville, NC 28786

Bruce O'Connell
(704) 235-8228

To experience what this magnificent part of the Smoky Mountains was like when only the Indians knew it, stay at the Pisgah Inn and absorb an unspoiled, breathtaking scene. Peering through the large windows of the dining room, from the deck or from any of the 51 rooms, one spans a 180-degree view of Pisgah National Forest, its peaks, balsam covered slopes, valleys and distant ridges silhouetted against an endless sky. Here on Mount Pisgah at 5,000 feet, the air is always fresh and crisp; in summer Mother Nature provides the air conditioning. Spring and fall bring their own glories, from April's early mountain laurel and flame azaleas to the rich, riotous foliage of autumn change.

The awesome beauty of the spot is truly biblical, as the name implies. According to Deuteronomy, it was to Pisgah Mountain that Moses was called to look in all directions for the "Promised

Land." For its natural beauty and diverse wildlife and to escape summer heat in the lowlands, people have been coming here since the early part of the century. The first Pisgah Inn, built in 1919, was a popular resort. Preserving the casual rusticity of the original, the present inn offers 51 rooms, all with private bath and with either porch or balcony overlooking the Pisgah Ledge. Rooms are comfortably furnished and convenient to the dining lodge. The Pisgah Room is extra large with fireplace and sectional sofa. Prices are very reasonable and the service, excellent: a laidback, informal inn for a comfortable, affordable family vacation.

If you are passing through the area or cruising the Blue Ridge Parkway anywhere close to marker 408, a meal here is a must. The grilled mountain trout is delicious, as is the chicken and other home-cooked specialties, and the setting one you'll never forget. Overnighters have a variety of hiking trails to explore, and the shops of Asheville are only about a half-hour away.

Location	*Follow the Blue Ridge Parkway about 14 miles south of Asheville. Turnoff to the inn is between mile markers 408 and 409*
Dining	*Breakfast, lunch, dinner, coffee shop open for quick snacks or full meals*
Season	*From early April to late November*
Children	*Yes*
Pets	*No*
Payment	*MasterCard, Visa, cash, check*
Rates	*Standard: $54 single, $65 double; deluxe: single $59, $69 double. Pisgah Room: $105; extra person $6. Children 12 years and younger in the same room with two adults are free*
Other Considerations	*Campground, camp store, laundromat, gift store on premises*

Up the long and winding road

THE SWAG

Rt. 2, Box 280-A
Waynesville, NC 28786

Deener Matthews
(704) 926-0430

Guests should prepare themselves for the driveway to The Swag. It climbs 1,200 feet in 2½ miles as it winds its way to this mountain-top inn. Wow!

"Many people thought the driveway couldn't be built," recalls innkeeper Deener Matthews. There was only a trail to the site when she and her husband Dan, an Episcopal minister, acquired the 250-acre property in 1969. Three bulldozers, a dynamite crew and 150 truckloads of gravel were needed to finish the task in 1970. Some guests may grumble at coming up to "the middle of nowhere," as Dan describes The Swag's location. Most, in fact, will come for just that reason and will look forward to seeing the remote, but romantic setting.

The Swag's name comes from a local term used to describe a dip on a ridge between two knolls. Designed by Dan, the inn's two lodges were built from old log buildings—some from the 18th century—that were disassembled and moved here from Tennessee, Kentucky and elsewhere in North Carolina. Adding the second building, the Chestnut Lodge, may have been the reason Deener ended up running an inn. "This was originally meant to be a second family home," she explains, "but when we wanted to add on the Chestnut Lodge for Dan's church group retreats, we decided to take in guests for one season to help finance the project." After the first season, so many guests asked to come back that Deener admits, "I was hooked. I couldn't stop."

There are a total of 12 rooms and two cabins, each with private bath. In addition to queen beds, three rooms have sleeping lofts ideal for children. Many have private balconies and fireplaces or woodstoves. All rooms have coffee mills, makers, decaf and regular coffee, herbal teas, hairdryers and terry robes. A popular honeymoon suite boasts a whirlpool tub with a view; it may be

The Swag. *Waynesville, North Carolina* © Cotten Alston

one reason most honeymooners return for subsequent anniversaries. Quilts and Early American furniture dominate the interior throughout the inn. The focal point of the main lodge is a huge mortarless rock chimney made of surface stones from dry creek beds. Large windows keep this room much brighter than one might expect in a traditional log building.

Other indoor amenities include a sauna, an underground racquetball and volleyball court, a library, a video loft and a small gift shop loft with one-of-a-kind items made by local craftspeople.

Outside, the Great Smoky Mountains National Park borders a mile of the inn property, and hiking the trails that lead throughout the park may be the favorite activity for Swag guests. At the inn, if croquet, badminton or horseshoes don't tempt, one can simply take in the scenery from the porches. On hot days, some guests swim in spring-fed Swag Pond. Others fish for trout.

All meals (pack lunches on request) are included in room rate. The accent is on healthful, low-cholesterol gourmet dishes. Lunch and dinner are open to the public by reservation.

Location	*North of Maggie Valley. From the Holiday Inn at the junction of US 19 and US 276, go north 2.3 miles to left turn onto Hemphill Road and follow signs 6.5 miles to The Swag. From I-40 Exit 20 go south on US 276 for 2.8 miles to right turn onto Hemphill Road and follow signs*
Season	*Memorial Day weekend through last weekend of October*
Dining	*All meals; average cost of dinner for two is $60*
Children	*Nursing babies and children seven and older*
Pets	*No*
Payment	*Cash, check, MasterCard, Visa*
Rates	*$150–$290 for two people, meals included. Additional persons in room $60 each; $50 off room rate for singles*
Other Considerations	*No smoking in the buildings; BYOB*

Glen-Ella Springs Hotel. *Clarkesville, Georgia*

GEORGIA

Chatsworth

A complete lodge with unrivaled scenery

COHUTTA LODGE AND RESTAURANT

500 Cochise Trail
Chatsworth, GA 30705

Floyd Franklin
(706) 695-9601

One comes to expect beautiful views in the hills. But you must prepare yourself to be especially dazzled by the scene from Cohutta Lodge on 145 acres high atop Fort Mountain in northern Georgia. The lodge's faraway resting place, 10 miles from the nearest town of Chatsworth, via a sinuous road, at an elevation of 2,800 feet that makes you feel as if you're on top of the world, expands the impact of the vista and strikes wonder in your mind and heart.

The lodge derives its name from the Cherokee word "gahu ta" which comes from "gahuta yi" and means "a shed roof supported on poles." For the literal, this is a bit of a misnomer because the lodge's 60 rooms, spread among the main lodge and two other buildings, are far nicer than the name implies. Each with private bath and air conditioning and most with a balcony mountain view, the rooms are very comfortably furnished with contemporary pieces and seasoned with country touches.

Given the remoteness of the lodge, guests may be surprised to find many recreational and social features. Built in 1974 and

GEORGIA

1 *Chatsworth*
2 *Clarkesville*
3 *Dahlonega*
4 *Mountain City*

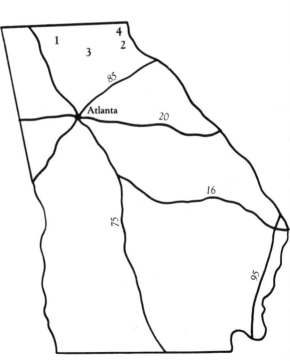

renovated in 1990, the old-English style lodge has tennis courts, an indoor pool, miniature golf, a volley ball court, horseshoes, horseback riding, a convention center and meeting rooms. Hiking and fishing are also available and, in winter, a nifty tobogganing course cuts through the woods. Southern cuisine, featuring steaks and seafood, is served in the lodge's large dining room in the glow of a hefty stone fireplace or with a view of the Chattahoochee National Forest.

Many points of interest near the lodge are related to the Cherokee Indians who once called these mountains home. There is the Chief Vann House, the restored home of the Cherokee Chief; New Echota, once the Cherokee National Capital; and the Red Clay Council Grounds, a Cherokee Council location. Other sites include the Fort Mountain State Park; Carter's Lake, Georgia's deepest lake; and the town of Dalton known as the carpet capital of the world.

Location	*The lodge is on Rt. 52, 10 miles east of Chatsworth*
Season	*Year round*
Dining	*Three meals served daily*
Children	*Yes*
Pets	*No*
Payment	*AmEx, Diner's Club, Visa, MasterCard, Discover, cash*
Rates	*For one or two people: 12/1–5/31, $49–$65; 6/1–11/30, $69–$85. For each extra person add $8. Call for group rates*

Clarkesville

New and different healing power

GLEN-ELLA SPRINGS INN

Bear Gap Rd., Rt. 3, Box 3304
Clarkesville, GA 30523

Barrie and Bobby Aycock
(706) 754-7295
(800) 552-3479

The newly rejuvenated Glen-Ella Springs Inn, peacefully hidden by trees and rolling hills in the Chattahoochee National Forest in Northeast Georgia—only a two-hour drive from Atlanta—is again greeting guests.

The inn sits on land that was once home to Georgia's Cherokee Indians. A 600-acre tract was awarded to a farming couple, Glen and Ella Davidson, in the 1830s as part of the great Cherokee land giveaway. The Davidsons built their two-story pine home here in 1875 and added on to it in 1890 and again in 1905 so that they could accommodate overnight guests. The guests came via the Tallulah Falls Railroad to enjoy the cool mountain summers, a spring believed to have healing powers, and other attractions such as Tallulah Falls. Glen Davidson met visitors at the train stop in Turnerville and brought them to his hotel in his horse-drawn wagon. By the early 1920s the hotel had stopped operating due largely to the damming of the falls for a hydroelectric plant and the end of the railroad. Davidson family members lived here until the 1950s when the property was purchased by a Methodist minister and used for two years as a home for orphan boys. The home later passed through several owners' hands before being rescued by today's innkeepers, Barrie and Bobby Aycock, in 1986.

Armed with Bobby's experience as a contractor and Barrie's desire to open a restaurant, the couple began the year-long process of bringing the old hotel and 17 surrounding acres back to life. Restoration work included re-doing the porches that line the front of the inn, refurbishing the heart pine walls, floors and ceilings (most of what you see is original) and, in the process, discovering delightful stacked stone fireplaces that had been hidden by stucco. The Aycocks added electricity and the first bathrooms to the inn, changing the original 27-room plan to make space for private baths for each of 16 guest rooms. At the rear of the inn they built a 20' x 40' swimming pool with large sundeck and perennial and herb gardens. They also made the inn handicapped accessible. Their fine restoration work won them top awards from the Georgia Society for Historic Preservation and the North Georgia Area Planning and Development Commission.

The comfortable, tastefully furnished guest quarters range from penthouse rooms with shared sitting rooms through suites with whirlpool baths and fireplaces. Rooms have twin, queen or king-sized beds. Equipped with telephone and air conditioning, each room boasts country period pieces and quilts that suggest the inn's early years. One room even has furniture original to the Davidson's hotel. An adjacent building serves as a meeting place for businesses and other groups.

The dining room offers dishes with emphasis on garden-fresh herbs and vegetables. Homemade breads and desserts are available for dinner. No alcoholic beverages sold. Guests are welcome to bring their own.

Location	*2½ miles off US Hwy. 441 between Clarkesville and Clayton, GA*
Dining	*Full breakfast daily. Dining room serves lunch Wednesday–Sunday; dinner Tuesday–Sunday, June–October. During winter months, dining room open based on demand. Please call ahead for reservations. Average price for dinner $20 per person*
Season	*All year*
Children	*In some rooms ($10 extra)*
Pets	*No*
Payment	*Cash, check, MasterCard, Visa, AmEx*
Rates	*$80–$145. Two-night minimum weekends, June through November*

Dahlonega

Decked out for easy living

MOUNTAIN TOP LODGE

Route 7, Box 150
Dahlonega, GA 30533
David Middleton
(706) 864-5257 or (800) 526-9754

Five miles outside of Dahlonega, the site of America's first gold rush, sits the newly built Mountain Top Lodge. On 40 acres and nestled among large oaks, pines and dogwoods, the lodge offers visitors a stunning panoramic view of the north Georgia mountains. Though there is plenty near here to occupy both history and nature buffs, the lodge itself, with its relaxed, casual atmosphere, is ideal for those who seek a quiet place that can give them the feeling of being away from it all.

Innkeeper David Middleton greets you personally with a warm welcome. Antiques, a wood-burning stove in the cathedral ceilinged great room, pine furniture and one-of-a-kind flea market finds combine to set a country tone. Decorated by brightly colored quilts, dust ruffles and pillow shams, each of the 13 comfortable guest rooms has a private bath. Some have queen-size beds, fireplaces and in-bath jacuzzi tubs. Two rooms, designated as suites, have their own sitting room and private deck. There's a library and card room loft for the use of all guests.

Outside, the lodge features unusually large decks for basking in the sun and taking in the view. You might wish to take a splash in the pleasant, heated outdoor spa or relax on the gazebo swing near its rock garden. Strolling on the lodge's walking paths may also have appeal. After all, you may feel compelled to work off the lodge's big country breakfast of two meats, eggs, grits, fruit, juice and homemade biscuits.

The town of Dahlonega has much to offer: Gold Rush Days in October, Old Fashioned Christmas, Wildflower Festival of the Arts in May and Family Day on July 4th are among the seasonal highlights. You can also visit the town's original 1836 courthouse,

Mountain Top Lodge. *Dahlonega, Georgia*

now a gold museum, shop for antiques and mountain crafts and even pan for gold. Rafting, hiking, fishing and horseback riding are near at hand as are The Chattahoochee National Forest and the Amicalola Falls and Vogel State Parks.

Location	*From Dahlonega go 3½ miles on 52W; turn right on Siloam Road and go ½ mile to Old Ellijay Road; turn right and go to end of road and turn left into entrance*
Season	*Year round*
Dining	*Full country breakfast*
Children	*Over 12*
Pets	*No*
Payment	*Cash, check, MasterCard, Visa, AmEx*
Rates	*$65–$125*

Glorious food atop a gold mine

THE SMITH HOUSE

202 S. Chestatee Street
Dahlonega, GA 30533

Freddy and Shirley Welch
(800) 852-9577 or (404) 864-3566

The Smith House, located one block from the town square in Dahlonega, GA, site of America's first gold rush, has been known for half a century for its outstanding traditional family style dinners. This unpretentious inn still serves up the best in good old-fashioned mountain hotel hospitality for hundreds of happy visitors every day except Monday.

If you have never before enjoyed this kind of dining experience, it is hard to imagine a better, more real introduction than what you will receive here. The meals are served on a first-come, first-served basis and they are so popular that before a recent dining room addition as many as 600 guests were known to have to wait outside. But don't worry, the dining room now seats 260 people at a time. It is not uncommon for the Smith House to serve up to 3,000 meals a day, especially on Sundays.

You will likely be seated at a large table with about a dozen strangers. Yet by the time all the introductions are made, huge platters of food will have arrived, breaking the ice. In fact, if ever there were a way to make a total stranger feel as if he were family or a friend it's this—being elbow to elbow with lots of old fashioned down-home cooking. Together you dig into fare that has changed little over the years. Fried chicken Smith House style, cured ham and lots of vegetables including beans, corn, okra, candied yam, turnip greens, black-eyed peas, rice and gravy are always offered, as are wonderful Angel biscuits, Smith House Rolls, fruit cobbler and strawberry shortcake. When you visit there might also be country fried steak, beef stew, squash casserole, banana fritters, catfish or shrimp on the table. You can count on three different kinds of meat and 12 to 14 different vegetables. Help yourself to as much or as little as you like!

You may think innkeepers Fred and Shirley Welch are sitting on a gold mine. They literally are. When site work for the home was being done in 1884 by Captain Hall, the original owner, a rich vein of gold ore was discovered by his son. However, Captain Hall was not permitted to capitalize on the lucky find. City officials would not allow a mine just one block from the public square. So Hall went ahead anyway, building his large two-story frame house with wide covered porches right on top of the gold.

In 1922, after Hall's death, Henry and Bessie Smith purchased the property and began operating it as an inn. Seven rooms were available for visitors then and the price for room and meals was $1.50 a day. The Welch family bought the Smith House in 1946. Fred, who grew up here, joined his family's business together with his wife Shirley in 1966. Since 1970, when they became the owners, they have continued to keep the Smith House tradition alive.

While the food is the focal point here, pleasant lodging is available as well. Sixteen guest rooms, each with private bath, are spread between the main house and the original columned carriage house. Some rooms have whirlpool tubs. With double, queen- or king-size beds, each room has air conditioning and cable TV but no phone. The style is pure country.

The Smith House has a pool, also a gift shop with items you'll likely want to take home such as homemade relishes, jams and jellies and a copy of the *Smith House Old Fashioned Mountain Cookbook.*

Location	*Fifty miles north of Atlanta. Take Highway 400N to end then turn left onto Highway 60. Continue 5½ miles. Smith House is on left just before town square*
Season	*Year round*
Dining	*Lunch and dinner Tuesday–Sunday, served family style. Continental breakfast available for guests*
Children	*Yes*
Pets	*No*
Payment	*Cash, Visa, MasterCard, Discover, AmEx*
Rates	*$45–$80 April–November; $30–$72 December–March*

Mountain City

Breakfast in bed

THE YORK HOUSE

P.O. Box 126
Mountain City, GA 30562

Jimmy Smith
(404) 746-2068 or (800) 231-9675

In the Little Tennessee Valley between Mountain City and Dillard lies one of northern Georgia's oldest mountain inns, the York House. Shaded by large trees, including huge hemlocks and rare, pre-Civil War Norwegian spruce, the inn offers visitors a special opportunity to soak up mountain serenity. Many guests have been so moved by its beautiful surroundings that they have chosen to be married here; a favorite spot for the ceremony is beneath the cathedral-like pines near the "Old Spring House." No doubt, the York House's romantic atmosphere has re-kindled many amorous sparks over the years between those already married. And if that isn't enough to entice you to visit, a full continental breakfast in bed should. The York House is one of few to offer it—and theirs comes to your door each morning on a silver tray.

The center part of the large frame house, a two story square-hewn log cabin, dates back to the late 1800s when it was home to "Papa Bill" and "Little Mama" York and their family. They had settled here on part of a 1,000-acre plantation deeded to them by "Little Mama's" grandfather. When the railroad came to the area, the Yorks began providing loading for those who worked on the line and later for summertime guests. Soon the inn had its own stop on the line, "York Siding," and visitors were taken by carriage the final one quarter mile to the inn. Over the years the inn was added onto to accommodate more guests. It stayed in the York family until the late 1970s and can still boast today that it has been in continuous operation since 1896. Other innkeepers have continued the tradition started by the Yorks, including the current owners, Phyllis and Jimmy Smith.

On the National Register of Historic Places, the York House features 13 guest rooms, all with private baths. Each room has its own entrance opening onto white-railed porches and breezeways. Some tasteful concessions to contemporary comfort and style include wall-to-wall carpeting, TVs in most rooms and air conditioning in some. But the genuine turn-of-the-century antiques, real wash basins and natural spring water plumbed into each room remind guests of the inn's rich past.

There is no shortage of things to do during your stay. Nearby you can hike trails in Black Rock Mountain State Park, Rabun Bald and Warwoman Dell, traverse Tallulah Gorge or linger at waterfalls. You can fish true native trout streams or try your luck in stocked lakes or ponds. (Six lakes and rivers are within one-half hour of the inn.) Horseback riding takes you over hilly trails with wonderful views. During the winter months, you can ski at the southernmost resorts in the country, Sky Valley and Scaly Mountain, only minutes away. And year 'round, shopping beckons from antique shops, galleries, art and craft studios.

Then again, after the luxury of breakfast in bed, if you so choose, you need go no farther for fun than to a rocking chair on the inn's covered veranda.

Location	*Between Clayton and Dillard, ¼ mile off Highway 441*
Season	*Year round*
Dining	*Continental breakfast, served to the room*
Children	*Yes (well behaved)*
Pets	*No*
Payment	*Check, MasterCard, Visa, AmEx, Discover*
Rates	*Weeknights: $64–$74 per couple. Weekends: $64–$79. Each additional person: $10. Continental breakfast included*

INDEX TO INNS
by State and Town

VIRGINIA

WEST VIRGINIA

KENTUCKY